After

After Grenfell

Violence, Resistance and Response

Edited by Dan Bulley,
Jenny Edkins and Nadine El-Enany

PLUTO  PRESS

First published 2019 by Pluto Press
345 Archway Road, London N6 5AA

www.plutobooks.com

British Library Cataloguing in Publication Data
A catalogue record for this book is available from the British Library

ISBN   978 0 7453 3960 3   Hardback
ISBN   978 0 7453 3958 0   Paperback
ISBN   978 1 7868 0460 0   PDF eBook
ISBN   978 1 7868 0462 4   Kindle eBook
ISBN   978 1 7868 0461 7   EPUB eBook

Typeset by Stanford DTP Services, Northampton, England
Simultaneously printed in the United Kingdom and United States of America

Contents

Acknowledgements

We would like to thank the contributors to this book for their willingness to offer their time, insight and research to make possible this small attempt to keep the violence of the Grenfell Tower fire in the public eye. Without their diligence and speed in responding to our requests, editorial comments and queries within such a tight time-frame, the book would never have been published by the second anniversary. Amongst the contributors, many have allowed us to use their previously published work with no fee, expressing the admirable desire that no one should profit from this atrocity.

Alongside the contributors, we have had the benefit of a wonderful editor at Pluto, Jakob Horstmann, who got the project off the ground, helped to contact contributors and piloted the book forward whenever it was in danger of running aground. The editorial board at Pluto has given us a great deal of freedom; this book would not have been a viable possibility at other publishing houses and we are very grateful for their commitment.

Bal Sokhi-Bulley suggested the title for the book and listened through all the difficulties of its journey. Wafa Iskander generously gave her time to transliteration. A range of other people have contributed in both big and small ways through conversations, suggestions, advice and encouragement. Thanks to James Brassett, Joseph Downing, Richard Dron, Lucy Easthope, David Edkins, Nisha Kapoor, Sarah Keenan, Renisa Mawani, Cian O'Driscoll, Fiona Owen, Colin Prescod, Sherene Razack, Andrew Russell, Carol Shergold, Andreja Zevnik and the members of the Global Politics, Economy and Society Research Centre at Oxford Brookes University, the Centre for Research on Race and Law at Birkbeck College and the Critical Global Politics cluster at the University of Manchester.

Finally, we are grateful for the permissions to republish the following work that previously appeared in other formats:

Parveen Ali photographs, some of which first appeared in Kathryn Snowdon, 'Grenfell Exhibition: New Photos of the Relief Effort to be Shown for the First Time', *Huffington Post UK Edition*, 10 June 2018, www.huffingtonpost.co.uk/entry/grenfell-exhibition-photos-relief-effort_uk_5b1ad7e4e4b09d7a3d724971. Reproduced by permission of Parveen Ali.

Sam Boal photographs first appeared in 'An Irish Photographer has Captured the Aftermath of Grenfell Tower', *The Journal*, 24 June 2017, www.thejournal.ie/grenfell-tower-sam-boal-photos-3460761-Jun2017/.© Photocall Ireland. Reproduced by permission of Photocall Ireland, Suite 31, Central Hotel Chambers, Dame Court, Dublin 2.

Yolanthe Fawehinmi photographs first appeared in Yolanthe Fawehinmi, 'The Grenfell Tower Fire Unveils How Power Operates in Great Britain: The Tale of the Haves and Have Nots', *Politicsmeanspolitics.com – The Blog*, 19 July 2017, https://blog.politicsmeanspolitics.com/the-grenfell-tower-fire-unveils-how-power-operates-in-great-britain-163ae2e424e5. Reproduced by permission of Yolanthe Fawehinmi.

Lowkey ft. Mai Khalil, *Ghosts of Grenfell*. The official music video can be found online at: www.youtube.com/watch?v=ztUamrChczQ. Reproduced by permission of Lowkey.

Ben Okri, 'Grenfell Tower, June, 2017', *The Financial Times*, 23 June 2017. © Ben Okri 2017. Reproduced by permission of Ben Okri, c/o Georgina Capel Associates Ltd, 29 Wardour Street, London, W1D 6PS.

Tony Walsh, *Equity*, originally commissioned as a video performance by ITN for Channel 4 News in August 2017 and introduced by Jon Snow as 'an ode to social housing'. The video can be found at: www.channel4.com/news/an-ode-to-social-housing. Reproduced by permission of Tony Walsh.

Figure 1.1: 'Notting Dale Area Classification' in Dan Bulley's chapter is credited to the Office for National Statistics, the Ordinance Survey and the Royal Borough of Kensington and Chelsea. It is reproduced from Royal Borough of Kensington and

Chelsea (2014) 'Notting Dale Ward Profile', RKBC Census 2011 profiles by ward, by permission of RBKC. At: www.rbkc.gov.uk/pdf/Notting%20Daledata.pdf.

Preface

Mobile phones have changed forever our shared experience of unfolding tragedy and disaster. In an instant and in real time, we bear collective witness to profound moments of suffering and death. I remember my first realisation of this – 5 February 2004, Morecombe Bay – the sea's coldest month of the year. Out on the treacherous sands in the freezing cold were migrant workers, their shift work determined by the ever-changing tides. Mainly from China's Fujian Province, backs aching and hands frozen, men and women living in the exploitative grip of ruthless gangmasters were trapped by the Bay's notorious fast-moving sea. Desperate phone calls were made, their last, to relatives across the globe as they were overwhelmed. Twenty-three drowned. The sheer horror of those phone calls I could only imagine. Now, a decade on, most people carry phones with high-resolution cameras.

Reflecting on witnessing tragedy and death, the 'ordeals of others', Susan Sontag (2003: 42) questions whether the 'only people with the right to look at images of real suffering of this extreme order are those who could do something to alleviate it'. She suggests that the 'rest of us are voyeurs, whether or not we mean to be'. It was this stark reflection by a woman who had recorded and exposed the full brutality and brutalisation of war that resonated as I watched, live on television, the horror of Grenfell Tower unfold. The dawning realisation that whether looking on from nearby streets or far beyond, 'we' as observers shared a collective helplessness. We watched silhouettes at windows. People like us who just minutes before had been sharing conversations, watching television or asleep in bed. Now they were making their final calls to their loved ones.

Morecombe Bay, Hillsborough, the *Marchioness*, Lockerbie, Grenfell Tower – people just like us. Men, women and children living typically complex lives, with diverse personal histories. Grenfell, a community within a community enriched by diversity, united by humanity. A tower block in which difference – cultural, religious, social, political, economic – was celebrated in lives coming together under one roof by chance and opportunity. A community of mutual respect regardless of life histories, in which differences in age and background were recognised, accepted and celebrated. Within days, however, the full impact of loss – of life, of home, of possessions, of futures – was compounded by a fabricated, purposeful enduring stripping of identity.

In the immediate aftermath, those traumatised by death and/or survival were subjected to a condemnatory discourse that doubted their legality, their citizenship and their validity. Like Morecombe Bay, it was buoyed by racist politics that questioned the lawful status of those who died depicting an 'enemy' queuing at the gates, 'aliens' at the ports. Kensington and Chelsea, a Royal borough and one of Europe's most affluent local authorities, revealed its binaries: of affluence and poverty; of inclusion and exclusion; of deserving and undeserving. At a moment of unimaginable pain, these binaries, both implicit and explicit, generated negative images of families and individuals who had lost everything including loved ones and friends. The questioning of the legitimacy and 'genuineness' of those who died was fired by a divisive Brexit-fuelled climate of 'insiders' and 'outsiders'.

National and local government failed immediately and spectacularly to respond to the complex needs of displaced, grieving families. In marked contrast, the community and those beyond organised and provided for their own. This is evident, starkly and angrily, in Ben Okri's profoundly personal yet collective cry of shared grief. In his poignant, angry words, power stands naked, stripped of the cloak of privilege. It is a telling response to the powerful, who stole legitimacy from the dead and dignity from survivors. The eclectic, interventionist collection that follows reveals their suffering and persistent marginalisation as an inevitable outcome of exploitation, privatisation, deregulation and the abdication of responsibility for safe, well-regulated social housing.

What should and could have been a containable, localised fire became one that engulfed the building. Within days, possibly hours, the devastating failures were starkly evident. The installation of combustible cladding and insulation panels together with ill-fitting windows were consequences of reducing costs to the lowest-priced options – trading safety and, ultimately, lives in an exploitative political economy. This is further evidenced by the structural failure to provide adequate means of escape for those living in medium-to high-rise blocks. No such compromises in the apartment blocks accommodating wealthy neighbours. That divide is well established throughout the chapters in this collection and has been exposed previously by critical analyses of housing policy and persistent privatisation – hallmarks of Thatcherism, adopted by New Labour.

They demonstrate the consequences of a political economy dependent on marginalisation and exclusion for its financial success, which, in working-class communities, purposefully and cynically has ignored local knowledge and personal experiences. In parallel, there has been the implicit, often explicit, dehumanisation of tenants as 'outsiders' fuelling a broader moral panic discourse regarding 'illegals'. From the early 1980s, inner-city uprisings against institutionally racist policing to the explicitness of hate crime on today's streets, neo-colonialist ideologies have sustained and nurtured a politics of fear, of dangerous places. What Grenfell demonstrates is that fear and danger are material realities; not of 'the other', 'the outsider', but the outworkings of a composite failure to provide and sustain safe, affordable homes for all.

Over a year on, these are early days in the long process of inquiry and investigation and it is difficult to draw informed conclusions regarding the full extent of private and public sector institutional culpability. In the first weeks of the public inquiry, however, deeply moving testimonies of those grief-stricken exposed the consequences – in lives lost and futures destroyed – of institutionalised racism in a class-riven society. Returning to Susan Sontag's words, in bearing witness to the 'ordeals of others', we are reduced to voyeurism unless we 'do something to alleviate it'. That is the priority. Grenfell Tower's epitaph is 'Change Must Come'.

Phil Scraton
Belfast 2018

Reference

Sontag, S. (2003) *Regarding the Pain of Others*. London: Penguin.

Introduction

Dan Bulley, Jenny Edkins
and Nadine El-Enany

The atrocity that struck the Lancaster West Estate in the early hours of 14 June 2017 was one of the most deadly preventable disasters in recent British history. From a simple refrigerator malfunction, a fire began which would turn Grenfell Tower, a 24-storey block built as social housing between 1972 and 1974, into a 'burnt matchbox in the sky' (Okri). At least 72 from Grenfell Tower were killed and at least 70 were injured. Over 200 people escaped as the tower blazed with suspicious speed and ferocity. It seemed that many who saw the fire, survivors, emergency services, locals and people watching the news in horror, were struck by a feeling of helplessness; a basic incapacity to *do* anything, to respond in the face of something so terrible that simply should not have happened, should not have been *allowed* to happen.

In the aftermath, survivors and first responders, community activists and neighbours, journalists and academics, politicians, international celebrities and human rights advocates sought to respond in their own ways. This sense-making was wide and various. It included simple acts of compassion, solidarity and community that gave solace and shelter. It often included anger, resentment and evidence of well-founded and deep-seated mistrust of local and national government. There were accusations of politicising what was so obviously an already political disaster. Investigations and reports were commissioned from a range of authorities. Journalists traced paper trails, contracts and sub-contracts. A public inquiry was announced that failed to take account of the needs and wishes of victims and survivors. And the community came together to contest the official response and to campaign for justice.

This book began as an attempt to bring together some of these voices, particularly those of activists, artists and academics from a variety of fields and disciplines. One thing unites all contributors:

the understanding that the Grenfell Tower fire was no unforesee-able accident. It was the result of a long history of violence. This violence is multifaceted. It has taken many shifting forms. The different responses therefore pick out and focus on particular types of violence, from the logics and legacy of colonialism, racism and xenophobia (see Chapter 3 by Nadine El-Enany, Chapter 5 by Sarah Keenan, Chapter 8 by Gracie Mae Bradley), the structural ways in which classed and racialised people are barred from legal justice (Chapter 7 by Patricia Tuitt), housing justice (Chapter 9 by Nigel de Noronha, Chapter 4 by Radical Housing Network [RHN]) and human concern (*Ghost of Grenfell* by Lowkey, Chapter 2 by Daniel Renwick, Chapter 10 by Monique Charles, *Equity* by Tony Walsh, *Grenfell Tower, June, 2017* by Ben Okri), the way they are repre-sented and spoken for (Chapter 6 by Anna Viola Sborgi, Chapter 4 by RHN), and the national and international spatial politics and neoliberal economic forces of cities and states (Chapter 9 by de Noronha, Chapter 1 by Dan Bulley). The response and resistance called for also carry different emphases, from community action in the face of dehumanisation and structural silencing (Chapter 10 by Charles, Chapter 2 by Renwick, *Ghost of Grenfell* by Lowkey, *Photo Essay* by Parveen Ali, *Photo Essay* by Yolanthe Fawehinmi), a stress on national equality and governmental policy changes (Chapter 8 by Bradley, Chapter 5 by Keenan, Chapter 9 by de Noronha, *Equity* by Walsh, *Photo Essay* by Sam Boal), to changes from the global to the individual level (Chapter 3 by El-Enany, Chapter 1 by Bulley, Chapter 6 by Sborgi, *Grenfell Tower, June, 2017* by Okri).

But none of us sees the Grenfell Tower fire as a regrettable accident that demands only policy tweaks, a public inquiry and then an act of memorialisation. The atrocity was preventable, and without attention to its structural causes, violence on the scale of the Grenfell Tower fire will happen again. The violence that produced this atrocity is too deep, too structural and too thoroughgoing for simple responses and solutions.

The Discomfort of Response

In seeking to introduce this volume, it is important to stress our discomfort of responding as editors. We are not from the North

Kensington area and are not members of the affected community. As Edkins' reflective essay puts it, we are 'interlopers'. This brings with it a danger of opportunism, using the label of Grenfell to further careers and push agendas. As Daniel Renwick writes in his chapter, 'Thousands now use Grenfell on their CV, there have been countless uses of its name'. And with this book we shall be amongst their number.

We have sought to combat the dangers of opportunism by not speaking for the victims, survivors or their families. We respond only in our own voices. We have aimed to include a wide range of views, some at the heart of the local struggle and some concerned to link it to broader themes. Only by doing so can we hope to balance the need to view what happened in the Lancaster West Estate as a devastating local event *and* part of wider forms of violence, broader expulsions and systematic injustices that are taking place across the world and often based on similar logics and structural power relations. This disaster is particular, specific to the North Kensington community *and* it reflects a situation echoed, to differing degrees, in all parts of the world. That situation is one in which some people are held to be more valuable, more worthy of protection, concern and attention while others are killed or allowed to die through neglect and intentional abandonment.

Nonetheless, the discomfort we feel in responding is important and reflects the way that a disaster can so easily become a commodity, turned into a product that can be bought and sold, generating profit. Related to this, even the cover art of this book – the green heart of Grenfell – is awkward and uncomfortable. On the one hand, it is a recognisable symbol that has become widely associated with inclusion and solidarity with those suffering and grieving. The Grenfell Action Group asked its supporters to wear 'green for Grenfell' on the one-year anniversary of the fire, as a symbol of 'unity, spirit and resilience' (Grenfell Action Group, 2018). However, on the other hand, it is a 'symbol that has been replicated many times, some in problematic and instrumental ways' (Renwick, Chapter 2). Associating the book with the green heart poses a danger of claiming credentials it possibly does not have. It can be interpreted as commodifying the symbol, appropriating it to sell books and profit from the ubiquity of its presence. In this way, the green heart and this book are potentially devalued, becoming part of the profit-seeking behaviour that many contributions (e.g. Lowkey, *Ghosts of Grenfell*; RHN, Chapter 4; Charles, Chapter 10; Bulley, Chapter 1; Renwick, Chapter 2; de Noronha Chapter 9) associate with the causes of the fire itself. Although this does not negate questions of commodification and opportunism, it is important to make clear that our authors have not been paid for their contributions. All royalties due to the editors will be donated directly to a Grenfell charity, as will an agreed percentage of the publisher's profits.

Ultimately, there is no solution to discomfort in the face of avoidable suffering. We *should* be uncomfortable and account for any complicity that may exist with the violence that killed 72 people and displaced over 200. As some of these contributions recognise, one way or another a vast number of people have benefited from the colonial logics of dispossession (El-Enany, Chapter 3), the politics of austerity and its low interest rates (Bulley, Chapter 1; Walsh, *Equity*), the 'right to buy' legislation and gentrification of areas such as North Kensington (RHN, Chapter 4; de Noronha, Chapter 9). Many of us are complicit and this needs to be acknowledged and accounted for, rather than avoided and erased.

Global Expulsions; Global Resistance

One of the particularly shameful episodes that emerged from the Grenfell fire was the shambolic governmental response. Over a year after the fire, several families have yet to be rehoused in appropriate local, long-term accommodation (RHN, Chapter 4). Their accommodation remains temporary and they cannot plan for the future. This is perhaps not surprising given the actions or inaction of the local council, the Royal Borough of Kensington and Chelsea (RBKC), in the immediate aftermath of the fire. After a Freedom of Information request from Channel 4 News, internal emails between councillors emerged which asked 'Who is in charge?' (Aggerholm, 2018). No one knew. But this begs a question: as the causes of the fire were partly global and diffused, can we expect response and resistance to be otherwise? This is to let RBKC off too lightly, as

Andrew O'Hagan sought to do in his *London Review of Books* essay (O'Hagan, 2018), but it speaks to an important issue of whether the activism in the North Kensington community can be linked to wider forms of resistance and response to injustice and displacement.

Beginning her 2014 book, *Expulsions*, Saskia Sassen argues that,

> We are confronting a formidable problem in our global political economy: the emergence of new logics of expulsion. The past two decades have seen a sharp growth in the number of people, enterprises, and places expelled from the core social and economic orders of our time.
>
> (Sassen, 2014: 1)

Such expulsions include the removal of vast numbers of people from social welfare and health insurance; ousting people from their homes due to debt and insolvency; the requisitioning of land and supplanting of people in the Global South by states and corporations to allow for mining, fracking and industrial farming; slum clearances and toxic industrial emissions making land uninhabitable.

Whether this is anything substantially new is called into question by many of the chapters in this volume, which focus on the colonial and capitalist logics of such expulsions (El-Enany, Chapter 3; Bradley, Chapter 8; de Noronha, Chapter 9; Bulley, Chapter 1; Charles, Chapter 10; Keenan, Chapter 5). It is hard to see Sassen's 'sharp growth' against the centuries of suffering and forced movement caused by the slave trade, colonial domination, the theft and settlement of land and partition of territories. Indeed, rather than being a break from feudalism, capitalism and racism emerged from it to create a 'modern world system of "racial capitalism" dependent on slavery, violence, imperialism, and genocide' (Kelly, 2017). Capitalism has from the very start operated through a need to accumulate, enclosing land, impoverishing people and casting them aside (Federici, 2004: 68–75). But these broader and long-term logics of expulsion speak to the fact that the Grenfell fire can also be seen in a wider context. If there is hope for a radical politics to emerge from the activism of Latimer Road, can it find common cause with expulsions that are continuing elsewhere?

While the global political economy is determining new ways to force people from their homes – and reviving old ways, of which fire is only one – it is also perhaps generating innovative forms of resistance in certain places. For instance, a wave of largely unfounded hope was discovered in the Arab uprisings, which saw the occupation of public space to protest against multiform violence and abuses of power. This inspiration spread across the world through the Occupy movement and its intentional misuse and redirection of squares, plazas, shopping malls and other 'commons'. More engrained and successful resistance has become institutionalised in other places. For instance, indigenous struggles in Mexico have produced 'counter-spaces of resistance' in Chiapas and Oxaca, spaces of non-capitalism that attempt to put rights and people ahead of appropriation and profit (Hesketh, 2017).

A Radical Politics of Response?

Unsurprisingly, Grenfell residents were and are well aware of what the global political economy does to them. Presenter of the documentary *Failed by the State*, Ishmael Francis-Murray (Ish), who was born in Grenfell Tower and lived there until he was 25, says at the start of the film:

> Grenfell burned for local *and* global reasons ... We talk politics now. And how we can take power, because we learned that we have to look after ourselves ... It's obvious global capital has no regard for people like me. It's the same story the world over, from Berlin to Rio, Madrid to New York ... What we had to live through could be a warning for you all.
>
> (Redfish, 2017)

He continues, 'Our local fight is against global enemies and structures. Eight guys have as much money as half the world because of the systems we are fighting' (Redfish, 2017). It is, again, unsurprising that local residents find common cause with struggles elsewhere, and recognise that global systems need to change.

In the immediate aftermath of the fire, the local community appeared on the streets. In the absence of any official support, or even a timely response by the larger charitable organisations, it fell to residents and survivors of the fire, those organisations already supporting them like the Radical Housing Network (RHN), and individuals who joined from elsewhere in solidarity, to organise help and assistance. These volunteers sorted the huge piles of donations that arrived from around the UK, organised emergency accommodation, helped those searching for missing relatives and friends or dealing with the media invasion, and comforted those traumatised by what had happened (Renwick, Chapter 2; Charles, Chapter 10; RHN, Chapter 4; Sborgi, Chapter 6). Parveen Ali's photographs in this volume, which were shown in an exhibition at St Clement's Church in Treadgold Street in June 2018, document the relief effort in which she participated as a resident (Snowdon, 2018).

For days and weeks afterwards, the North Kensington community was visible in all its unity and power (Charles, Chapter 10), contradicting stereotypes and showing itself capable of taking charge in the absence of central or local government or any other form of outside assistance. The people of the area were demonstrably politically engaged, thoroughly capable organisationally, and united across religious, political and other externally imposed divides. The contrast with the absence, incompetence and disorganisation of local and national government was stark. A largely working-class community, with a high proportion of black and minority ethnic members, living in housing estates was not supposed to be like this. They did not fit the stereotype of what Robbie Shilliam calls 'the undeserving poor'. They didn't have the characteristics that elites regularly attribute to certain groups in order to justify their social and economic exclusion (Shilliam, 2018). Nevertheless, those in authority refused to hear them, before or after the fire.

Given the history of this particular area of London, the strength of the community, its unity and its awareness should not have come as a revelation to the media, though it seemed to. The area has a long tradition of organising and resistance, from the founding of the Carnival in 1959, through the Republic of Frestonia, to the Save our Silchester campaign (Charles, Chapter 10). Community was built and resistance strategies honed in the course of these struggles. Indeed, 'community' became 'ComeUnity', as people came together once more from June 2017 onwards. There was a different politics afoot (Renwick, Chapter 2): youths of the area (and others) self-organised for a radical alternative, commandeering space to refashion for their activism. However, it did not succeed. One reason was the lack of a pragmatic plan; another was that radical organising has been rendered mute by the neoliberal context in which it finds itself (Renwick, Chapter 2).

Has a radical politics been forming in the grounded, local activism before and after Grenfell? What do we even mean by a 'radical politics'? For us it means a politics that challenges the system itself, that seeks to dismantle rather than reform it. What about justice? Is there justice in a narrow legal or radically transformative sense to be had? Probably not through the inquiry, with its judge-led structure, its lack of community representation and its inability to deal with long-standing and racialised oppression (Tuitt, Chapter 7). A list of demands does not exhaust the meaning of justice either. But even when no demands are voiced, as in the silent march, 'the call for justice is being enacted: the bodies assembled "say" ... "we are still here, persisting, demanding greater justice"' (Butler, 2015: 26). Writing of his experiences during the uprising in Greece in 2008, Hara Kouki notes how, by forming neighbourhood assemblies and solidarity groups, 'we were transformed from invisible solitary figures rambling around in our urban misery into political subjects who managed to challenge, not the solutions that had to be applied to the situation, but the situation itself' (Kouki, 2011). It seems the residents of North Kensington have long understood that this is how the power of local, community action works.

Colonial Legacies, Racialisation, Immigration

Despite the demise of the British Empire, Britain remains racially and colonially configured. Racialised descendants of colonised and enslaved people, regardless of when they arrived in Britain, are made disproportionately vulnerable to harm and premature death (Gilmore, 2006: 28). The majority of the Grenfell fire victims were racialised, many of whom were Muslim (Rice-Oxley, 2018). Across the world, millions have died and are daily exposed to violence, poverty and insecurity as a result of continuing British imperialism, often masked in the language of humanitarian intervention. The vast majority of victims of recent imperial attacks have been Muslim. In Iraq, 2 million people are estimated to have been killed as a result of the US-British-led 2003 invasion (Benjamin and Davies, 2018). The ongoing material consequences of colonialism, along with imperial invasions and unequal trade and debt arrangements continue to cause people to be displaced from their homes and to make dangerous, often deadly, journeys in search of safety. Over half the adult victims of the fire had arrived in Britain since 1990 (Rice-Oxley, 2018). Sarah Keenan notes the first victim of the fire to be identified was 23-year-old Syrian refugee, Mohamed Alhajali, who fled the war in Syria, only to die in Grenfell Tower (Chapter 5). His fate was widely covered in the mainstream media, but what became a tragic 'human interest' story served to distract attention and anger away from wider issues of imperialism and racialised and classed exclusion (Edkins, 2019).

Britain's colonial history and legacies of racial exclusion are central to understanding the context in which the fire took place. Any attempt to deny the relevance of race and colonial legacies to our understanding and response to the fire must be challenged (El-Enany, Chapter 3; Keenan, Chapter 5; Bradley, Chapter 8). One such casual erasure can be seen in media attempts to explain why people 'wear green for Grenfell'. Reporting on the one-year anniversary memorial services, the *Sunday Express* claimed 'It is thought that Grenfell is an adaptation of the words "green field" – the tower block was built on a green before the sprawl of the city took over' (Whitfield, 2018). In fact, as Gracie Mae Bradley notes, Grenfell Tower took its name from the nearby Grenfell Walk, which itself was named after Field Marshall Lord Grenfell who fought in numerous colonial wars throughout Africa before commanding British troops in their colonial occupation of Ireland (Chapter 8). Lord Grenfell's career, in fact, provides a useful mirror for the area around Notting Hill, much of which was initially built by Irish settlers and became deeply segregated by race and class (Bulley, Chapter 1). But by propagating a much more pleasant myth of 'green fields', the media are able to whitewash this colonial past and present of North Kensington, as well as the fire itself. In contrast, the contributions of this book help to tie this back together, demonstrating the connections between the fire and colonial practices and logics (El-Enany, Chapter 3), the hostile environment that has produced a 'border in every street' (Keenan, Chapter 5) and the Windrush scandal, which has seen racialised groups expelled from their homes (Bradley, Chapter 8).

Housing, Regulation, Safety

The need for struggle and resistance is apparent in the very practical questions of housing provision. Much of the attention of the North Kensington community in the aftermath of the Grenfell fire was rightly focused on these questions: on the need for tenants and lease-holders to be represented on bodies managing estates or considering regeneration; on the requirement for regulations that guarantee building quality; and, most pressing of course, on provision for residents' safety. It became clear early on in the evidence to the inquiry that Grenfell Tower had been altered from a tower block constructed in the 1970s with fire safety as a priority, to a 'refurbished' building with, among other things, flammable cladding, ill-fitting windows, underspecified fire doors, poor access for emergency vehicles and unusable equipment for fire fighters (Lane, 2018).

The history of housing provision in England over the last 100 years, from the programme to build 'homes fit for heroes' in 1919, to the present where state and local authority responsibility has been surrendered to the market and property developers' profits, is charted by Nigel de Noronha (Chapter 9). Even when local authority house building was taking place, programmes were based on exclusion, whether of tenants unable to afford higher rents, or racialised Commonwealth citizens facing discrimination (de Noronha, Chapter 9). From Grenfell, where cladding was installed to make the building look more acceptable to rich neighbours, it is easy to see how 'gentrification' works: first, estates and their inhabitants are stigmatised, and then they are moved on to make way for private developers and the market (Bulley, Chapter 1; de Noronha, Chapter 9). At the same time, deregulation and cuts in resources mean that building regulations and safety are no longer adequately enforced.

Social and economic deregulation and reducing 'red tape', including fire safety regulations, is part and parcel of making the privatisation and marketisation of what were previously public services more profitable for corporations (Shilliam, 2018: 177–179). The state prioritises profit for the private companies it contracts to provide 'public' services over the needs of the people served. The results are far-reaching and the immediate impact on those who experience the direct effects of this agenda, like the residents of Grenfell Tower, was plain: 'in the rush to deregulate, to cut costs for business, the statutory provisions for fire safety became poorly defined and their interpretation uncertain' (Bhandar, 2018). Deregulation has often resulted in not just fewer regulations, but a confusing landscape of provisions. This morass became clear in one of the first reports to be released to the Grenfell Inquiry, that of Dr Barbara Lane (2018). It means that companies can take advantage of loopholes and supply non-compliant materials.

Fighting these processes is not easy, especially in a context where the main UK political parties are implicated in deregulation, regeneration and marketisation. The Radical Housing Network, of which Grenfell Action Group is a member, describes how it formed in an attempt to connect and share experiences and resources across organisations from all parts of London engaged in this struggle (RHN, Chapter 4). The fight for accountability is made even harder by the intricacy and global spread of those corporations involved in regeneration and social housing projects in London, whether as developers, contractors or suppliers of building materials (Bulley, Chapter 1). Although there are volunteer organisations offering legal support in the aftermath of Grenfell, like the North Kensington Law Centre or Citizens Advice Kensington & Chelsea, the legal route may not be the most effective way to tackle long-term discrimination, oppression and injustice. The law only recognises certain forms of wrong; it does not see, nor offer remedies for, the slow violence of inadequate and unsafe housing provision (Tuitt, Chapter 7). In the end, resistance needs to find ways to address the system itself, rather than focus solely on seeking remedies within it.

The Organisation of the Volume

The book is not organised around discretely grouped themes of violence, power or resistance. Certainly, as suggested at the start of this Introduction, important topics of race, class, social housing, abandonment, community and resistance do appear throughout. But these themes are overlapping and intersecting, emerging and re-emerging as each contributor identifies their core areas of concern. This is because we, as editors, did not approach people to write on specific topics. Rather, we started out by searching for existing responses to the Grenfell Tower fire in various forms of media (television, newspapers, blogs and academic conferences). We selected and approached those that we thought shared our central claim: that this fire was not a regrettable accident but a foreseeable result of various forms of negligence, violence and structural inequalities. In many cases, we did not know what the result of our inquiries would be, or how powerful the response would become. Putting this volume together, and reading each contribution, has taught us much we did not know when we began.

In some cases, however, we did know. The poems of Ben Okri and Tony Walsh, as well as the lyrics of Lowkey's formidable *Ghosts of Grenfell* appealed on a visceral level. The poem by the Nigerian writer Ben Okri, *Grenfell Tower, June 2017*, first appeared in the unlikely setting of the *Financial Times* on 23 June 2017. He was later interviewed on Channel 4 News, and a video reading of the poem was posted (Channel 4 News, 2017a). A year later, he reflected on how he made his way to North Kensington, an area close to where he once lived, three days after the fire. What he saw brought back memories of his 'lost childhood on the edges of a civil war'; it all 'became in some mysterious way personal' (Okri, 2018). Tony Walsh's *Equity* begins with his childhood, battling rheumatic fever in a privately rented house. His life was saved and his future transformed by a move to social housing. At that time, in the 1960s, council houses were places of hope and respectability for those with access to them. Walsh is a performance poet and his poem, commissioned by Channel 4, was a video from the start (Channel 4 News, 2017b), as was Lowkey's *Ghosts of Grenfell*. The latter especially needs to be seen in that form to be appreciated (Lowkey, 2017). The vocals of Mai Khalil and Niles 'Asheber' Hailstones, with the refrain 'Did they die or us? Did they die for us?', are haunting. The video closes with members of the community reciting the names of those who were missing, demanding 'Where are they?'.

Similarly, the photo essays of Parveen Ali, Sam Boal and Yolanthe Fawehinmi have been chosen because they provide a very different record of events from that in much of the media. Ali and Fawehinmi are local residents; Boal is not, and his images reflect the ambiguity he feels in taking on the role of photographer in this context. Ali's photographs show the quiet dignity and resilience on the streets in the immediate aftermath, as people try to carry on with their everyday lives, and the gargantuan efforts of those organising the relief effort. Fawehinmi's images record the anger and grief expressed in posters, T-shirts and notices attached to the railings around Grenfell. The images and the poems punctuate and counterpoise the academic and activist voices in this volume.

One deadly disaster with its causes based in social and political violence and injustice – Hillsborough, where 96 Liverpool football fans were killed – was held by relatives in the public eye from 1989 until some form of justice was finally achieved in 2016 (Scraton, 2016). The academic and campaigner at the forefront of supporting this movement, Phil Scraton, has written our Preface. The fight for an official inquiry into Hillsborough and justice for the 96 lasted until inquests were rerun 27 years afterwards. A verdict of unlawful killing led finally to criminal prosecutions. A campaigner from Liverpool spoke of their strong feeling of connection with those in Grenfell at the monthly silent march (Zylbersztajn, 2018), and Liverpool fans travelling to Chelsea for an away match unfurled a banner demanding Justice for Grenfell (Pearce, 2018).

Robbie Shilliam's work on the legacies of European colonialism and the logics of separating the deserving and undeserving poor, as well as his writings specifically on Grenfell, have been an important influence on the inception and development of this book. Shilliam is another academic, like Scraton, with a long history of activism and engagement, in his case with various Rastafari and black communities in London, among others. His book, *Race and the Undeserving*

Poor, traces the way in which different groups have been painted as 'undeserving' in moments of struggle in British imperial history, from enslavement and poor law reform, to present-day welfare conditionality. He writes that 'race is class ... there is no politics of class that is not already racialized' (Shilliam, 2018: 180). He has strong links with Grenfell activists, and his Afterword concludes this volume.

References

Aggerholm, H. (2018) 'Grenfell Tower: Kensington and Chelsea Councillors Emailed to ask who was "in Charge" After Tragedy'. *The Independent*, 9 June. www.independent.co.uk/news/uk/home-news/grenfell-tower-fire-royal-borough-kensington-chelsea-emails-council-nick-paget-brown-a8390956.html (websites in this list last accessed November 2018).

Benjamin, M. and Davies, N. J. S. (2018) 'The Iraq Death Toll 15 Years After the US Invasion'. *Common Dreams*, 15 March. www.commondreams.org/views/2018/03/15/iraq-death-toll-15-years-after-us-invasion.

Bhandar, B. (2018) 'Organised State Abandonment: The Meaning of Grenfell'. *The Sociological Review Blog*, 19 September. www.thesociologicalreview.com/blog/organised-state-abandonment-the-meaning-of-grenfell.html.

Butler, J. (2015) *Notes Toward a Performative Theory of Assembly*. Cambridge, MA: Harvard University Press.

Channel 4 News (2017a) 'Ben Okri's Heartfelt Poem: Grenfell Tower 2017'. 26 June. www.facebook.com/Channel4News/videos/10154977083871939/.

Channel 4 News (2017b) 'An Ode to Social Housing'. 3 August. www.channel4.com/news/an-ode-to-social-housing.

Edkins, J. (2019) *Change and the Politics of Certainty*. Manchester: Manchester University Press.

Federici, S. (2004) *Caliban and the Witch*. New York: Autonomedia.

Gilmore, R. W. (2006) *Golden Gulag: Prisons, Surplus, Crisis, and Opposition in Globalizing California*. Berkeley, CA: University of California Press.

Grenfell Action Group (2018) 'Green for Grenfell Day'. 8 June. https://grenfellactiongroup.wordpress.com/2018/06/08/green-for-grenfell-day/.

Hesketh, C. (2017) *Spaces of Capital/Spaces of Resistance: Mexico and the Global Political Economy*. Athens, GA: University of Georgia Press.

Kelley, R. G. D. (2017), 'What Did Cedric Robinson Mean by Racial Capitalism?'. *Boston Review*, 12 January. http://bostonreview.net/race/robin-d-g-kelley-what-did-cedric-robinson-mean-racial-capitalism.

Kouki, H. (2011) 'Greece: A Short Voyage to the Land of Ourselves'. *Critical Legal Thinking*, 10 January. http://criticallegalthinking.com/2011/01/10/a-short-voyage-to-the-land-of-ourselves/.

Lane, B. (2018) Report of Dr Barbara Lane to the Grenfell Tower Inquiry, 18 April. www.grenfelltowerinquiry.org.uk/evidence/dr-barbara-lanes-expert-report.

Lowkey (2017) *Ghosts of Grenfell* (Official Music Video) featuring Mai Khalil. 8 August. www.youtube.com/watch?v=ztuamrchczq.

O'Hagan, A. (2018) 'The Tower'. *London Review of Books*, 40(11). www.lrb.co.uk/v40/n11/andrew-ohagan/the-tower.

Okri, B. (2018) 'Ben Okri on Grenfell and Writing About Calamity'. *Financial Times*, 8 June. www.ft.com/content/44484824-6a44-11e8-b6eb-4acfcfb08c11.

Pearce, J. (2018) 'Liverpool Fans Praised for Grenfell Tower Gesture at Chelsea'. *Liverpool Echo*, 30 September. www.liverpoolecho.co.uk/sport/football/football-news/liverpool-fans-praised-grenfell-tower-15219339.

Redfish (2017) *Failed By The State: The Struggle in the Shadow of Grenfell*. Co-producers Ish and Daniel Renwick. Part 1 10:24min. 16 November. https://youtu.be/9tFPCUgjbfA.

Rice-Oxley, M. (2018) 'Grenfell: The 72 Victims, Their Lives, Loves and Losses'. *The Guardian*, 14 May. www.theguardian.com/uk-news/2018/may/14/grenfell-the-71-victims-their-lives-loves-and-losses and www.theguardian.com/uk-news/ng-interactive/2018/may/14/lives-of-grenfell-tower-victims-fire.

Sassen, S. (2014) *Expulsions: Brutality and Complexity in the Global Economy*. Cambridge, MA: Harvard University Press.

Scraton, P. (2016) *Hillsborough: The Truth*, revised edn. London: Mainstream Publishing.

Shilliam, R. (2018) *Race and the Undeserving Poor: From Abolition to Brexit*. Newcastle: Agenda Publishing.

Snowdon, K. (2018) 'Grenfell Exhibition: New Photos of the Relief Effort to be Shown for First Time'. *HuffPostUK*, 10 June. www.huffingtonpost.co.uk/entry/grenfell-exhibition-photos-relief-effort_uk_5b1ad7e4e4b09d7a3d724971.

Whitfield, K. (2018) 'Grenfell Tower Anniversary: Why is Green for Grenfell?'. *Sunday Express*, 14 June. www.express.co.uk/news/uk/974345/grenfell-tower-fire-anniversary-why-green-for-grenfell.

Zylbersztajn, D. (2018) 'Grenfell Tower Silent March'. 14 October. www.youtube.com/watch?v=ooqy_Hhg2GE.

Grenfell Tower, June, 2017
Ben Okri

It was like a burnt matchbox in the sky.
It was black and long and burnt in the sky.
You saw it through the flowering stump of trees.
You saw it beyond the ochre spire of the church.
You saw it in the tears of those who survived.
You saw it through the rage of those who survived.
You saw it past the posters of those who had burnt to ashes.
You saw it past the posters of those who jumped to their deaths.
You saw it through the TV images of flames through windows
Running up the aluminium cladding
You saw it in print images of flames bursting out from the roof.
You heard it in the voices loud in the streets.
You heard it in the cries in the air howling for justice.
You heard it in the pubs the streets the basements the digs.
You heard it in the wailing of women and the silent scream
Of orphans wandering the streets
You saw it in your baby who couldn't sleep at night
Spooked by the ghosts that wander the area still trying
To escape the fires that came at them black and choking.
You saw it in your dreams of the dead asking if living
Had no meaning being poor in a land
Where the poor die in flames without warning.
But when you saw it with your eyes it seemed what the eyes
Saw did not make sense cannot make sense will not make sense.
You saw it there in the sky, tall and black and burnt.
You counted the windows and counted the floors
And saw the sickly yellow of the half burnt cladding
And what you saw could only be seen in nightmare.
Like a war-zone come to the depths of a fashionable borough.
Like a war-zone planted here in the city.

To see with the eyes that which one only sees
In nightmares turns the day to night, turns the world upside down.

Those who were living now are dead
Those who were breathing are from the living earth fled.
If you want to see how the poor die, come see Grenfell Tower.
See the tower, and let a world-changing dream flower.

Residents of the area call it the crematorium.
It has revealed the undercurrents of our age.
The poor who thought voting for the rich would save them.
The poor who believed all that the papers said.
The poor who listened with their fears.
The poor who live in their rooms and dream for their kids.
The poor are you and I, you in your garden of flowers,
In your house of books, who gaze from afar
At a destiny that draws near with another name.
Sometimes it takes an image to wake up a nation
From its secret shame. And here it is every name
Of someone burnt to death, on the stairs or in their room,
Who had no idea what they died for, or how they were betrayed.
They did not die when they died; their deaths happened long
Before. It happened in the minds of people who never saw
Them. It happened in the profit margins. It happened
In the laws. They died because money could be saved and made.

Those who are living now are dead
Those who were breathing are from the living earth fled.
If you want to see how the poor die, come see Grenfell Tower
See the tower, and let a world-changing dream flower.

They called the tower ugly; they named it an eyesore.
All around the beautiful people in their beautiful houses
Didn't want the ugly tower to ruin their house prices.
Ten million was spent to encase the tower in cladding.
Had it ever been tested before except on this eyesore,
Had it ever been tested for fire, been tried in a blaze?

But it made the tower look pretty, yes it made the tower look pretty.
But in twenty four storeys, not a single sprinkler.
In twenty four storeys not a single alarm that worked.
In twenty four storeys not a single fire escape,
Only a single stairwell designed in hell, waiting
For an inferno. That's the story of our times.
Make it pretty on the outside, but a death trap
On the inside. Make the hollow sound nice, make
The empty look nice. That's all they will see,
How it looks, how it sounds, not how it really is, unseen.
But if you really look you can see it, if you really listen
You can hear it. You've got to look beneath the cladding.
There's cladding everywhere. Political cladding,
Economic cladding, intellectual cladding – things that look good
But have no centre, have no heart, only moral padding.
They say the words but the words are hollow.
They make the gestures and the gestures are shallow.
Their bodies come to the burnt tower but their souls don't follow.

Those who were living are now dead
Those who were breathing are from the living earth fled.
If you want to see how the poor die, come see Grenfell Tower
See the tower, and let a world-changing deed flower.

The voices here must speak for the dead.
Speak for the dead. Speak for the dead.
See their pictures line the walls. Poverty is its own
Colour, its own race. They were Muslim and Christian,
Black and white and colours in between. They were young
And old and beautiful and middle aged. There were girls
In their best dresses with hearts open to the future.
There was an old man with his grandchildren;
There was Amaya Tuccu, three years old,
Burnt to ashes before she could see the lies of the world.
There are names who were living beings who dreamt
Of fame or contentment or education or love
Who are now ashes in a burnt out shell of cynicism.

There were two Italians, lovely and young,
Who in the inferno were on their mobile phone to friends
While the smoke of profits suffocated their voices.
There was the baby thrown from many storeys high
By a mother who knew otherwise he would die.
There were those who jumped from their windows
And those who died because they were told to stay
In their burning rooms. There was the little girl on fire
Seen diving out from the twentieth floor. Need I say more.

Those who are living are now dead
Those who were breathing are from the living earth fled.
If you want to see how the poor die, come see Grenfell Tower.
See the tower, and let a world-changing deed flower.

Always there's that discrepancy
Between what happens and what we are told.
The official figures were stuck at thirty.
Truth in the world is rarer than gold.
Bodies brought out in the dark
Bodies still in the dark.
Dark the smoke and dark the head.
Those who were living are now dead.

And while the tower flamed they were tripping
Over bodies at the stairs
Because it was pitch black.
And those that survived
Sleep like refugees on the floor
Of a sports centre.
And like creatures scared of the dark,
A figure from on high flits by,
Speaking to the police and brave firefighters,
But avoiding the victims,
Whose hearts must be brimming with dread.
Those who were breathing are from the living earth fled.

But if you go to Grenfell Tower, if you can pull
Yourselves from your tennis games and your perfect dinners
If you go there while the black skeleton of that living tower
Still stands unreal in the air, a warning for similar towers to fear,
You will breathe the air thick with grief
With women spontaneously weeping
And children wandering around stunned
And men secretly wiping a tear from the eye
And people unbelieving staring at this sinister form in the sky
You will see the trees with their leaves green and clean
And will inhale the incense meant
To cleanse the air of unhappiness
You will see banks of flowers
And white paper walls sobbing with words
And candles burning for the blessing of the dead
You will see the true meaning of community
Food shared and stories told and volunteers everywhere
You will breathe the air of incinerators
Mixed with the essence of flower.
If you want to see how the poor die, come see Grenfell Tower.

Make sense of these figures if you will
For the spirit lives where truth cannot kill.
Ten million spent on the falsely clad
In a fire where hundreds lost all they had.
Five million offered in relief
Ought to make a nation alter its belief.
An image gives life and an image kills.
The heart reveals itself beyond political skills.
In this age of austerity
The poor die for others' prosperity.
Nurseries and libraries fade from the land.
A strange time is shaping on the strand.
A sword of fate hangs over the deafness of power.
See the tower, and let a new world-changing thought flower.

1

Everyday Life and Death in the Global City

Dan Bulley

In the wealthier countries a mediocrity that hides the horrors of the rest of the world has prevailed. When those horrors release a violence that reaches into our cities and our habits we're startled, we're alarmed. Last year I was dying of fear and I made long phone calls to Dede, to Elsa, even to Pietro, when I saw on television the planes that set the towers in New York ablaze the way you light a match by gently striking the head. In the world below is the inferno.

Elena Ferrante, *The Story of the Lost Child*

The response to the 9/11 attacks in New York has been wide, violent and long-lasting, including an unwinnable global war and the deaths of hundreds of thousands across the world. Despite the burning of Grenfell Tower bearing many similarities to that of the World Trade Center – an intense fire in a high-rise; victims forced to jump to their deaths; a confused emergency response; and the solidarity of a local community – the reaction to the two events has been markedly different (Edkins, 2019). For Grenfell, the response has been thoroughly domesticated. Both the causes of the fire and the ways of holding those responsible to account have been consistently kept within the confines of the UK as a state, society and legal system. As the MP and campaigner David Lammy puts it, the fire resulted from 'a nation where the social contract between the state and the individual [has] broken down'; the response must be 'putting those responsible for the horror in the dock of the Old Bailey' (2017). What this ignores is the way that both events took place in global cities that pride themselves on drawing in and reaching out to the rest of the world. Whatever happens in London and New York has global origins and implications. When the 'horrors of the rest of the world' reach into 'our' cities, 'our' cities have also stretched out to produce those very horrors, both there and far beyond.

One way in which the response has been similar, however, has been the characterisation of both as exceptional events: 9/11 was quickly interpreted as a rupture in world politics (Booth and Dunne, 2002). In a different register, even a year on from what we know was a predictable and preventable fire, news agencies and media outlets continued to characterise Grenfell as a 'tragedy'. Tragedy implies something beyond intentionality, something to which any response is inadequate as it escapes the ways in which we try to make sense of the world (Zehfuss, 2018: 37–38). A tragedy is unexpected and inexplicable, exceeding everyday life and business-as-usual. Such a characterisation of Grenfell effectively hides the fact that it was foreseen by residents (Platt, 2017). Far from the opposite of business-as-usual, the Grenfell Tower fire was the anticipated result of a long history of everyday decisions, errors, exercises of power and violence. This deadly blaze was the outcome of a more banal inferno in the world below.

The danger of accepting these two characterisations of Grenfell – as domestic and as exceptional – is that they are simplifying, restricting our ability to respond to wider causes and forces at work. Confronted with an exceptional tragedy, we search for a singular or collective villain, someone or something who is ultimately accountable. And as a domestic disaster, we look to the state and its legal system to hold them liable. In contrast, this chapter argues that as an everyday product of global political, economic and social forces, we need to supplement this with a much broader response. The chapter proceeds by first outlining how global politics and economics are always implicated in life and death in cities such as London. The second and third sections will tie this in to the Grenfell Tower fire, exploring how migration, racial segregation, the orthodoxy of international political economy and multinational corporations materially constituted it. The final section will conclude the chapter by turning to accountability and responsibility, demonstrating how these are even more refracted, complex and difficult to trace through an array of international corporations, institutions and networks than has been acknowledged in much of the existing journalistic and academic commentary. Faced with this, the promise of inquiries and man-slaughter trials at the Old Bailey seem insufficient. In addition (*not* instead), a much broader and deeper response is required, reflecting our own complicity in global political and economic structures that allows, feeds upon and erases the everyday struggles of life and death.

Life, Death and the Everyday

The 'everyday' is so mundane because it is characterised by repeti-tions, some of which are cyclical and others linear (Lefebvre, 1987: 9–10). Whilst the linear refers to the 'repetitive gestures of work and consumption', the cyclical repetitions include those of night and day, work and rest, hunger and its satisfaction, life and death. The particular ways in which these repetitions are performed – the jobs we have; what we consume and how; the hours we work; the leisure activities available; what we eat; where we live and in what type of housing; how we die and when – are a product of various forces that are particular to time and place. Our banal everyday existence is not a naturally occurring, uniform phenomenon; it is a *product* of political and economic decisions which are rarely within our control, or even within that of the city or state in which we live.

It is commonly observed in academic scholarship that everyday life in cities such as New York, London and Tokyo is the result of global flows and movements that includes goods, services, labour, ideas, finance and capital (Dürrschmidt, 2000; Eade, 1997). Major cities have long been spaces in which these flows meet, cross and diverge – where the repetitions of the everyday are especially affected by global forces. Some cities also function with a capacity for commanding and controlling the flows of international finance, labour and capital, and this is what helps define truly 'global' cities (Sassen, 2001). Such global cities did not occur naturally, however. They are the product of decisions made primarily from the 1980s to deregulate Western economies, allowing the free flowing of capital across borders, priva-tising public services and prompting innovation in the legal, banking, business, financial services and insurance industries (Massey, 2007:

29–53). Due to the UK being at the forefront of this neoliberalising wave, London was able to take a significant role in commanding these global flows. This ability is also part of what draws more people in to London, from all over the world, further feeding the production of the global-urban, where the local and the global are closely entangled. In such an environment, the repetitions and material needs of everyday life – including food and drink, jobs, transport, infrastructure, health care and shelter – are met or not met, but are always affected by transnational movements (Amin and Thrift, 2002: 70–71).

However, whilst the global nature of everyday life in many cities is commonly accepted, far less attention is given to the global production of death. How we die and when appears a strangely local, private and apolitical affair – determined only by home-grown health politics, economics and inequalities. There are two obvious exceptions to this: when death is intentionally produced through the physical violence of war, massacre or terrorism; and when it is the outcome of spectacular environmental catastrophe. In the former case, such as 9/11, the London bombings of July 2005 or the Paris attacks of November 2015, there is a great deal of effort to externalise the death, to make its cause appear foreign, the unstable outside reaching in to our cities (Bulley, 2017: 147–155). In the latter case, such as the Asian Tsunami of 2004 or the 2010 Haitian earthquake, it is the lack of intentionality and human agency that warrants international attention and aid efforts (Zack, 2009: 1–5). But when premature death is more mundane, seemingly the result of individual, corporate or government errors, it is comfortably domesticated, more or less easily insulated in its causes and effects from the outside world. However, if everyday life in the global city is made possible by transnational forces, it is odd to think that the same does not apply to death. Even at the most practical, end of life care in the West is often provided by people from elsewhere, especially mobile women (Raghuram, 2016), and this fact is intensified in global cities. In London, 56 per cent of care assistants were foreign-born by 2004/2005, compared to only 11 per cent nationally (Wills et al., 2010: 42–43).

The ignorance of premature mortality is problematic because its patterns reveal important elements of the social, ethical and political world, mapping relations of class, (dis)ability, inequality, violence, gender and race (Therborn, 2013). I shall explore this in the next section, with specific reference to the Royal Borough of Kensington and Chelsea (RBKC). Yet, whilst everyday death requires more attention, it is hard to characterise the deaths of Grenfell Tower residents as mundane and banal. As noted, this was a major event and was covered as such by news networks around the world. However, by treating it as a one-off event, we obscure the fact that it is the product of everyday global forces that come to ground in the global city. We domesticate it and search for responsibility and accountability at the national level. The next two sections will therefore concentrate on drawing out how routine, complex, transnational power relations operated within the locale of RBKC to engender this apparently singular event.

The Global Production of North Kensington

Reflecting on the changing nature of North Kensington, former local resident Ed Vulliamy (2017) describes a constantly changing space formed by successive waves of migration. He describes how much of the area was settled and even built by Irish in the nineteenth century, later supplemented by refugees from Franco's Spain in the 1940s. Over subsequent decades, many others fleeing wars of independence (e.g. Bangladeshis in the 1970s), ethnic cleansing (e.g. East African Asians in the 1970s) and failed uprisings (e.g. the 2011 Arab uprisings) would find refuge in the area. In the 1950s, North Kensington received the Windrush generation, supplying the labour that literally allowed the city to reproduce itself (many found work in the NHS) and circulate its labour and goods and services (London Transport was another major employer). This multicultural mix would be supplemented by white Bohemians seeking alternative lifestyles in the 1960s. As housing became increasingly commodified in the 1980s, however, property speculators began to regenerate the area, raising rent and property prices. What Vulliamy calls a 'social cleansing' led to hundreds of families leaving altogether, whilst others were pushed further north into social housing around Latimer Road and Golborne 'if they were lucky'.

Movement into RBKC and London more broadly, however, did not stop with these rising property prices. Indeed, the neoliberal orthodoxy of political economy of which property speculation was a part may have started in the UK and North America, but its biggest impact was felt by 'developing' countries in the Global South, which were forced by international organisations to adopt a deregulating market economy, friendly to business and hostile to stable labour relations and permanent employment. The result was a massive increase in movement from South to North, with people seeking greater socio-economic security and post-colonial governments happy to offload surplus labour (Wills et al., 2010: 2–17). Global cities, with their constant need for a cheap labour supply, their transient and settled migrant populations and willingness to turn a blind eye to migration status, proved a 'natural' destination. They facilitated everyday life, allowing work and leisure alongside people in a similar situation, while the anonymity of global cities made them an accommodating choice. However, in wealthy boroughs such as RBKC, the only environment where housing could be found was the more deprived wards, such as Notting Dale, to which the foreign-born and less affluent residents had already been pushed.

Given this history and present, it is hardly surprising that the victims of the Grenfell Tower fire moved to the area from all over the world: Afghanistan, Australia, Bangladesh, Dominican Republic, Egypt, Eritrea, Ethiopia, Gambia, India, Iran, Ireland, Italy, Lebanon, Morocco, Philippines, Sierra Leone, Sudan, Syria, the UK and possibly Nigeria (*The Guardian*, 2018).[1] Many of the victims and survivors were a tiny proportion of London's 3.2 million border-crossing people, nearly half of whom reside in the mere 319 square kilometres of differentially deprived inner London (Rienzo and Vargas-Silva, 2017: 4). It is crucial to bear this variable deprivation in mind in demonstrating the global production of the Grenfell fire. After all, RBKC as a whole has one of the most diverse populations in the UK; more than half of its people moved to the UK from elsewhere. Yet whereas nearly a quarter of RBKC residents were born in North America and Europe, this proportion is halved again for Notting Dale – the Ward that includes Grenfell Tower. In contrast, Notting Dale has twice the proportion of people from the Caribbean and African regions (Baker, 2012: 3; RBKC, 2014: 4). Compared to the wider borough, Notting Dale's population is raced substantially darker.

These figures are mirrored by the deprivation statistics, with Notting Dale consistently appearing twice as socio-economically deprived as RBKC and London overall (RBKC, 2014: 6). What emerges in the borough's Strategic Needs Assessment is a graphic mapping of the area (see Figure 1) in which the south and centre are described as 'Aspiring and Affluent', whilst four northern wards are designated an overwhelmingly 'Endeavouring Ethnic Mix'. The latter term refers to a region with a high proportion of Bangladeshis (relative to more affluent Indians), with a majority of social housing (71 per cent), where 'overcrowding is more prevalent, and public transport more commonly used to get to work' (RKBC, 2014: 6). Though a modern, cosmopolitan global city, London's everyday spatial politics is based on a form of racial and socio-economic segregation that replicates the colonial philosophies of urban planning in British and French Africa (see Njoh, 2008).

Unlike colonial urban planning, this segregation may not be intentional – there is no authority explicitly orchestrating it from

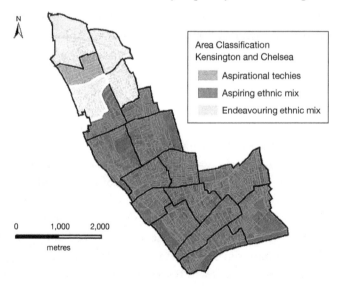

Figure 1.1 Notting Dale Area Classification – 'Endeavouring Ethnic Mix' (RKBC, 2014: 6) (© Crown copyright and database rights 2014 Ordnance Survey 100021668)

above, based in a theoretical model of racial and class hierarchies. But neither is it accidental – it is part of what Nadine El-Enany refers to as the colonial logic of the fire (Chapter 3). This logic is, in my reading, beyond intentionality, an underlying rationale engrained within countless small decisions of government and business-as-usual. What it demonstrates is the way that the techniques of colonial domination are being applied to everyday life in the global city with deadly effects (Davies, 2016: 22). The city produces and reproduces itself through the cyclical and linear repetitions of production and consumption, living and dying, drawing migrants in from the Global South and sheltering them in diverse communities where they can be contained and neglected, separated from the super-wealthy by invisible barriers. Through these everyday repetitions, functions and flows, the global city contributes to the replication of everyday life and death in the other societies and markets to which it is connected through the movements of capital, goods, services, dominant ideas and policies that it directs. The differences in housing, wealth and health between Notting Dale and RBKC are in many ways 'broadly representative of a global reality in which racialized "Others of Europe" remain largely impoverished, spatially marginalised and excluded from dignified housing in cities across the world' (Tilley and Shilliam, 2018: 534–535).

The Global Production of Grenfell Tower

Migration and segregation show how human transnational move-ments contributed to the make-up of this disaster, but the material causes of the fire are also global in their scope. Indeed, much media attention was drawn to the migration status of victims and survivors, but the role of multinational corporations has been comparatively underplayed. These corporations played a range of different roles, from the most immediate but banal to the more detached but significant. The former group would most clearly include Whirlpool Corp, the US-based company that owns the Hotpoint brand of fridge-freezer which malfunctioned, causing a fire. However, when this particular model (FF175BP) was manufactured between 2006–2009, Hotpoint had been owned by an Italian company, Indesit, which built them in

8

Italy, Poland and the UK (Morales and Ryan, 2017). This gives an immediate sense of how the material goods, such as fridge-freezers, that support everyday life (as well as death) are the outcome of global supply chains, manufacturing, branding and ownership.

However, ultimately such a comparatively minor fire should not have caused a major loss of life and this drew investigators' attention to the reasons the fire spread so quickly and trapped residents without an escape route – how a site of everyday life became a death trap. Most media attention has focused on the refurbishment of the Tower between 2015–2016 that prompted several complaints from residents, which ultimately foretold the potential of a major fire (Platt, 2017), though the public inquiry has not yet reached the refurbishment at the time of writing. While Kensington and Chelsea Tenant Management Organisation (KCTMO) oversaw this work, four contractors were appointed to manage and undertake it, including the French-owned cost-cutting specialist, Artelia, a global project management consultancy group (Davies, 2017). The lead contractor however, was the British firm, Rydon. The Rydon group then subcontracted major elements of the refurbishment to a wide range of multinationals, who often further subcontracted them, such that by April 2018 Scotland Yard were apparently investigating up to 500 different companies and organisations (Cohen, 2018).

Most controversially, Rydon paid Harley Facades Ltd over £2.5 million (over a quarter of the entire budget) to provide and install the tower's new cladding (Davies, 2017). Harley bought the ACM (Aluminium Composite Material) panels used on Grenfell from Omnis Exteriors, a group with subsidiaries in the UK and USA, but the particular ACM panels used, known as Reynobond PE (poly-ethylene), were manufactured in France by Arconic, an American multinational. The more expensive version of this panel (£2 extra per square metre), known as Reynobond FR (fire resistant), was passed-up in favour of the non-fire retardant variety (Davies, Connolly and Sample, 2017). These border-crossing panels are thought to have played a key role in the spread of the fire, but especially when combined with the layer of insulation behind the panels and the way they were installed by Harley. The cavity between the panels and the insulation appears to have been too big at 50 mm, creating a 'chimney effect', providing oxygen and channelling smoke and fire up through the building (Booth and Grierson, 2017). Meanwhile, the insulation material, called RS5000, was bought by Harley from another multinational, Celotex. According to a BBC (2018) *Panorama* investigation, the RS5000 insulation supplied by Celotex was deliberately mis-sold to Harley, despite Celotex knowing it had not passed the requisite safety tests when combined with non-fire resistant panels and that its plastic foam constitution would give off toxic cyanide fumes when burnt. These decisions and materials are especially significant; most of the victims died of smoke inhalation.[2]

Ultimately, the cost-savings provided by these choices would allow Artelia to bring the budget for the refurbishment down from £9.2 million to £8.65 (Booth and Grierson, 2017). Whilst these choices may demonstrate the global causes of the fire and its deadliness, they do not account for the causes of those causes. Why such a confusing array of contractors and subcontractors? Why was a private organisation, KCTMO, overseeing the refurbishment? Why didn't RBKC carry out its own renovation with a proper budget? After all, Rydon were only appointed after the initial contractors approached refused, due to the paltry £10m budget (Apps, 2017a). The causes of the causes have their roots in decisions taken years and sometimes decades earlier, many justified in terms of the neoliberal economic orthodoxy begun in the 1980s, which sought to make the UK a less regulated, more competitive venue for foreign investment and global corporations. A range of ideologically driven reforms in this period saw competition introduced into protected and heavily regulated industries and freed up the financial flows that, as noted above, helped make London into a truly global city (Tilley and Shilliam, 2018; Massey, 2007).

Crucially in this context, competitive market mechanisms reached public sector housing provision by the 1990s, with 'compulsory competitive tendering' allowing private firms to bid for public service delivery in an attempt to reduce costs and improve efficiency (Apps, 2017c). Central government required councils to contract out the management of their housing stock by 1999, leading to a huge stock transfer to housing association management across the UK. The aim was to reduce the size of the welfare state, justified through a 'logic of no alternative' in the context of a competitive globalised political economy (Hay, 1999). Under this logic, globalisation cannot be stopped or negotiated; all a state can do is make their economy more lean and flexible, reducing taxes and government expenditure, keeping wage inflation and interest rates low, and competing for foreign investment to increase productivity. The everyday life of social housing was thus privatised and RBKC lost control due to the same neoliberal decisions that saw London transformed into a global financial hub and an accommodating host for mobile people. However, this valuable housing stock was to be protected from being sold-off by a housing association through the creation of private organisations called tenant management organisations (TMO) – non-profit companies that would give tenants and leaseholders the responsibility for managing their own estates and homes in exchange for council management and maintenance fees.

KCTMO was therefore set up in 1996 as the only such borough-wide body in the UK, managing over 9,000 homes, with any major works (over £400,000) requiring approval from the council. This was a complex process, driven by ideological claims about making the UK competitive in the global market place. But it is what ultimately brought RBKC and KCTMO to the legally required tendering of bids for the renovation of Grenfell Tower. The need for cost-cutting, however, was deepened by more recent decisions. Under a renewing of the 'no alternative' claims generated by the global financial crisis of 2008, the coalition government imposed austerity measures, which included a cap on local government borrowing from 2012 (Apps, 2017b). This meant that even infrastructure investment, such as the Grenfell renovation, needed to be financed by the sale of assets. The work was therefore largely financed by the sale of RBKC-owned basements in Fulham, generating £8m, nearly the entire budget (Apps, 2017a).

This cost-cutting, the capping of borrowing, the introduction of competition and privatisation of housing stock was obviously not *intended* to produce a major conflagration and loss of life. Just as with the spatial politics and racial segregation of RBKC described earlier, the fire was not an intentional outcome, but neither can it be characterised as an accident. It was rather a predictable if unnecessary outworking and everyday implementation of decades-old decisions, global financial climates, poor regulation, complex webs of transnational subcontracting, planning, design and installation errors. The Grenfell Tower fire was an intricate product of an international political economy, partially directed from the global city of London, that prized cost savings over human life. Intentionally or otherwise, the flows that constitute the city had the power to determine everyday life and death: who lived, who died, where and how. But where does responsibility lie in this picture? And how does its globality affect our ability to respond to Grenfell as an unintentional but non-accidental atrocity?

Responding to the Fire

The baffling layers of decisions, transnational subcontracting and manufacturing involved in major infrastructure projects in cities produces a tangled web of responsibility which makes accountability very hard to determine. We could see this in the immediate aftermath of the fire. Harley's website quickly included a brief statement acknowledging its role in the refurbishment but also noting that the ACM panels used were common within the industry and not manufactured by themselves (Harley Facades, 2017). Likewise, Omnis Exteriors issued a statement five days after the fire through its subsidiary, CEP Architectural Facades, stressing that they neither manufactured Reynobond PE, nor did they select it for the job: 'CEP's role was limited to fulfilling the order for components to the specification, design and choice of material provided by the design and build contracting team' (2017). Arconic's response was to withdraw Reynobond PE from sale to high-rise refurbishments worldwide, claiming that this was due to 'inconsistency of building codes across the world' (in BBC, 2017). Whirlpool Corp quickly released a statement noting that they had not manufactured the Hotpoint fridge-freezer that began the fire (Morales and Ryan, 2017). Even the financial liability for the fire was not straightforward: whilst Grenfell Tower was insured by Protector Forsikring, a Norwegian company, the cost will largely be covered by Germany's Munich Re, which is liable through a reinsurance process (Skonnord, 2017; Taruc, 2017).

Whilst a tracking and tracing of legal accountability and responsibility remains of the utmost importance, putting companies 'in the dock of the Old Bailey' cannot be the limit of our response. Nor, I would suggest, is it enough to engage in moralising critiques which determine who *ought* to be held morally accountable, regardless of strict legal liability. This would be to tackle the immediate causes of the fire, but not the everyday causes of those causes – the structures of global political economy, which both enable life and allow people to die. It would be to domesticate our response, treating Grenfell Tower as if it were an exceptional one-off, but one that could be handled through the traditional legal avenues and comforting bureaucracy provided by the state, such as a public inquiry, corporate manslaughter charges and reviews of building regulations and fire safety laws. Yet, as we have seen, this conflagration was the product of a much wider 'inferno below', an everyday inferno that spans continents and cannot be so easily contained by the state.

This inferno created a situation in which people came from all over the world to a global city, were offered social housing in an exceptionally wealthy, racially and socio-economically segregated borough, only to be killed through a combination of abandonment and disregard emerging from multinational industry, government and globally sanctioned policy choices. The seduction of the everyday and its repetitions lies in its ability to generate an 'organized passivity', where we become observers of events, accepters of decisions taken elsewhere (Lefebvre, 1987: 10). Relying on trials and inquiries leaves us as just such passive observers; instead, we can take this opportunity to reflect on how Grenfell might shake us out of this passivity, considering a much broader response to how the atrocity was produced. I would suggest that this broader response would require at least four elements, developing on and adapting Susan Marks' exploration of how to draw out the root causes of massive human rights abuses (2011: 74–78).

First, we may benefit from an anti-moralistic account which considers that, while perhaps unintentional, these catastrophes like Grenfell would not occur if they weren't benefiting some groups, just as they destroy others (Marks, 2011: 69). Instead of asking what governments, TMOs and contractors *should* be doing then, we need to ask why they are doing some things and failing to do others; who is benefiting from these arrangements, such as austerity policies, the segregation of boroughs, the mis-selling of products and a lax regulatory regime? The directors of Rydon, Harley and Celotex make money from cutting corners, but what about stock-holders? What about those of us who benefit from the low interest rates on mortgages, maintained by austerity politics, or the rising property prices of gentrified areas? Asking these questions could be profoundly uncomfortable for many of us who do not feel implicated in the Grenfell fire, as it involves questioning our personal roles within property and mortgage markets, the use of urban space, the insurance industry, patterns of voting and community activism, as well as the investment of our pension funds. Have we benefited from the precarious life and death of Grenfell victims and those like them across the globe? I am sure I have.

Second, we need to pay closer attention to the 'relational character of social phenomena'. For Marks, this means exploring not just victims and perpetrators, but also beneficiaries, as noted above (2011: 76). But we can also push this relationality further, in different directions. Global cities, their spaces, populations and infrastructure are produced through interactions and flows of people and things from all over the world. The city depends upon these flows in order to reproduce, feed and shelter itself; they enable the repetitions of everyday life. But the city, and the state within which it is embedded, appears to take little responsibility for the way these flows affect other spaces elsewhere, nor for how the interactions internal to the city are organised and arranged to exclude and exploit, liberate and constrain, making live and letting die. As Doreen Massey (2004) argues, the relational character of social phenomena demands wider 'geographies of responsibility', including an account of London's parasitical reliance on the Global South (initially through coloni-alism and slavery, subsequently through exploitation of irregular migrants and the brain drain of medical professionals). Likewise, a broader response would detail the way in which the wealth of South Kensington depends upon the mundane, repetitious labour of the areas of 'endeavouring ethnic mix' to the north. We need to widen our frames of responsibility.

Therefore, a third aspect of responding to Grenfell would place an emphasis on *materialist* explanations (Marks, 2011: 76). This includes exploring how the socio-economic conditions that led to damaging ideas – such as austerity, marketisation and the logic of no alternative – gaining influence and acceptance, in order to challenge their material outcomes. But it also involves investigating how everyday life in the global city is materially sustained – through food, water, transportation, health care, infrastructure – and what international ties of obligation and responsibility this generates towards the people who produce that food, provide that care, clean those offices. How does London contribute to the material socio-economic conditions (including inequality, scarcity and conflagrations) across the globe through its role as a sustaining node of 'command and control' within global flows of capital, goods, finance, ideas and labour?

Finally, any such broader response would require a *'repoliticizing* thrust'. For Marks, this is about strategy, the task of 'channelling grievances into organized and coherent action' (2011: 76–77). This may involve attempts to link the Notting Dale community's activism (see Renwick, Chapter 2; Charles, Chapter 10; and RHN, Chapter 4 in this volume) to campaigns for adequate social housing and justice for victims and survivors of 'accidental' urban expulsions across the world. It may not involve any such grand, unifying strategy, but rather aim in a number of smaller-scale ways to disorganise the passivity and numbing effects of everyday urban existence. This could include a variety of minor actions – from mortgaging and pension decisions to the occupations, protests – that seek to repoliticise the local in the global and vice versa, to disturb the foundations of indifference, the domestication of response and the reliance on the state to determine liability. Any adequate repoliticisation would be about making it harder for atrocities based in segregation, carelessness and disregard to happen again by keeping a forensic eye on the relational character of everyday life and death in the global city.

Notes

1. The nationality of Vincent Chiejina, 60 years old when he died, is unknown. These *Guardian* (2018) pen portraits identify Alexandra Atala and Victoria

King as British, although Australia's Department of Foreign Affairs and Trade claimed them as Australian citizens (ABC, 2018).

2. These were by no means the only failings involved in the refurbishment (see Cohen, 2018; Slawson, 2018; Barnes, 2018; Booth, 2017). They are emphasised here because of the role played by multinational corporations and the culture of subcontracting.

References

ABC (2018) 'Two Australians among Grenfell Tower Victims, DFAT Confirm'. *ABC News*, 26 April. www.abc.net.au/news/2018-04-26/two-australians-among-grenfell-tower-blaze-victims/9698564 (all websites in this list last accessed November 2018).

Amin, A. and N. Thrift (2002) *Cities: Reimagining the Urban.* Cambridge: Polity Press.

Apps, P. (2017a) 'Grenfell: The Paper Trail'. *Inside Housing*, 11 August. www.insidehousing.co.uk/news/news/grenfell-the-paper-trail-51907.

Apps, P. (2017b) 'Grenfell Refurbishment Budget was Limited by Borrowing Cap'. 11 August. www.insidehousing.co.uk/news/grenfell-refurbishment-budget-was-limited-by-borrowing-cap-51906.

Apps, P. (2017c) 'A Look at the History of KCTMO'. *Inside Housing*, 7 September. www.insidehousing.co.uk/insight/insight/a-look-at-the-history-of-kctmo-52300.

Baker, D. (2012) 'Census 2011: Kensington and Chelsea'. The Royal Borough of Kensington and Chelsea, 11 December. www.rbkc.gov.uk/pdf/Census%20 2011%20key%20statistics.pdf.

Barnes, S. (2018) 'Morning Briefing: Grenfell Tower Fire Prompts Gas Safety Investigation'. *Inside Housing*, 12 April. www.insidehousing.co.uk/news/news/morning-briefing-grenfell-tower-fire-prompts-gas-pipe-investigation-55739.

BBC (2017) 'Grenfell Tower: Cladding Firm Ends Global Sales for Tower Blocks'. *BBC News*, 26 June. www.bbc.co.uk/news/uk-40409981.

BBC (2018) 'Grenfell Tower Insulation 'Never Passed Fire Safety Test'. *BBC News*, 21 May. www.bbc.co.uk/news/uk-44200041.

Booth, K. and T. Dunne (eds) (2002) *Worlds in Collision: Terror and the Future of Global Order.* Basingstoke: Palgrave Macmillan.

Booth, R. (2017) 'Flammable Grenfell Tower cladding "passed" by council officer in 2015', *The Guardian*, 14 July. www.theguardian.com/uk-news/2017/jul/14/grenfell-tower-cladding-passed-by-council-officers-in-2015.

Booth, R. and J. Grierson (2017) 'Grenfell cladding approved by residents was swapped for cheaper version', *The Guardian*, 30 June. www.theguardian.com/uk-news/2017/jun/30/grenfell-cladding-was-changed-to-cheaper-version-reports-say.

Bulley, D. (2017) *Migration, Ethics and Power: Spaces of Hospitality in International Politics.* London: Sage.

CEP Architectural Facades (2017) 'Statement from CEP Architectural Facades'. 19 June. http://omnisexteriors.com/division/statement-cep-architectural-facades/.

Cohen, D. (2018) 'Leaked Grenfell Dossier Reveals How Disastrous Refurbishment Turned Tower into a "Tinderbox"'. *Evening Standard*, 16 April. www.standard.co.uk/news/london/shock-grenfell-dossier-reveals-disastrous-refurbishment-turned-tower-into-a-tinderbox-a3814866.html.

Davies, M. (2016) 'Everyday Life as Critique: Revisiting the Everyday in IPE with Henri Lefebvre and Postcolonialism'. *International Political Sociology*, 10(1): 22–38.

Davies, R. (2017) 'Complex Chain of Companies That Worked on Grenfell Tower Raises Oversight Concerns'. *The Guardian*, 16 June. www.theguardian.com/uk-news/2017/jun/15/long-builder-chain-for-grenfell-a-safety-and-accountability-issue.

Davies, R., K. Connolly and I. Sample (2017) 'Cladding for Grenfell Tower was Cheaper, More Flammable Option'. *The Guardian*, 16 June. www.theguardian.com/uk-news/2017/jun/16/manufacturer-of-cladding-on-grenfell-tower-identified-as-omnis-exteriors.

Dürrschmidt, J. (2000) *Everyday Lives in the Global City: The Delinking of Locale and Milieu*. London: Routledge.

Eade, D. (ed.) (1997) *Living the Global City: Globalization as a Local Process*. London: Routledge.

Edkins, J. (2019) *Change and the Politics of Certainty*. Manchester: Manchester University Press.

The Guardian (2018) 'The Lives of Grenfell Tower'. *The Guardian*, 14 May. www.theguardian.com/uk-news/ng-interactive/2018/may/14/lives-of-grenfell-tower-victims-fire.

Harley Facades (2017) 'Statement from Harley Facades Limited'. *Harley*, 14 June. www.harleyfacades.co.uk/page/8031/article/727.

Hay, C. (1999) *The Political Economy of New Labour: Labouring Under False Pretences?* Manchester: Manchester University Press.

Lammy, D. (2017) 'Those Responsible for the Grenfell Tower Fire Must Face Trial'. *The Guardian*, 26 December. www.theguardian.com/commentisfree/2017/dec/26/grenfell-tower-fire-david-lammy.

Lefebvre, H. (1987), 'The Everyday and Everydayness'. *Yale French Studies*, 73: 7–11.

Marks, S. (2011) 'Human Rights and Root Causes'. *Modern Law Review*, 74(1): 57–78.

Massey, D. (2004) 'Geographies of Responsibility'. *Geografiska Annaler*, 86B(1): 5–18.

Massey, D. (2007) *World City*. Cambridge: Polity Press.

Morales, A. and C. Ryan (2017) 'Whirlpool Fridge Started London's Grenfell Tower Fire that Killed at least 79'. *Insurance Journal*, 26 June. www.insurancejournal.com/news/international/2017/06/26/455673.htm.

Njoh, A. J. (2008) 'Colonial Philosophies, Urban Space, and Racial Segregation in British and French Colonial Africa'. *Journal of Black Studies*, 38(4): 579–599.

Platt, E. (2017) 'Grenfell Tower: Chronicle of a Tragedy Foretold'. *New Statesman*, 9 October. www.newstatesman.com/politics/uk/2017/10/grenfell-tower-chronicle-tragedy-foretold.

Raghuram, P. (2016) 'Migration and Feminist Care Ethics', in A. Sager (ed.), *The Ethics and Politics of Immigration: Core Issues and Emerging Trends*. London: Rowman & Littlefield, 206–225.

Rienzo, C. and C. Vargas-Silva (2017) 'Migrants in the UK: An Overview'. 6th Revision, *Migration Observatory briefing*. COMPAS, University of Oxford, 21 February. www.migrationobservatory.ox.ac.uk/wp-content/uploads/2017/02/Briefing-Migrants_UK_Overview.pdf.

Royal Borough of Kensington and Chelsea (RKBC) (2014) 'Notting Dale Ward Profile'. RKBC Census 2011 profiles by ward. www.rbkc.gov.uk/pdf/Notting%20Daledata.pdf.

Sassen, S. (2001) *The Global City: New York, London, Tokyo*, 2nd edn. Princeton, NJ: Princeton University Press.

Skonnord, O. P. (2017) 'Grenfell Tower Insurer, Protector Forsikring, Raises Claims Estimate to $65m'. *Insurance Journal*, 10 July. www.insurancejournal.com/news/international/2017/07/10/457071.htm.

Slawson, N. (2018) 'Kensington Council to Spend £3.5m Replacing Fire Doors after Grenfell'. *The Guardian*, 30 May. www.theguardian.com/uk-news/2018/may/30/grenfell-kensington-chelsea-council-replace-fire-doors-social-housing.

Taruc, P. (2017) 'Grenfell Tower Reaction: Insurers Mulling Higher Rates for Substandard Tower Blocks'. *Insurance Business UK*, 25 October. www.insurancebusinessmag.com/uk/news/breaking-news/grenfell-tower-reaction-insurers-mulling-higher-rates-for-substandard-tower-blocks-82859.aspx.

Therborn, G. (2013) *The Killing Fields of Inequality*. Cambridge: Polity Press.

Tilley, L. and R. Shilliam (2018) 'Raced Markets: An Introduction'. *New Political Economy*, 23(5), 534–543.

Vulliamy, E. (2017) 'Apartheid London: Social Cleansing Ruined the Minestrone Streets I Grew Up In'. *The Observer*, 18 June. www.theguardian.com/uk-news/2017/jun/17/apartheid-notting-hill-grenfell-tower-development-social-cleansing.

Wills, J., K. Datta, Y. Evans, J. Herbert, J. May and C. McIlwaine (2010) *Global Cities at Work: New Migrant Divisions of Labour*. London: Pluto Press.

Zack, N. (2009) *Ethics for Disaster*. Lanham, MD: Rowman & Littlefield.

Zehfuss, M. (2018) *War and the Politics of Ethics*. Oxford: Oxford University Press.

2

Organising on Mute

Daniel Renwick

The role of the nation-state changed from that of a mediator between a national capitalist class and its labour force to a transmission line between global capital and a local population.

(Kundnani, 2007)

Power concedes nothing without a demand, Frederick Douglass famously said. These words were echoed in the wake of the fire by community journalist and film-maker Ishmahil Blagrove, as he addressed a rally at the end of the first silent march (see Blagrove, 2017). They were again stated on the steps of North Kensington Library by Lowkey, as the council conceded to the demands of the community, and kept the building a public asset and library after community campaigns. It took the fire for them to bend to community demands. Despite the gains made in the wake of the fire, the compassion and humanity, the green heart and all it represents, a politics of contempt remains at the heart of governance, at a local and national level. Demands made before the fire were muted, after the fire they were not understood. An abandoned community, aghast at how poorly treated they were by the state, were used and instrumentalised by a universe of interlopers, who sought to make Grenfell an object of their struggle. Narratives framed Grenfell. Pre-established political paths were proscribed. What so many could not comprehend is that 'there is a politics in stories told truthfully', as A. Sivanandan once said.

When the redevelopment at Grenfell Tower began, residents organised to be heard. A community, ballasted by a proud local history, pursued 'truth and justice'[1] in creative fashion. They were rational, genteel and inclusive. The Grenfell Action Group had already formed, due to long-standing issues. After the redevelopment began to blight lives and angered residents, a larger group began to have meetings. They formed Grenfell Unite (not to be confused with Grenfell United, the group for survivors and bereaved formed after the fire), a group composed to fight for the rights of residents of the tower. They fought both through and against the local Labour Group. Their activism got them a meeting with their MP of the time, the Conservative Victoria Borwick, who forced the group to become a compact, a subsidiary structure to represent the interests of the tower, under the Lancaster West Residents Association (LWRA). They lobbied local power. Vocal residents blogged and held the council (The Royal Borough of Kensington and Chelsea, RBKC), and their landlord (Kensington and Chelsea Tenant Management Organisation, KCTMO) to account. They called for an independent investigation into the tower's redevelopment, by organisations with no links to RBKC or the KCTMO. They were rebuffed. The TMO investigated themselves. The council reviewed the redevelopment through the scrutiny committee, their conclusions were careless, commending the contractor Rydon and seeking to mitigate the 'inconveniences' of the refurbishment for residents (Johnson, 2016). Organised residents had petitioned for a professional body to assess the works, a document that now haunts. If their voices had been heeded and proper health and safety work undertaken, not a single life would have been taken. Instead, at least 72 people were killed.

The chair of the tower's compact was David Collins, a white professional, who works to advise large organisations around health and safety. Even he faced the structured prejudice of class contempt as he met with authorities. His appeals, protestations and demands were as muted as the rest, who were not voiceless, rather, preferably unheard and unseen, as Arundhati Roy so eloquently put it. So to make themselves heard, some broke conventions and confronted those who they felt were not listening. There was humour in their resistance at points. On one action where the community confronted the deputy leader of the council, protesters donned chicken suits. But the spectacle couldn't break through. Fateful decisions were made against the community, for the community. And the media did not care to report what was all too local, until it became global.

The callous contempt of institutional indifference can be found at all levels in the task of analysing Grenfell and the events around it. The fateful and deadly redevelopment of the tower came with the building of a school for North Kensington, the Kensington Aldridge Academy (KAA). Many saw the school's construction as a cynical attempt to circumvent the huge catchment of North Kensington at Holland Park School, a school that has been 'gentrified' according to former student Reis Morris, who recollects with a wry smile how rowdy the school was, and how he contributed to that environment. Whatever the decision-making around the procurement process was – and there is no denying how broken the chain was, given three project managers oversaw the work – KAA's development was not the same as the tower's. The tower was fatally underfunded, while the school's construction and evacuation procedures were, and remain, first rate (FDS Consult, 2018).

The first bone of contention for residents of the estate and the wider area when the developments began was Lancaster Green being eaten up. The green pitches, infamous in the area as a meeting spot and a place to kick ball for free, were also swallowed. Locals were not consulted about the development, nor were their wishes catered to. When refurbishment of the tower began, it was an inconvenience. Shoddy workmanship became obvious, though its consequences were not. Residents felt like objects in the place they lived. When they objected, they were treated as irritants and impediments. Some felt bullied (Grenfell Public Inquiry, 3 October 2018),[2] others were sent legal documents warning them to desist or face defamation proceedings. Where once there was space around the tower, there was no more. The tower's vehicular access was greatly diminished, while the disastrous decisions that were putting them at increasing risk were hidden behind a facade. Not all residents were as disturbed by the council and TMO as others, but all spoke up on their concerns and pressed to be heard.

Any discourse of preventability around Grenfell hinges on the voices of truth speaking and those in power acting. Yet, for all of the contrition and guilt expressed in the wake of Grenfell, most famously articulated by Channel 4's Jon Snow, who spoke passionately on his desires to amplify local voices in the future, this struggle has not been undertaken in earnest. Thousands across the country are at risk, in similar conditions to Grenfell Tower. They remain on mute. We may see them block a road on London Live or read of their activism in *Manchester Evening News*, but we don't hear their voices on national media, nor the politics forged by the expression of their truth. The logics that bred Grenfell doggedly persist, both in the state and the battle for justice.

Building with Petrol – Callous Indifference and the Market State

The raw matter that collided to create the disaster of Grenfell still crashes around, threatening life in ways that cannot be quantified, belying the statistical analysis of state, which read the decrease in deaths from fire to be due to fire safety standards. Grenfell showed there to be no such standards. Many across the country now know viscerally that the market state doesn't fulfil its duties and they are at risk.

Almost 500 public buildings, amongst them hospitals and schools – but mostly homes – are wrapped in the equivalent of solidified petrol in England and Wales (Tobin, 2018). None are in Scotland. An ambiguity in a housing regulation lets business do its own safety tests, away from any labs. These 'desktop studies', coupled with a disintegration and privatisation of the regulatory frameworks, led to a huge public health crisis that portends a far deeper political crisis. Not only is there a huge risk of infernos at a national level, there are the long-term health effects of the toxins released when insulation and plastics burn.[3]

Austerity alone does not account for Grenfell. The very nature of regulation in the era of neoliberalism must be questioned, as *Inside Housing*'s 'Paper Trail' demonstrates (Apps, Barnes and Barratt, 2018). The coalition government's statement in 2011, One in One Out, puts it simply. The government pledged to 'remove or simplify regulation that impedes growth', while promising to only regulate as 'a last resort' (HM Government, 2011). Cracks in the system were bred by design. With regulation seen as anti-business, rolling back regulations and the state's control was taken as good economics. These attitudes antedate the Tories being in power. It was a small change in phrasing in fire regulations, put into wording by New Labour, that allowed for desktop studies, which was exploited by the private sector. Flammable cladding was sold by the ton, under the watch of both sides of the House of Commons. Once applied to blocks, structurally sound buildings – some new – became death traps. After the fire at Grenfell, when forensic tests were conducted on the materials clad to buildings across the country deemed potentially dangerous, there was a 100 per cent fail rate (Sparrow, 2018).

Despite thousands of people being at risk of death, power could not see, hear or feel the extremities before Grenfell burned. The London Fire service did not consider cladding and insulation to present significant risk. They knew of fires in the UK and abroad spread through cladding. Consequently, duties to perform fire safety checks mentioned building exteriors, only they were advisory, Dany Cotton told the public inquiry. Despite advisements to check potential breaches of compartmentation (the way that fire is contained in high-rise buildings) – including cladding – the commissioner told the inquiry that the extensive list could not be performed by a service under so much strain (Grenfell Public Inquiry, 27 September 2018). Moreover, she argued, the fire services could not oversee what lay behind the cladding. What they couldn't see, they didn't question, and, therefore, didn't train for. They assumed that the regulation within the industry would safeguard against highly flammable materials being clad to a building, with an air gap.

The bereaved and survivors who formed Grenfell United have lobbied the government determinedly in a bid to prevent another inferno. It is a role they have played, from necessity, which shames this government. Natasha Elcock, a survivor of the fire, and now Chair of Grenfell United, told MPs 'we shouldn't be fighting for what is right for other people.' The government should have. In the immediate aftermath of the fire, Sajid Javid, at the time minister for housing, pledged to remove the cladding and insulation. Philip Hammond told the country the materials were 'technically illegal'. Yet, governmental action has been glacial since. At the Tory party conference, James Brokenshire finally announced a ban, 15 months after the fire. The survivors and bereaved had called for it immediately.

The government's moves to address the issues do not go far enough, firefighters, campaigners and architects have expressed. As Ahmed Elgwahry, a bereaved family member who lost his mother and sister at Grenfell, said in his *Inside Housing* piece: '[o]n its own, and without more, it falls well short of the root-and-branch change needed in the way fire risk assessors, designers and contractors approach fire safety' (Elgwahry, 2018). The devil is in the detail and any ambiguity allows for private interests to stretch wording to maintain their profit margins. Any lack of clarity is by extension a lack of control, and can be exploited. The Royal Institute of British Architects called for a complete ban on combustible exteriors, along with the retrofitting of sprinklers into blocks and the construction of a second means of escape (Apps, 2018). The government has not done anything close to this. In her government commissioned review, Dame Judith Hackitt called for a new regulatory framework to be created (Hackitt, 2018). The bereaved and survivors echo calls for a new testing regime that is stringent enough to prevent anything resembling the conditions at Grenfell being replicated or maintained. The recently announced ban is not retrospective. Moreover, it only applies to buildings above 18 metres, from 2020 onwards. Schools and hospitals clad with flammable and combustible materials, but below 18 metres in height, are not within its scope.

It was only after the efforts of campaigners that the government announced £400 million of public money had been made available to remove the dangerous cladding and insulation from high-rise blocks. They took the funds from the general housing budget. The cost of safer housing therefore became less homes and an inflated cost of living; the profits are still taken by a scattered network of outsourced companies. In many cases, the same companies that installed the cladding in the first place (Bergin, 2017).

Any party at 'the centre' has had to be willing to abandon the cumbersome burdens of state, and allow it to be a profitable enterprise for others. When costs are cut, and responsibility is outsourced, duty is jettisoned. As Adel, a bereaved family member, eruditely put it, 'it's health and safety culture gone mad'. The government, in essence, allowed for fuel to be doused upon buildings. In many cases, the interiors of said buildings were kindling to fire, due to underfunding and non-compliance in the procurement of materials. The cutting of red tape, forged with a mind to preserving life, can be taken as an act of violence, especially when coupled with austerity. In the case of RBKC, this was needless austerity, as they were the richest borough in London.

Processes of managed decline typified the management of social housing in North Kensington, as MP for Kensington, Emma Dent Coad, explained in *Failed by the State* (Redfish, 2017). The 'shoddy job' she suspected has already come to light in the Grenfell Public Inquiry. Nothing could stop the flames once the fire started at Grenfell. Even the fire doors were not fireproof. As detailed in Barbara Lane's extensive and expert report to the Public Inquiry, there was a 'culture of non-compliance' in regard to fire safety and prevention at Grenfell Tower (Lane, 2018). Safety in housing is a complex web, so multiple fail-safe mechanisms are inbuilt to avert disaster. Grenfell was a catastrophic failure. The cladding and insulation were the fuel for the fire, but compartmentation was breached in a number of ways.

Dany Cotton told the inquiry that any preparation for Grenfell that could have been done was of little consequence (Grenfell Public Inquiry, 27 September 2018). The fire could not have been fought. Andrew O'Loughlin, the most senior member of the fire service present at the fire, told the inquiry that people should not have been allowed to live there (24 September 2018). The fire service were profoundly shocked by the fire at Grenfell. On the night, senior officers maintained a stay put policy, which told residents to stay in the building, for an hour and twenty minutes after compartmentation had been breached, Barbara Lane's (2018) report states. They had never had a night like Grenfell. The heroism of the service members who fought the fire is recognised by all. Many are members of the community and are tormented by the open questions and wounds that remain. O'Loughlin told the inquiry 'my expectation was people who were safe in their flats should stay safe in their flats.' The fire service had never trained or planned for such a catastrophic failure. To have done so, Dany Cotton told the inquiry, would have been seen as absurd. The fire lifts did not work. The dry risers did not work. Their ladders were too short. The fire spread in ways never witnessed before. Where the fire could be fought with hoses, the rain screening of the cladding prevented the water from extinguishing fire.

The testimonies heard at the inquiry expose a lack of prepared-ness for risks that should have been known and foreseen, before disaster. The fault is not the fire service's alone. They are not the agents responsible for making a building that was safe, unsafe. The policy of 'stay put' was the right advice for Grenfell, right up until the cladding and insulation was attached. Lives had been saved through this practice prior to the fire. The market's callous indifference to life changed that. The conditions that maintain life were fatally undermined by a number of private companies, who were facilitated by national legislation and local government malfeasance. To date, no corporation or governmental body has faced justice. This led the poet Potent Whisper to dub the UK 'Grenfell Britain': a country where when the safety of people is breached, power is so compartmentalised that nobody is responsible (Potent Whisper, 2018).

Migrants, Criminals and the Rabble

According to the Grenfell Action Group, it was only the economic crisis that prevented the demolition of their homes.[4] The redevelop-ment followed, but master plans for the area continued to be drawn. Battles to maintain the conditions for working-class life were made all the harder in 2015 when Lord Adonis released his 'City Villages' report for the Progressive Policy Think Tank (the Institute for Public Policy Research). His ideas, embraced by the Conservative-led government, were to tear down the 'sink estates' and create new villages from the wreckage. As a consequence, Notting Dale's social housing was under mounting pressure. Silchester, the neighbouring housing estate to the Lancaster West Estate, faced redevelopment. Residents, inspired by the struggles at Grenfell, campaigned. Only after the fire at Grenfell and the world's attention being placed upon the local authority were they assured of their future in the area.

Despite the inspirational struggles waged around Grenfell, those who lived in the tower and kept power in check faced pernicious attacks upon their character, the details of which have yet to be disclosed through the public inquiry. Tenacious activism was dismissed as ramblings and ravings, and lurid depictions were made of community activists by local councillors. 'If you're talking about class or race and are from North Kensington, you are the great unwashed to them,' Niles Hailstones, a community activist and touring musician, told me. Hailstones constantly challenges the council and its local functionaries for institutional racism and ill-gotten wealth, which he traces all the way back to the trading of enslaved Africans.

Paradoxically, before the fire, the former leader of the council, Nicholas Paget-Brown, claimed it was the resistant community who were engaging in class warfare. At a full council meeting, attended by community activists, the council leader brushed aside contentions following the council's deal with a local private school to lease them the local library building. The public, listed building – which had been a community asset since 1891 – is a site of significance for locals. It stands in the centre of Ladbroke Grove and is seen as a testament to the municipal values of yesteryear, in an area where wealth divides are astronomical. For 127 years, it has had public use. When Paget-Brown heard words to this effect, he dismissed them as 'quaint heritage'. The library's reallocation and the historic building being handed over to private education seemed a fait accompli. Yet, despite contemptuous attitudes and defeatist logic, the Save North Kensington Library campaign has succeeded in saving the building, both as a community space and as a library. But activists know this was only because of Grenfell. In the council's letter pledging to keep the building for the foreseeable future, the letter begins by acknowledging how the disaster necessitated a change in the council's attitude and policies in North Kensington. They have changed tack to soothe the mood, but they haven't engaged in any process of reform to tackle the issues that bred the inferno.

Before the fire, a number of campaigns formed to fight their community assets being stripped.[5] They sought to save community provisions from a rapacious process of redevelopment. Various community organisations accused the local authorities of engaging in a process of arrested development, asset stripping and social cleansing. The fire vindicated some at unimaginable cost. Ed Daffarn of the Grenfell Action Group, who predicted a major disaster like a fire being the only thing to shine a light on his mistreatment, called for the council to engage in reparative processes and give back community assets. The council have conceded to this demand in a number of struggles. The case of the sale of Kensington and Chelsea College's Wornington Road campus highlighted fundamental issues in leadership and accountability in the local authority; Kroll, an international risk assessment centre, engaged by the college, concluded in October 2018. The issues were highlighted consistently in the Grenfell Action Group blog. Yet, even as the fire smouldered, the group were cast by their local ward councillors as the boy who cried wolf (Blakeman, 2017).

Casting off statutory responsibility necessitates dehumanisation. In the wake of riots, 'feral rats' bred by 'sink estates' took the blame. For the housing crisis, it is the 'benefit scroungers' and 'migrants' liable; a hostile environment created. Punitive measures were introduced across all spectrums of society, any provision for undocumented or irregular migrants a criminal act. And, then, there was terrorism. A number of young men from North Kensington went to Syria during the war, leading the national press, both broadsheet and tabloid, to dub the area a 'hotbed of extremism' (e.g. Evans, Harley and Brookes-Pollack, 2014). Attempts to undermine community activism led to the recycling of these stories, fictions and facts in the wake of fire.

All of this was compounded by the post-Brexit environment, where a London-centric mode of governance was blamed for breeding the forces that birthed Brexit. A new discourse of 'left behind' was peddled from the left and right, which denied extreme poverty and precarity in the 'cosmopolitan cities', especially London. The xenoracism and nativism that Brexit swelled, Grenfell should have compressed. Everything about Grenfell should have been a turning point in the country, opening up to the universality of the threat presented by the moment, as Robbie Shilliam argued (Shilliam, 2018). Instead, the far-right dined on the smorgasbord of contempt and prejudice. Katie Hopkins and Tommy Robinson told their huge followings that Grenfell was a state conspiracy. They decried its attention, and spoke of the cover up to mask the number of undocumented killed in the fire. Hopkins even insinuated the fire was started by people playing with combustible materials to commit terrorist attacks. Such logics, though absurd, may provide some explanation as to why the Metropolitan Police decided to send armed officers with automatic weapons patrolling the area in the immediate aftermath of the fire. The contemptuous attitudes to life in the area manifested with a gratuitous act on 5 November 2018, when at a gathering in a South London back garden fireworks display, Grenfell Tower, with black and brown children at the window, was burned to cinder.

Citizens of Nowhere and the Count

The far-right and radical left contend that the state's death toll from the fire is a cover up. To the right, the 'take over of London by illegals' explains the government's alleged crimes, whereas to the left, it is the hostile environment that unpeopled so many that they don't even count in the death toll. In the immediate aftermath, there was no signage in any language other than English for weeks. Statutory sites were ring-fenced by workers who were legislatively bound to extend a hostile environment. The government's amnesty amounted to little more than a stay of deportation. NGOs like the Red Cross took weeks to facilitate spaces outside of the state's scope. The police throughout the month of June made clear they hadn't been able to access certain sections of the community. Amidst the chaos, Grenfell was widely reported as 'the worst disaster of post-war Britain'. Given how many died in Aberfan, the Tower Hamlets stampede and Hillsborough, many took this to mean a true death toll was in the hundreds. The BBC's *Panorama* that was released a week after the fire, on 21 June 2017, estimated the occupancy of Grenfell to be 500 people. If this were true, hundreds would be dead.

The conditions of the fire meant many bodies were incinerated. It was communicated by Fiona McCormick in June 2017 that 'true death toll may never be known' (Bannerman, 2017). The police announced later that 87 human remains were removed from the tower, however, they stressed this was not indicative of the death toll. The number was reported as 'at least 79' until forensic work identified 70 missing people from the remains taken from the tower (one of the deceased had died in hospital). After a number of fraud cases concluded, the police announced that the number 'was very unlikely to change from

71'. Then the 72nd victim passed, Maria del Pilar 'Pily' Burton. She had suffered a serious deterioration of health following the fire, and it was upon the community's insistence that her name was added to the toll.

Because of the failures of administration on the part of RBKC and the KCTMO, there was no accurate list of residency to work off in the immediate aftermath. Moreover, for days, at key sites listed in the media as refuge centres, the lists of missing were being constructed by volunteers, or by the survivors themselves. Because of a lack of formal structure, and an issue around language, the transliteration of names meant many were triple counted. Excel spreadsheets being worked on at community centres listed hundreds of people missing, assumed dead. The state's discourse around the death toll confused matters. For the first few days, for reasons probably justified around social order, the death toll was downplayed. The cynicism of the state led people to think the worst.

Because of the peculiarities of this inquiry, the inquests have not been concluded at the time of writing. The state's coroner Dr Fiona Wilcox has a very good reputation amongst the bereaved and survivors. Her work has identified all those who are known to be missing. There are no new missing posters being put up, nor are there any reports of people coming into the community speaking names beyond the count. So, therefore, the assumption is that the state has done its job, and 72 is the official figure. Yet, for reasons implicit and explicit in this piece, at least 72 remains the most accurate phrasing.

Britain is a country where deaths take place beyond the state's count, bred by the processes of abandonment and callous indifference (Bhandar, 2018). It remains a possibility that there are names unspoken, who were lost in the fire. They, however, will not be as numerous as the fringe voices, speaking hyperbolically from abstraction, make out. The hysteria of the early days was predicated upon the state's incapacity, the conditions bred by the state's abandonment and indifference. What those outside, who are sceptical of the state, miss is that local consciousness of the fire's realities must develop in the area; continued conspiracy breeds distrust and feeds the worst elements of post-disaster politics.

'Confetti at a Whore's Wedding?'

Despite the hostile environment residents found themselves in, something set Grenfell apart from other post-disaster environments, especially where the state is culpable. When asked about the fire, locals blamed the redevelopment, which they placed within a broader context of social cleansing. They held the KCTMO and RBKC directly responsible for the fire and demanded justice. The truth, we are assured, will come out in the public inquiry. Extrapolations to form a general analysis, however, have not taken a back step since the fire started. Many are problematic. None more so than the *London Review of Books'* Andrew O'Hagan, who sought to undermine the 'narrative' supposedly constructed by the Grenfell Action Group and other concerned residents, and upheld by the media (see O'Hagan, 2018).

In a move of post-modern buggary, masked as empirical reasoning, O'Hagan blended fact and fiction. When locals spoke of how senior members of the council were engaged in a programme of social cleansing and large-scale redevelopments that made them disregard their duties of care, O'Hagan thought of himself as the man to join the fray. He wrote to community members that he is the right man to get to the bottom of this all. He told people he 'was hated by the right-wing media' and wore it as a badge of honour. But his piece came out as an apologia for the council and a wider defence of the patrician elite structures of Toryism. He cast those who opposed the council as career activists 'throwing accusations into the air like confetti at a whore's wedding.' At best, they were victims of a mob mentality, bred by a false narrative, that was misreported by the media. He smugly points out that on a basis of analytic truth, the catastrophe foretold by the activists, particularly Edward Daffarn, was not the one that struck.

The cladding and insulation were not cited as a fire risk by residents of the tower in their external and internal communications. Rather, it was the state of the building, the storage of provisions, the blocking of corridors, the movement of the boilers, the exposed pipework that disturbed them. This is all true. The prophetic nature of the 'Playing with Fire' Grenfell Action Blog post on the 20 November 2016, which read: 'only a catastrophic event will expose the ineptitude and incompetence of our landlord, the KCTMO, and bring an end to the dangerous living conditions and neglect of health and safety legislation that they inflict upon their tenants and leaseholders' (Grenfell Action Group, 2016) is therefore undermined, O'Hagan contends. Only the Grenfell Action Group (GAG) had put in a Freedom of Information request regarding the cladding, but were denied knowledge of the details. Unlike statutory authorities, extreme negligence led them to the conclusion that only eternal vigilance would keep them safe. David Collins told me that GAG always operated with a mind on the worst of all possible outcomes, such was their view of the KCTMO, who they dubbed 'an evil, unprincipled, mini-mafia'.

Andrew O'Hagan never spoke with the Grenfell Action Group before writing his piece. His attempt to contact both Ed Daffarn and Grenfell United were made just days before his article went to print. Whatever the methodological reason was, the attempt to undermine the community through the Grenfell Action Group blog has not worked out for the author. The victory of the campaigns for the library and the Wornington College have vindicated the group's work. Moreover, as detailed in the inquiry and explained briefly above, the disaster at Grenfell was due to a confluence of factors. Market state logics from the national government and managed decline and needless austerity from local authorities. The only stairwell at Grenfell Tower was non-compliant, on top of the litany of violations and failures that have already emerged. The people who lived in the tower – including but by no means exclusively Ed Daffarn – knew something was not right, their intuition led them to make demands. If those demands had been met, lives would have been saved. Instead of telling this story, O'Hagan tells a story of contrarian malcontents who wrongfully targeted a white man with the best of intentions. North Kensington doesn't need this story. The world doesn't need this story. The only person who stood to benefit from this unprecedented intervention were councillors he sought to absolve, in particular former Deputy Leader Rock Feilding-Mellen, who locals blame more than anyone else for the catastrophe at Grenfell. In their attempt at reparative work, the council have had to work very hard to untie the knots of Feilding-Mellen.

Using Grenfell

Those versed in the struggles of yesteryear pontificated to those on the Lancaster West Estate in the days after the fire, when they should have listened. Few had ever been there before. They held that a crude voluntarism must not be allowed to sprout, that politics is about commitment, not the experience of being burnt from house and home. So, they sought to organise above those most affected. Much of the early activism around Grenfell was unilateral, invasive and unwelcome, especially as few had versed themselves in the history of the actions around the redevelopment and resistance.

Beyond the sound-bite commentary picked from the testimony of locals by news crews, led by the diktats of their editors, the framing of Grenfell fell to voices outside of the area, who talked for, not with, the community around Grenfell Tower. Their politics imposed national solutions, blaming May and Cameron. They hailed Labour's Jeremy Corbyn as the magic elixir, who had a miraculous stature after the shock election result. This blighted the development of resistance. Politics which does not work from what was revealed from the fire serves the state. A politics which doesn't work from the groundwork already laid is destined to run afoul. Yet, it has been the modus operandi for much of the organised left.

As the fire was still alight, political commentators took a cursory glance at the Grenfell Action Group's blog, through which, they lampooned the KCTMO and RBKC. The chaos and anarchic atmosphere on the streets deepened the council's crisis; they were perceived as absent, which entrenched their pariah status. The incompetence of the local authority in the immediate aftermath was the ostensible reason for the resignations of Leader of the Council Nicholas Paget-Brown and Deputy Leader Rock Feilding-Mellen. With their resignations came a reshuffle in the council's cabinet with Elizabeth Campbell the new facade on a council that had no will to do anything but change perceptions. The people seethed. But, with the cosmetic changes, and the complications of local politics, national attention waned.

Commentators of the left took a macro look at deregulation and named the names of neoliberal Britain's architects, who presided over the bonfire of regulations (Monbiot, 2017). These were key interventions to frame Grenfell, but they did not account for the fire, nor empower the community. The usual suspects of the left came to the base of the tower and sought to empower through co-option. The acronyms took up their soapboxes. The Socialist Workers Party held private caucuses before filling rooms and panels with members from front organisations. Labour, cast as the proverbial white knights of the situation, saw the solution as a change in government. But the Tories did not fall because of the fire; not locally, not nationally. And as the instrumental value of Grenfell diminished, so did engagement.

The council's vacuum in the wake of the fire necessitated self-organising. The communities of North Kensington ran services themselves. As statutory duties were not being met, ad hoc protocols came into play. The withering away of governmental structures, services and departments at a national level extended the callous indifference further. The scandalous reality of the post-disaster environment shocked even seasoned politicos, whether they worked inside or outside the system. But, national and international solidarity bred conditions by which aid could be offered, and work could be done, without state structures. Weeks, and in some cases months, of autonomous work began.

The summer of 2017 saw forms of organising unparalleled in modern Britain. Because of a chain of resistance in the area, there was a politics implicit in the humanitarian aid effort, which resembled a system of mutual aid. An appetite for a new political formation ran deep. Numerous projects began with an intention of taking power from RBKC, whether in a limited or more fundamental sense. Dreams of developing a new administration, run by and for the locals of North Kensington, led to the seizing of community spaces for community use. When Ishmael Francis-Murray, Redfish and I made *Failed By The State*, we sought to historicise and articulate this mood (see Redfish, 2017). After the long, hot summer, a cold, desolate winter loomed. Fair weather friends of the community began to leave. This was a pivotal moment. The frenetic activity on the streets was coming to a close and dust was beginning to settle. Aid was being liquidated into funds and distributed to survivors. Grenfell was still bare and exposed to the elements. To all around, it was a reality of dystopian proportions.

'The City' and its Limits

On the day of the fire, underneath the Westway, at Bay 56, Acklam Village, a space was taken for community need. It was already a site of significance in the area, having been an adventure playground, a yard for steel pans and a pop-up cinema. For years, it had been kept in a state of arrested development, primed to become a retail space in a radical reshaping of the area. When its doors were opened to Niles Hailstones, due to the gargantuan relief effort, tonnes of aid came in within hours. It became a central node in the aid effort. 'The Village', as it came to be known, was a space of relentless activity in the summer months. But with the autumnal shifts, and aid being managed by the bereaved and survivors, the semi-outdoor and unheated occupation looked attritional. When a former college was found abandoned, the keys were offered to Hailstones, who administers The Village. He saw an opportunity for a reparative process. He organised community members involved in The Village, and took them to what he dubbed 'The City'.

It was four months after the fire, in October 2017, when community groups got access to The City. It is a huge space beneath the Westway. It had been designated for redevelopment to become a site of adult social care. Three statutory services were to be moved there, their previous offices primed for redevelopment. By the very nature of the occupation, council redevelopments could be stopped. But the community dreamed bigger. The idea of an independent administration was an ember of the fire. The possibilities for a space for training, learning and realizing dreams led to scores of young people refurbishing the building. They wanted to build the space to provide the services and opportunities they never felt they had.

Many of the boys who filled The City came from the street life of the area and would be classified as 'at risk' by the state. Some had lost family members in the disaster at the tower. They brought their bravado with them and the anarchic atmosphere allowed for their worst sides to find space. But despite all the machismo, they refashioned the building, they painted walls and spent the vast majority of the cold winter months seeking to prepare the space for either a grand launch or for the day the doors would be permanently open to the community. Those days never came.

The City was a throw of the dice; it was a gamble for a radical change in the immediate aftermath. It failed. Although some individuals have been blamed, it was destined to fail, due to the limitations structured into the moment. Few political visionaries engaged with the space, some popped their heads in or came to the attempted grand openings after the monthly silent march, but where organisational discipline was needed, there was no radical ideology to structure an alternative. Even with the will, there was no way.

There's something that is often missed when analysing Grenfell. A tower block burned. Blocks are as central to street culture as anything, the basis of pirate radio, the place to plot. So when Grenfell burned, youths across the country felt it deeply. If those in North Kensington who tried to build something better had decided to burn and loot in response, the whole country would have felt it. The youths of the area knew their power and they tried to build a radical alternative, but they did it with an ideology steeped in neoliberal doctrines and the cut-throat capitalism of the streets. Their labour could fashion the space, but space became a void. Appeals were made for assistance, but the struggle was not taken up.

The Panthers ten-point programme was not a philosophic doctrine. The demands had been made before, in similar methods. But it provided a backbone to struggle. No such doctrine emerged in North Kensington. Where there was activism before the fire, and to a large extent after it, it was reactive. Community spaces were defended. The community fought to maintain the gains of the past. The question was begged: what are we for? Substantive and collective demands have not been made officially by the myriad groups. To find unity in a solution is a tough endeavour. Yet, from all of the campaign groups, and all those who responded from their heart, it is clear to see that the community want their needs met and the spaces that better their life maintained. They want their rights and responsibilities respected. They want a state worthy of the trade-offs they make to live in Britain. As Antonio Roncolato, a survivor of the inferno, told the Public Inquiry 'after all we are paying our dues and it is our lives'.

Thousands now use Grenfell on their CV, there have been countless uses of its name. But for all the good will, a political vision could not be realized, even one nourished in grassroots, on land that is common. With the dream deferred, the remaining endeavours of the community are, by necessity, dependent upon the state or the charitable structures it uses.

Charity as a Conduit of State

Within North Kensington, as Anthony Wilks tells in his documentary, there is a culture of using charity as a conduit of state. This he dubs the 'Failed Experiment', which Grenfell punctuated (Wilks, 2018). Grenfell, and all the controversies that fall from it, are placed within a context of the local authority using charity in this locality to serve the community. However, this reading of history is culturalist and broad. The idealism that drives the narrative is that charitable, patrician logics persisted for over a century in the administration of North Kensington. However, this analysis lacks any explanation of the changes within charity in a world of globalised finance. Changes to board structures and constitutions mutated even recent organisations, like the Westway Trust, beyond reckoning. The scope of these organisations – who they serve and who they answer to – demands a materialist analysis, one that sees the financialised logics of profiting without producing, particularly land banking, as playing a role.

Within the Grenfell Action Group's blog lay far more than prophecy and agitation. The blog spoke against the asset stripping, arrested development and managed decline that defined governance in the area. Three organisations were seen as working in an informal alliance, dubbed 'the unholy trinity' (Grenfell Action Group, 2016; 2017). Two of these organisations have faced much scrutiny, RBKC and KCTMO. The Westway Trust, however, has managed to maintain the perception that they are a benign charity, acting to enable and empower the local community. They are anything but.

Anyone familiar with West London will know the Westway. It is a six-lane flyover that dissects North Kensington. What locals knew viscerally from their experiences could not be sensed by those who came to the area in the aftermath of the fire. The Westway Trust administers the community's land beneath the A40. Much of the land, now adorned with post-Grenfell art, has taken on new significance. Yet, plans to redevelop spaces, like the Maxilla Wall of Truth, have not been redrawn. Subtly, the Westway Trust have re-exerted their control and fuelled tensions, with long-term plans seeking to take back land taken for community endeavours and projects after the fire.

In the 40 or so years that the community's land has been held in trust, two-thirds of its 23 acres have been let for commercial use. The revenues generate millions. Yet, they distribute less than 10 per cent of their revenues to the community. The locals have protested, accusing the organisation of being in cahoots with big developers and complicit in the violence of social cleansing. Many articulated a sense of erasure, especially when images of their proposed redevelopment at Portobello Road showed only white people. In response the Westway23 formed, which fought to return the land beneath the six-lane London artery to the commons.[6] When the Westway was built, at a time when the area was known for its poverty and rebelliousness, the land was derelict. The community repurposed it, which led to the forming of the North Kensington Amenity Trust (the embryo of the Westway Trust). Throughout the years of neoliberalism and financialisation, the charity mutated from something that worked for the community interest to something that works against it, the first director of the Trust, Anthony Perry, said in his last interview before he passed away.

There were tipping points that the community should have seen and responded to, Ed Daffarn told me: 'When Rock Feilding-Mellen joined the board of the Westway Trust, alarm bells should have sounded.' It is alleged by a number of prominent community activists, that Angela McConville, the departed and disgraced CEO of the Westway Trust (who left while under internal investigation for institutional racism), worked hand in glove with Feilding-Mellen in plans to redevelop North Kensington. McConville made her dream of making the Westway a 'top ten London destination' well known. Her plans were to use the land as a link to the White City and Westfield developments. Her endeavours were historicised by the community, who rallied to oppose her plans, as within a line of class warriors who sought to make North Kensington rich again.

When the impressive houses around Ladbroke Grove were built, they were never intended to be working-class homes. The area became the melting pot it is through war, depression and histories of migration, through which the mansions became tenements. When Anthony Perry, the first director of the North Kensington Amenity Trust, sought to act in the interests of the population of North Kensington in the 1970s, he was met with resistance from his peers, who loved the area, but loathed the presence of the people.[7] Many charities and third sector organisations formed through struggle in North Kensington, some with radical roots. However, over the years, the organisations have widened the scope of their purpose, diluting their potency or becoming complicit in wider processes that have priced so many out of the area.

Charitable structures in times structured by the market absorb doctrines and discourses that undermine their purpose. The Westway Trust's discourse regarding its plans for redevelopment adopted market logics. The community were best served, they held, by increased footfall and more spending. The Trust therefore sought to develop a land that would entice those who have to dip into their pockets. Two consecutive Annual General Meetings were shutdown by angry North Kensington residents after the Trust unveiled their plans. Residents contend that the proposals afoot would fundamentally alter the geography, both social and physical, of the historic area.

As the inquiry enters its second phase, RBKC will fall back on the charities it supports in the area to argue its hidden hand was there. They will argue that their work enabled charity, they will argue they led from behind through the rich tapestry of organisations that supported the community in the aftermath of the fire. On their telling of history, the lionising of the community is the pardoning of the state, because the people filled spaces that the council or its functionaries had a hand in. What needs to be seen, understood and analysed is how intermeshed charitable structures are with the state. A politics is demanded which transcends the limitations of the moment, which can at least articulate the lived experience of those at the coalface of struggle.

Grenfell as a Rupture

Grenfell was a rupture, an event,[8] which exposed truths otherwise hidden from view. Something of the magnitude of Grenfell disturbs and reveals all, exposing similarities in differences and bonds of unity, formed through the state's disregard. The risk to life extends equally to all, cutting across the lines of division from the state's count and classification.

Indifference to life has been met with stoicism and silence. Above all else, the bereaved and survivors, who through necessity have remained campaigners, value their dignity. They bring the heart to a heartless system, and the voice of truth, but they have been kept on mute. The silent march is therefore a poignant form of protest. It takes place on the 14th of every month and will continue for the foreseeable future. The numbers attending has waned of late, but thousands still attend, respecting the community's demand for silent and dignified remembrance. On the march to commemorate a year since the disaster, tens of thousands attended.

But where the bereaved and survivors want to be heard, they remain silenced. 'The inquiry is taking place in the heart of lawyerland,' Natasha Elcock, the chair of Grenfell United told me. The bereaved and survivors are being made to bend around the conveniences of the legal structures. 'Do not speak unless spoken to,' the British judiciary say down their noses. The atmosphere has made the vast majority of those most affected detach themselves from the space. 'The bereaved and survivors merely ask that they be done right by, for once,' Elcock told me as she stood outside Holborn Bars. The Grenfell community want the venue moved. Two survivors have found spaces in Hammersmith, a neighbouring borough and a short train ride away. They were dismissed by the legal authorities. Compounding issues around the venue, the lawyers of the bereaved and survivors have yet to have full disclosure of evidence. Objections have been made publicly and privately, but remain muted. Marx's explanation for the Napoleonic era comes to mind: 'first as tragedy, then as farce'.

The Heart is Where the Battle is

Throughout North Kensington, the heart is now ubiquitous, representing community solidarity and grief. It is an all-inclusive symbol
that has been replicated many times, sometimes in problematic
and instrumental ways. Keeping people's attention on the issues
and campaigns around Grenfell has led to the building of a broad-
based coalition. Empty signifiers therefore assist the moral appeal
to keep up awareness. But more is being asked for, and therefore a
more subversive reading of the heart comes to mind. The American
writer Upton Sinclair once said: 'I aimed at the public's heart, and by
accident I hit it in the stomach.' This piece never aimed for the heart.
Heads must roll for what happened.

The great black radical Kwame Ture (formerly known as Stokely
Carmichael) publicly criticised Martin Luther King's activism for
making the fallacious assumption his oppressor had a heart (see
Carmichael, 1967). Appealing to the moral sensibilities of a system
so structured around the market is a fool's errand. North Kensington
cannot. It knows this viscerally, from experience, as do those at risk
of death across the country. To hear their stories hits both the heart
and the stomach, but it should hit the heads of authority. The heart,
by my reading, is therefore representative of the love that is found
when people come together in the face of state abandonment. It
represents the duty of care that only community can provide. It is a
moral symbol in an immoral world, representing the politics forged
by building the systems of care that no longer exist in authority.

Serious political questions fall out of Grenfell and the crises
around it. Statutory services must meet people's rights and needs,
but the structures to fulfil these duties are not fit for purpose. In
Cracks in the System, a film about the scandalous public health crisis
on the Ledbury Estate, made by the Rainbow Collective (2018), the
question is asked, 'are councils and local authorities, filled, as they
are with politicians from a particular demographics, the best bodies
to have statutory responsibility for life?' In North Kensington, the
local authority knows they have betrayed their purpose. They know
the people do not trust them. Any covenant or contract with the
residents of North Kensington is kept in place by force. But such

feelings are mirrored across the country, in a huge number of wards and local councils.

Neoliberalism has challenged the state's structures so much that defending council housing has meant defending the system of its provision. Very few would endorse their local authority or tenant management organisation as the ideal. The fire and the failure at Grenfell exposed profound issues that require fundamental redress. One of the major avenues would be to legislate so that discrimination against those who require state subsidies is punishable. The 2010 Equality Act unites all bills protecting those from prejudice and discrimination. In its draft form, the bill considered class a protected characteristic, but parliament decided against it. Class is not an identity and is very hard to define. But class is real, it is relational and it needs addressing.

In response to the state's callous indifference towards life, communities across the country want the power to look after themselves. Amplifying these voices could subvert what 'taking back control' really means. If a council can be punished for substandard services and failing in its duty of care, it would radically change the dynamics of power. Politics must address the needs of people across the country. Too many feel they are being unpeopled by those in power – locally and nationally. The conditions that maintain their lives have been fatally changed, some by austerity, some simply by the logics of the times. In such a moment, real politics must make those who count for nothing come to count for everything. Grenfell, we felt, changed everything. Only it didn't. It does nothing on its own. To assume change on the basis of death makes the same fallacious assumption that was called out by Ture.

The changes Grenfell demands are implicit within every power dynamic it exposed. The media need to look long and hard at their processes, where all the labour hours and wages went and where all the unused testimony they extracted from traumatised people now sits. The state must address, at root, where it has failed in its duty of care. Politicians must reflect on how they attempted to instrumentalise Grenfell. In the immediate aftermath, Grenfell was cast by Jeremy Corbyn and those around him as the outcome of austerity. He told Prime Minister Theresa May in the House of Commons that Grenfell came from 'disregard for working-class communities, the terrible consequences of deregulation and cutting corners' (see Merrick, 2017). But corners were cut by his party, who were complicit in the deregulation drive. When May volleyed this in response, the cycle of buck-passing continued and political commentators quipped about it. As we hurtle towards Brexit, such flippancy is dangerous.

With regulation read as anti-business – not pro-life – the Tories, supported by a motley crew of nationalists and nativists, won the right to depart from the European Union. On the current trajectory, gaping holes will be left in legislation. There are huge concerns about the consequences of this as, when redrafting legislation and regulations in a market state, poor wording can kill. The battle to defend life necessitates a language that preserves or rebuilds the conditions that maintain life and a government willing to challenge business to fight for the right to life for its citizenry.

Across the country, people are organising to be heard. They are seldom recognised for their actions, but when they are, their moving image is taken, but their voices have been kept on mute, apart from a few selected sound-bites according with a pre-established script. A man speaks over their action, with a narrative arc that makes everything OK, if incredibly sad. The country keeps calm and carries on. There's evil in this process. Complacency is not justifiable. A proper reckoning is demanded, where contrition is expressed from all parties involved in this injustice. Grenfell was a state crime. The work of redress which must be undertaken in its wake is infinitely demanding, but necessary. A politics is brewing beneath the mounting failures and cynical uses. If those in power don't listen, the voice of the unheard will speak, and there will be no dictating the terms of the discourse.

Notes

1. This was the language used prior to the fire, in Newsletters sent out by the Grenfell compact to update residents on their actions.
2. The Grenfell Public Inquiry website is www.grenfelltowerinquiry.org.uk/.
3. At the time of writing, the residents of North Kensington have had their fears regarding the toxicity of the fire and its health impacts confirmed. A report by Professor Anna Stec found 'huge concentrations' of potential carcinogens in soil up to two-thirds of a mile away from the tower. Like in

so many situations that have blighted the community of North Kensington, intrigue prods, pokes and re-traumatises. The release of this information was through a *Guardian* article, which released Anna Stec's research before she could confirm her findings, leaving the community with an information gap and anxiety. When authorities spoke, they in essence put concerns down to hypochondria and hysteria.

4. See Grenfell Action Group blog: https://grenfellactiongroup.wordpress.com.
5. Beyond the Grenfell Action Group and the North Kensington Library campaigns, there were battles to Save Wornington College, return Maxilla Nursery beneath the Westway, allow West London Stables to operate once again at its site on Stable Way.
6. See Westway23 website: www.westway23.org/.
7. Wyn Baptiste has recorded a long interview with Anthony Perry, which was his last before dying in 2016. The video is only privately available at this moment.
8. I mean this in the philosophical as well as everyday usage.

References

Apps, P. (2018) 'RIBA Hits Back at Government Expert's Suggestion of Limits on Combustible Materials Ban'. *Inside Housing*, 16 July. www.insidehousing. co.uk/news/news/riba-hits-back-at-government-experts-suggestion-of-limits-on-combustible-material-ban-57219 (all websites in this list last accessed November 2018).

Apps, P., S. Barnes and L. Barratt (2018) 'The Paper Trail: The Failure of Building Regulations'. *Inside Housing*. No specific date. https://social. shorthand.com/insidehousing/3CWytp9tQj/the-paper-trail-the-failure-of-building-regulations.

BBC (2017) 'London Tower Fire: Britain's Shame'. *Panorama*, aired 21 June.

Bannerman, L. (2017) 'We May Never Know True Number of Those Who Died in Grenfell Fire, Police Warn'. *The Times*, 24 June. www.thetimes.co.uk/article/we-may-never-know-true-number-of-those-who-died-in-glenfell-fire-police-warn-3thv99znw.

Bergin, T. (2017) 'After Grenfell Fire, Same Builders Rehired to Replace Dangerous Cladding, Reuters Finds'. *Reuters*, 13 December. https://uk.reuters.com/article/uk-britain-fire-cladding-exclusive/exclusive-after-grenfell-fire-same-builders-rehired-to-replace-dangerous-cladding-reuters-finds-idUKKBN1E714Z.

Bhandar, B. (2018) 'Organised State Abandonment: The Meaning of Grenfell'. *The Sociological Review Blog*, 19 September. www.thesociologicalreview.com/blog/organised-state-abandonment-the-meaning-of-grenfell.html.

Blagrove, I. (2017) Justice for Grenfell Rally, 19 June. www.youtube.com/watch?v=jvVQKWqPINw.

Blakeman, J. (2017) Email from Councillor Judith Blakeman to Kensington Labour Groups, 14 June.

Carmichael, S. (1967) Speech. www.youtube.com/watch?v=TqNk83otce8.

Elgwahry, A. (2018) 'The Ban on Combustibles is Welcome, But What Comes Next Matters'. *Inside Housing*, 5 October. www.insidehousing.co.uk/comment/comment/the-ban-on-combustibles-is-welcome-but-what-comes-next-matters-58509.

Evans, M., N. Harley and T. Brookes-Pollack (2014) 'Estate Where Suspected Terrorist Lived was a "Hotbed of Extremism" Locals Warn'. *The Telegraph*, 9 October. www.telegraph.co.uk/news/uknews/terrorism-in-the-uk/11150061/Estate-where-suspected-terrorist-lived-was-a-hotbed-of-extremism-locals-warn.html.

FDS Consult (2018) *Kensington Aldridge Academy, London W10 – Fire Safety Review*, June 2018. https://kaa.org.uk/wp-content/uploads/2018/07/180611-Kensington-Aldridge-Academy-Fire-Safety-Review-Issue05-KAA-referenced.pdf.

Grenfell Action Group (2016) 'KCTMO – Playing with Fire!'. 20 November. https://grenfellactiongroup.wordpress.com/2016/11/20/kctmo-playing-with-fire/.

Grenfell Action Group (2017) 'KCTMO – Feeling the Heat!'. 14 March. https://grenfellactiongroup.wordpress.com/2017/03/14/kctmo-feeling-the-heat/.

Hackitt, J. (2018) *Building a Safer Future – Independent Review of Building Regulations and Fire Safety: Final Report*, Cm 9607, May. London: HMSO.

HM Government (2011) *One-in, One-out: Statement of New Regulation*, April. www.gov.uk/government/publications/one-in-one-out-rule-regulations-1-january-to-30-june-2011.

Johnson, L. (2016) *Grenfell Tower Report by the Director of Housing*, The Royal Borough of Kensington and Chelsea Housing and Property Scrutiny Committee Report, 11 May.

Kundnani, A. (2007) *The End of Tolerance: Racism in 21st Century Britain*. London: Pluto Press.

Lane, B. (2018) *Grenfell Tower – Fire Safety Investigation Report*. Presented to Grenfell Tower Inquiry, 12 April. www.grenfelltowerinquiry.org.uk/evidence/dr-barbara-lanes-expert-report.

Merrick, R. (2017) 'Jeremy Corbyn Blames Government Cuts for Grenfell Tower Fire Sparking Angry Tory Protests in the Commons'. *The Independent*, 28 June. www.independent.co.uk/news/uk/politics/jeremy-corbyn-grenfell-tower-fire-government-pmqs-cuts-blame-tory-protests-commons-conservative-mps-a7812146.html.

Monbiot, G. (2017) 'With Grenfell Tower, We've Seen What "Ripping up Red Tape" Really Looks Like'. *The Guardian*, 15 June. www.theguardian.com/commentisfree/2017/jun/15/grenfell-tower-red-tape-safety-deregulation.

O'Hagan, A. (2018) 'The Tower'. *London Review of Books*, 40(11). www.lrb.co.uk/v40/n11/andrew-ohagan/the-tower.

Potent Whisper (2018) 'The Rhyming Guide to Grenfell Britain'. www.youtube.com/watch?v=JzGgtztLU-A.

Rainbow Collective (2018) *Cracks in the System*. Ledbury Estate Documentary. Preview. www.youtube.com/watch?v=QT3hJE7boMw.

Redfish (2017) *Failed by the State: The Struggle in the Shadow of Grenfell*. Co-Producers Ish and Daniel Renwick. Part 1: www.youtube.com/watch?v=9tFPCUgjbfA. Part 2: www.youtube.com/watch?v=VxggXo-4UEU. Part 3: www.youtube.com/watch?v=xnBrvCTlayA.

Shilliam, R. (2018) *Race and the Undeserving Poor: From Abolition to Brexit*. Newcastle: Agenda Publishing.

Sparrow, A. (2018) 'Grenfell Fire: 100% Failure Rate After Cladding Tested on 75 Blocks'. *The Guardian*, 14 February. www.theguardian.com/politics/blog/live/2017/jun/26/brexit-eu-nationals-theresa-may-to-meet-arlene-foster-in-hope-of-finalising-torydup-deal-politics-live.

Tobin, O. (2018) 'Almost 500 Buildings in the UK have Same Cladding as Grenfell Tower, Government Report Reveals'. *Evening Standard*, 30 June. www.standard.co.uk/news/london/almost-500-buildings-in-the-uk-are-using-the-same-cladding-as-grenfell-tower-government-report-a3875396.html.

Wilks, A. (2018) 'Grenfell: The End of an Experiment?'. *London Review of Books*, 30 May. www.lrb.co.uk/2018/05/30/lrb-film/grenfell-the-end-of-an-experiment.

Photo Essay
Samuel Boal

Feeling the heat on the ground gave me the slightest glimpse into what it may have felt like in the tower on the night of the fire. Looking up, I could feel the looming shadow of this huge blackened tower and around me the picture upon picture of faces, the missing residents, whole families presumed dead.

As I held my camera, I knew I was about to impinge on what was not only a sobering story but a raw reality of loss that had fiercely visited people in their homes on an ordinary night. I wanted to respect and give dignity to what I saw. I wanted my pictures to reflect the worth of each person so that this tragedy would be recorded and not forgotten.

The moment I arrive, I work in a circle, photographing as I go around the circumference of the police cordon. I wanted to remain almost anonymous and not to infringe on the sense of grief I could feel all around me. I was keenly aware of not being from the area. As an outsider, I was deeply moved by what I saw.

When covering these events, a photographer is looking at the light to guide the eye, not too guide it away from the reality but to enhance the senses of emotion and focus it. The sunlight was reflected off another tower block and no one could realistically walk past all the tributes and 'missing' posters without becoming emotional.

I don't know if the man in this photograph was a local, family member or a member of the public from somewhere else, but it was his raw, silent emotion I endeavoured to capture.

This picture best shows the social inequality of the area; wealth rubbing shoulders with deprivation. Here I could see aspects of London life that speak of those who have and those who do not.

This final photograph shows one of those moments where people may think that photographers and journalists have no respect, but it is so hard to record these moments whilst blanking out the emotion.

3

Before Grenfell

British Immigration Law and the Production of Colonial Spaces

Nadine El-Enany

I am always conflicted about writing and speaking about Grenfell, cognisant of some media outlets' exploitation (de Gallier, 2018), misrepresentation (Barratt, 2018) and re-traumatisation of survivors. In this contribution, I set out a critique of academic responses to the fire that exceptionalise it as an object of study and argue that we must not lose sight of its structural causes. It was only a matter of days after the Grenfell Tower fire of 14 June 2017 that an academic call for papers analysing the fire emerged. It ignored Britain's colonial configuration and its legacy of racism as a factor in what made the victims of the fire, the majority of whom were racialised, many of them Muslim (Rice-Oxley, 2018), disproportionately vulnerable to violence and premature death (Gilmore, 2006: 28). I responded at the time by writing a short piece about why we cannot ignore the racial and colonial dimensions of the atrocity (El-Enany, 2017a). Since the fire occurred, it has been the subject of multiple academic events across Britain. The tendency in the neoliberal academy to define 'new' research areas and to engage with topics attracting a high level of media attention has led to the exceptionalisation of the Grenfell fire as an object of study which hinders our understanding of its structural causes (El-Enany, 2018a). The relevance of racialisation and racial discrimination are also issues that are left unaddressed in the terms of the public inquiry into the fire, which began in May 2018. Although official inquiry documentation is available in Arabic and Farsi as well as English, indicative of the racialisation[1] of the majority of the victims, racial discrimination is not an issue under investigation. I argue that this omission is a glaring one. In this contribution, I make the case that in order to understand what happened at Grenfell Tower on 14 June 2017, we must be cognisant of the colonial and racial dimensions of the atrocity.

The Grenfell fire embodies a double meaning of atrocity. It was not only a sudden, terrifying occurrence, its roots lie in slow violence. Slow, or structural, violence is more difficult to identify than the sudden violent spectacle. Yet, in the case of the Grenfell fire, the violence and disintegration that preceded the horrifying spectacle of the fire was perceptible. It was perceptible to its eventual victims and survivors, but they and their calls for help in making their homes safe were marginalised, silenced and ignored until it was too late. Crises tend to be declared, and action called for, when white middle-class people are affected. What would it mean for times of 'crisis' to be declared, attention paid and preventative action taken when racialised people are at risk of harm? In the designation of last decade's financial crisis as being 'of 2008', for example, erased was the moment of violence for predominantly poor black Americans who saw their houses repossessed across Southern California, Arizona, Nevada and Florida in 2007. David Harvey thus locates the crisis for capital as beginning in 2008, but describes the 2007 spate of housing repossessions as being 'the primary epicentre of the crisis' (Harvey, 2010). We might similarly ask when the violence of the Grenfell fire began? Was it the night of 14 June 2017, or can its origins, its causes be located further back in time?

I consider the epicentre of the fire to be located in European colonialism and transatlantic slavery. Ideas of race and racial inferiority served to justify practices of profit-induced exploitation, subjugation and control of populations, with disastrous and ongoing consequences for people with ancestral or geographical histories of slavery and colonisation. Many of the Grenfell victims and their ancestors suffered the dispossessing effects of European colonialism. They lived and fled not only the lasting material consequences of colonisation, but also the economic decline caused by global trade and debt arrangements that ensure the continued impoverishment and dependency of Southern economies on those of the North. Understanding the violence of the Grenfell Tower atrocity demands a historical and contextualised analysis. I will reflect in what follows on the colonial and racial logic of the Grenfell Tower fire, in part through an analysis of British immigration law in the context of Britain's colonial history as well as its ongoing colonial configurations.

Immigration control in Britain is intricately connected to the ebb and flow of Britain's imperial ambitions and attachments (El-Enany, 2017c; El-Enany, 2019). In 1948, the British Nationality Act rolled out a secondary status of 'Citizenship of the United Kingdom and Colonies' to include nationals of independent Commonwealth countries and those of British colonies – a status which included a right to enter and remain in Britain (Lord Goldsmith, 2008: 15). This granting of a right of entry to Commonwealth citizens was principally an attempt to hold together what remained of the British Empire, and was not expected to be used by racialised Common-wealth citizens (El-Enany, 2019; Hansen, 1999). British politicians accepted the migration of racialised people from colony and Com-monwealth countries into Britain as a trade-off, an unfortunate but necessary by-product of maintaining the relationship between Britain and the Old (white) Dominions (El-Enany, 2019; Hansen, 1999). The principal beneficiaries of the British Empire's system of sub-jecthood were white Britons, who could move and settle throughout the Commonwealth pursuant to sponsored emigration facilitated through agreements with Australia, South Africa, New Zealand and Canada (Hansen, 1999: 76).

Despite the legislators' lack of enthusiasm for non-white immi-gration from the colonies, the 1948 Act's provisions had the effect of facilitating the arrival in Britain of around 500,000 racialised people. These arrivals and those who followed were not only exercising rights granted to them under the law, but were escaping economic hardship and an absence of employment opportunities (Phillips, 2001: 264), along with other dispossessive effects of slavery and colonialism (see Payne, 1983; Wint, 2012). Post-war arrivals from Jamaica, for example, were leaving a country profoundly marked by both the transatlantic slave trade and colonialism. By the time the British colonised Jamaica in the seventeenth century, the country's 'indigenous peoples had already been wiped out by the Spanish, and

[it] was populated mainly by enslaved Africans and white settlers' (Hall, 2002: 67–68).

It was not until 1962 that the Commonwealth Immigrants Act brought all Commonwealth citizens formally under immigration control. The exceptions were the (majority white) citizens who had been born in Britain or Ireland, or who held a British or Irish passport issued by either one of these governments (Lord Goldsmith, 2008: 15). The Act was designed to restrict the entry of racialised Commonwealth citizens. In the late 1960s, Britain saw an increasing number of East African Asians enter the country, many of whom possessed a British passport issued by Kenyan authorities. This movement followed the introduction of policies discriminating against Asians in Kenya by President Kenyatta. The 1968 Commonwealth Immigrants Act further narrowed the exceptions to control. Rights of entry were limited to Commonwealth citizens born in Britain, or with at least one parent or grandparent born or naturalised in Britain. The effect of the 1968 Act was to discriminate against Commonwealth citizens on racial grounds. The legal restrictions on entry of Commonwealth subjects was a response to the perceived and symbolic threat which non-white immigration posed to white British supremacy at home. As Paul Rich has written,

The loss of empire came as a profound psychological shock to a society that had grown used to having colonial possessions, despite its ignorance of their nature and extent. The sense of imperial mission and 'trusteeship' and governance over 'backward races' extended, however, only to the colonial sphere and became difficult to reapply back within the imperial metropolis itself once a series of black communities, with links back to former colonial possessions, had begun to emerge in its midst.

(Rich, 1990: 11)

According to Dennis Dean, new arrivals were 'expected "to go it alone" and fend for themselves'. British government ministers argued that legislation outlawing racial discrimination would be 'unworkable and unenforceable' (Dean, 1993: 58). The Cabinet Committee on Commonwealth Immigration feared that providing housing and other support and advice services to new arrivals would encourage more racialised people to travel to Britain. It stated that,

> as long as immigration remained unrestricted, the use of public funds for that purpose could only serve as an added attraction to prospective immigrants and would frustrate the efforts we were encouraging Commonwealth and Colonial governments to make to reduce the rate of emigration from their territories to the United Kingdom.

(Dean, 1993: 59)

This is the reason the Committee refused to provide the necessary funds to housing trusts to ameliorate accommodation problems in places such as Notting Hill (Dean, 1993: 59), a stone's throw away from where Grenfell Tower was to be built a decade later. At the same time as lawmakers were working hard to write colonial subjects and Commonwealth citizens out of the British welfare state, British rulers were raising revenue through exploitation and extraction in colonised countries. The British had long been levying taxes on colonies as a means of swelling government coffers. This was achieved through a tactic of the British colonial administration, which was to forge alliances with elites in colonised countries and 'to use them to collect taxes and maintain political order' (Lange, Mahoney and vom Hau, 2006: 1430). In spite of this, the very people who had contributed to building the British welfare state were not only denied access to it, but were constructed as being a drain on public funds.

While British legislators considered how to reduce the numbers of racialised people in Britain, they monitored developments taking place in the United States with respect to the civil rights movement (Dean, 1993: 67). Fears about similar uprisings in Britain led to increased support among politicians for the introduction of immigration controls. The then Home Secretary, Rab Butler, speaking in May 1961, stated that, '[i]t was now accepted by government supporters generally that some form of control was unavoidable if there was not to be a colour problem in this country on a similar scale to that of the USA' (Dean, 1993: 67). Rather than see racial violence and hatred in the USA and in Britain, such as the 1958 Nottingham and Notting

Hill attacks by the far-right on West Indian communities, as being products of the racist subjugation used to justify transatlantic slavery and European colonialism, British politicians considered racism to be the result of the presence of racialised people in majority-white societies.

The historical context outlined above is important if we are to understand the structural causes of the Grenfell Tower fire. Britain is today a space of domestic colonialism: a space of control and exclusion in which racialised populations are disproportionately subject to state violence, a violence which is uninterrogable by the law (El-Enany, 2019). In the course of the changes to British immigration law outlined above, as Britain transitioned from an empire to a nation-state, effectively federating as a white nation, the entitlement of racialised people to enter and remain in Britain was halted. The presence of those already on the British mainland was questioned through multiple institutionalised practices of racial control and exclusion. This was manifested spatially with the confinement of racialised populations to sites of extreme deprivation, predominantly in the inner cities. Ongoing disproportionate vulnerability of racialised populations to violence in Britain must be understood as 'lingering expressions of empire' (Jackson, 2016: 205). Racialised people experience extreme hostility in Britain today. When she was Home Secretary, Theresa May said explicitly that her Immigration Law reforms of 2014 and 2016 were designed to 'create a hostile environment' for migrants. We have seen the effect of this hostile environment on long-settled former colonial subjects who have been deported, detained and denied access to health care, housing and other vital support services (Gentleman, 2018; Keenan, 2017; 2018; Chapter 5 in this volume). The 2016 referendum on Britain's EU membership has both amplified and legitimised racist hatred in Britain. The Leave campaign won on a mandate of 'taking back control', and making Britain a better place to live for Britons, conceived in large part, as white (Emejulu, 2016; El-Enany, 2016; 2017b; 2017c; 2018b).

The Grenfell Tower fire is perhaps the most extreme instance in which people with geographical or ancestral histories of colonisation have been unable to escape their condition of coloniality in contemporary Britain. We can see in the burnt shell of Grenfell Tower the persistent and ongoing colonial practices of state-sanctioned racial hierarchy in Britain. State-sanctioned insecurity and a denial of rights is a long-standing and everyday experience for poor racialised people living in Britain (Dean, 1993). The mostly brown, black and Muslim Grenfell residents whose faces smiled back at us from 'Missing' persons posters could not escape their condition of coloniality and vulnerability to racial state violence. It haunted them, confining them to lives of poverty in a dangerous building in one of the wealthiest places in the world. In this way, in Sherene Razack's words, 'colonisation has continued apace' (Razack, 2002: 127).

Officially, 72 people are confirmed to have died in the Grenfell Tower fire, although on the ground, the death toll is said to be higher. According to the Emergency Events Database, it is the deadliest fire in Britain since at least 1900. The fire spread rapidly up the building due to highly flammable exterior cladding that had been installed primarily to enhance the aesthetics of the building for the predominantly white wealthy people living in the surrounding area. There was only one stairwell, and no sprinkler or alarm system. Scapegoating of migrants and those racially profiled as such frequently manifests itself in the lie that they live in council flats that white British people are entitled to occupy. The Grenfell atrocity cuts viscerally through this construction of the unjustly enriched and privileged migrant. Racialised people are systematically and disproportionately made vulnerable to harm and premature death, to draw on Ruth Wilson Gilmore's conception of racism (Gilmore, 2006: 28). The statistic that children who live above the fourth floor of high-rise blocks in England are more likely to be black or Asian is striking in a country that is 87 per cent white (Dorling, 2011). In Britain, '[p]overty rates are lowest among the white population – at about 20 per cent – while 50 per cent of people of African descent live in poverty. Overall, two-fifths of ethnic minorities live in a household earning below average income' (Foster, 2017). Akwugo Emejulu and Leah Bassel have demonstrated the differential impact of austerity policies, which disadvantage minority women disproportionately, exacerbating existing inequalities (Emejulu and Bassel, 2017).

We can identify contemporary colonial practices in the state-sponsorship of spatially unjust zones like North Kensington. To draw again on Razack, 'the presence of the racial Other in white space gives rise to a careful management of boundaries within the urban space. Projects [in a British context, council housing] ... are created, cordoning off the racial poor' (Razack, 2002: 129). Despite the Ronan Point high-rise collapse in Newham East London in 1968 and the ensuing loss of public confidence in high-rise residential buildings, Grenfell Tower was approved for construction by the local council in 1970 as part of the Lancaster West Development Project designed to clear slums in the area. The marginalised poor housed in Grenfell Tower could not escape their heightened vulnerability to harm and premature death, a condition intensified as a result of rapid gentrification in the area, and the council's prioritisation of the needs of new, predominantly wealthy white residents. Gentrification entails the over-policing of racialised communities to enhance the desirability of an area and to ensure property prices are not devalued (Hudson, 2015). Khadija Saye, a photographer who was killed in the Grenfell fire, could not telephone for help on the night of the fire because she had recently been wrongfully arrested and the police had not returned her phone to her (Tropping, 2017).

The hyper-segregation and differential quality of life of North Kensington residents mirrors practices of the colonial era when British authorities instituted spatial ordering on the basis of ideas and practices of racial hierarchy and white European supremacy. Razack has documented the way in which the end of the colonial era combined with 1950s and 1960s urbanisation policies of segregation to replicate the spatial zones produced by colonisation whereby 'slum administration replaces colonial administration' (Razack, 2002: 129). These practices, rooted in colonialism, are implemented and sustained through processes of regulation and deregulation, which serve to legitimise and de-politicise the painful, fraught and sometimes disastrous consequences for racialised people. People come to inhabit adjacent worlds that are materially drastically different.

A refusal to understand contemporary British politics in the context of Britain's colonial history determined the attitude of the local council to the demands for fire safety from Grenfell residents.

Colonial violence has not only allowed for the theft of land and resources, but has allowed societies enriched through processes of colonisation to consider themselves entitled to colonial spoils (Razack, 2002: 129). Some Grenfell survivors reported that 'they felt the implicit message from everyone they contacted before the fire for help with the building was "you are a guest in this borough, and a guest in this country, you have no right to complain"' (Foster, 2017). Not only were Commonwealth citizens deprived of their rights of entry and stay throughout the 1960s and 1970s, but those who entered Britain, and their children, have since been treated as underserving of access to basic resources and safety. In an act of administrative violence, the local council in Kensington offered a tax rebate of £100 to wealthy citizens in the borough, rather than investing in making Grenfell Tower safe for its residents. According to Razack, '[w]hat a spatial analysis reveals is that bodies in [what are deemed] degenerate spaces lose their entitlement to personhood through a complex process in which the violence that is enacted is naturalized' (Razack, 2002: 155). The absence of history and the abstraction of day-to-day life in Britain from the country's colonial history that determined the presence of many racialised people in Britain today means the state and local government cannot 'be seen in the colonial project in which [it is] embedded' (Razack, 2002: 126). In this way, the council tax rebate offered to the predominantly wealthy dwellers in the borough can be seen as mirroring imperial societies' 'historic participation in and benefit from [the] dispossession and violence [of colonialism]' (Razack, 2002: 127).

Britain's geography is marked by spaces of colonial control and exclusion in which resources are withheld from people living in conditions of spatial and temporal precarity. Hanging over the lives of the Grenfell residents was the assumption that they were taking up space. Their presence was all that stood in the way of profitable real estate ventures. Our understanding of the Grenfell atrocity is marred by the abstraction of day-to-day life in Britain from the country's colonial history. Absent is an understanding of the relationship between British immigration law and the country's imperial history and constitution. The reality of Britain's colonial history continues to be denied (El-Enany, 2017c) along with the fact that certain sections of society continue to benefit from it. The result is a failure to connect both the presence of many racialised people in Britain today to the destruction and dispossession of European colonisation, as well as the existence of modern state infrastructure, including the welfare state, to resources acquired through colonial conquest.

Note

1. In acknowledgement of Britain as a white supremacist context, I use the term racialised to refer to people who are non-white. Following Cheryl Harris, I adopt the definition of white supremacy as posited by Frances Lee Ansley:

> By 'white supremacy' I do not mean to allude only to the self-conscious racism of white supremacist hate groups. I refer instead to a political, economic, and cultural system in which whites overwhelmingly control power and material resources, conscious and unconscious ideas of white superiority and entitlement are widespread, and relations of white dominance and non-white subordination are daily reenacted across a broad array of institutions and social settings.
>
> (Frances L. Ansley, cited in Harris, 1993: 1714)

References

Barratt, L. (2018) Twitter Feed, 30 May. https://twitter.com/lukewbarratt/status/1001764126392242176 (all websites in this list last accessed November 2018).

De Gallier, T. (2018) 'London Review of Books Used Quotes Without Consent in Grenfell Article, Interviewee Claims'. Talk Radio, 5 June. talkradio.co.uk/news/exclusive-london-review-books-used-quotes-without-consent-grenfell-article-interviewee-claims.

Dean, D. (1993) 'The Conservative Government and the 1961 Commonwealth Immigrants Act: The Inside Story'. *Race and Class*, 35(2): 57–74.

Dorling, D. (2011) *So You Think You Know About Britain*. London: Constable.

El-Enany, N. (2016) 'Brexit as Nostalgia for Empire'. *Critical Legal Thinking*, 19 June. http://criticallegalthinking.com/2016/06/19/brexit-nostalgia-empire/.

El-Enany, N. (2017a) 'The Colonial Logic of Grenfell'. *Verso Blog*, 3 June. www.versobooks.com/blogs/3306-the-colonial-logic-of-grenfell.

El-Enany, N. (2017b) 'Empire en Vogue'. *Red Pepper*, 24 June. www.redpepper.org.uk/empire-en-vogue/.

El-Enany, N. (2017c) 'Things Fall Apart: From Empire to Brexit Britain'. *IPR Blog*, University of Bath, 2 May. http://blogs.bath.ac.uk/iprblog/2017/05/02/things-fall-apart-from-empire-to-brexit-britain/.

El-Enany, N (2018a), 'Grenfell and the Academic Gaze'. *Pluto Blog*, June 2018. www.plutobooks.com/blog/remembering-grenfell-tower-fire-one-year/.

El-Enany, N. (2018b) 'The Next British Empire'. *IPPR Progress Review*, 25(1): 30–38.

El-Enany, N. (2019) *(B)ordering Britain: Law, Race and Empire*. Oxford: Hart Publishing.

Emejulu, A. (2016) 'On the Hideous Whiteness Of Brexit: "Let us be Honest About Our Past and Our Present If We Truly Seek to Dismantle White Supremacy"'. *Verso Blog*, 28 June. www.versobooks.com/blogs/2733-on-the-hideous-whiteness-of-brexit-let-us-be-honest-about-our-past-and-our-present-if-we-truly-seek-to-dismantle-white-supremacy.

Emejulu, A. and L. Bassel (2017) *Minority Women and Austerity: Survival and Resistance in France and Britain*. Cambridge: Polity Press.

Foster, D. (2017) 'Would a White British Community Have Burned in Grenfell Tower?'. *The New York Times*, 20 June. https://mobile.nytimes.com/2017/06/20/opinion/london-tower-grenfell-fire.html?referer=.

Gentleman, A. (2018) '"My Life is in Ruins": Wrongly Deported Windrush People Facing Fresh Indignity'. *The Guardian*, 20 September. www.theguardian.com/uk-news/2018/sep/10/windrush-people-wrongly-deported-jamaica-criminal-offence.

Gilmore, R. W. (2006) *Golden Gulag: Prisons, Surplus, Crisis, and Opposition in Globalizing California*. Berkeley, CA: University of California Press.

Hall, C. (2002) 'Histories, Empires and the Post-Colonial Moment', in I. Chambers and L. Curti (eds), *The Postcolonial Question: Common Skies, Divided Horizons*. London: Routledge.

Hansen, R. (1999) 'The Politics of Citizenship in 1940s Britain: The British Nationality Act'. *Twentieth Century British History*, 10(1): 67–95.

Harris, C. I. (1993) 'Whiteness as Property'. *Harvard Law Review*, 106(8): 1701–1791.

Harvey, D. (2010) 'The Enigma of Capital and the Crisis this Time'. American Sociological Association Meeting, Atlanta, 16 August. http://davidharvey.org/2010/08/the-enigma-of-capital-and-the-crisis-this-time/.

Hudson, A. (2015) 'How Punitive and Racist Policing Enforces Gentrification in San Francisco'. *Truthout*, 24 April. https://truthout.org/articles/how-punitive-and-racist-policing-enforces-gentrification-in-san-francisco/.

Jackson, N. M. (2016) 'Imperial Suspect: Policing Colonies within "Post"-Imperial England'. *Callaloo*, 39(1): 203–215.

Keenan, S. (2017) 'A Border in Every Street'. *The Disorder of Things*, 29 June. https://thedisorderofthings.com/2017/06/29/a-border-in-every-street/.

Keenan, S. (2018) 'A Prison Around Your Ankle and a Border in Every Street: Theorising Law, Space and the Subject', in A. Philippopoulos-Mihalopoulos (ed.), *Handbook of Law and Theory*. London: Routledge.

Lange, M., J. Mahoney and M. vom Hau (2006) 'Colonialism and Development: A Comparative Analysis of Spanish and British Colonies'. *American Journal of Sociology*, 111(5): 1412–1462.

Lord Goldsmith QC (2008) 'Citizenship Review: "Citizenship: Our Common Bond"'. http://image.guardian.co.uk/sys-files/Politics/documents/2008/03/11/citizenship-report-full.pdf.

Payne, A. (1983) 'The Rodney Riots in Jamaica: The Background and Significance of the Events of October 1968'. *The Journal Commonwealth & Comparative Politics*, 21(2): 158–174.

Phillips, C. (2001) 'The Pioneers: Fifty Years of Caribbean Migration to Britain', in *A New World Order*. New York: Vintage.

Razack, S. (2002) *Race, Space and the Law: Unmapping a White Settler Society*. Toronto: Between the Lines.

Rice-Oxley, M. (2018) 'Grenfell: The 72 Victims, Their Lives, Loves and Losses'. *The Guardian*, 14 May. www.theguardian.com/uk-news/2018/may/14/grenfell-the-71-victims-their-lives-loves-and-losses and www.theguardian.com/uk-news/ng-interactive/2018/may/14/lives-of-grenfell-tower-victims-fire.

Rich, P. B. (1990) *Race and Empire in British Politics*. Cambridge: Cambridge University Press.

Tropping, A. (2017) 'Khadija Saye: Artist on Cusp of Recognition When She Died in Grenfell'. *The Guardian*, 17 June. www.theguardian.com/uk-news/2017/jun/17/khadija-saye-artist-was-on-cusp-of-recognition-when-she-died-in-grenfell.

Wint, T. A. S. P. (2012) '"Once you Go You Know": Tourism, Colonial Nostalgia and National Lies in Jamaica'. Report to the Faculty of the Graduate School of the University of Texas at Austin. https://repositories.lib.utexas.edu/bitstream/handle/2152/ETD-UT-2012-05-5846/WINT-MASTERS-REPORT.pdf?sequence=1&isAllowed=y.

4

Struggles for Social Housing Justice

*Radical Housing Network, Becka Hudson
and Pilgrim Tucker*

*Written by members of the Radical Housing Network (RHN), with
contributions from Lancaster West Estate residents, this chapter sets
Grenfell in the context of wider struggles around housing. The Radical
Housing Network is a network of 30+ housing groups and campaigns
from across London, ranging from boaters to council tenants, estate
leaseholders to those battling fuel poverty, students to private renters.
The Grenfell Action Group, a group based at Grenfell Tower who
worked for many years to expose the contempt with which residents were
treated by their landlord and the council, and the poor and dangerous
standard of their housing, were members of this network in the years
leading up to the fire. Looking at RHN's work with estate and tower
residents before the fire, as well as in its aftermath, the chapter sets
the struggles of estate residents in the context of ongoing experiences of,
and efforts to counter, regeneration and austerity in West London – and
across the capital.*

On the morning of 14 June 2017, emails, texts and posts ricocheted
around the loose online community of housing campaigners in
London. It took some time, waking in those early hours, to piece
together what was happening. As the first pictures of the fire
emerged, someone named the building. On activist email lists, people
started sharing their knowledge of the history of the building and its
landlord, and the politics of the borough in which it stood. As some
Radical Housing Network (RHN) members attempted to contact
those they knew who lived there, shock, grief and anger began to take
hold. Though a name not known across the world before that day, the
struggle at Grenfell Tower on the Lancaster West Estate against the

cowboy actions of their landlord the Kensington and Chelsea Tenant Management Organisation (KCTMO), and the local council, the Royal Borough of Kensington and Chelsea (RBKC), were well known by some. In the local area, this included the loved ones of those who lived there, and many who had for years been fighting assaults on their own safety and housing rights, across London, with every tactic from letters to theatrical sit-ins.

And so Grenfell was a fire that shocked us all in its horror, but did not entirely surprise. Many – those who lived there, those who campaigned, and those who lived in similar circumstances – knew that such a horror was probable considering how social housing tenants had been treated, institutionally, and for many years. Indeed, housing activists in London had long struggled against estate demolition and what is often referred to as 'managed decline' – the decades long abandonment and disinvestment – of their estates. Borough after borough had seen promises of regeneration mutate into danger and displacement, with councils and developers collaborating to directly expel people from affordable homes after leading them into states of disrepair, often to access the land beneath. Years of austerity, of closing community facilities, shrinking services and slashing access to any public funds had pushed those whose homes were under attack into even further difficulty.

From that morning on, the pain of Grenfell has marked a step change. It was a new landscape of grief and urgency for many involved in housing campaigns. Residents, activists and commentators repeated calls for justice, as well as for such an atrocity to never take place again. It was urged over and over that Grenfell must mark a turning point in how the UK houses those on its land. Those struggling against the dramatic, brutal and ongoing shifts in the city's housing – its availability, its affordability and its safety – if adamant before, were now unshakeable. Yet those first days, that fell quickly into months, were also marked by extreme media scrutiny. Amidst much of the frenzied emotion, and the mammoth tasks that lay before a string of communities facing near total state abandonment, intense, disjointed and often misrepresentative media attention became a fixture. Within RHN alone, despite Network members being dispersed across London and its work only adjacent to those who had been living in and around the tower, this meant hundreds of calls and emails from journalists and broadcasters for days, with several media requests a week coming through even six months later. Disorienting enough, the largely voluntary activist groups that characterise RHN, and the UK's housing campaigns more generally, are sparsely funded and supported. The work of everyday life often takes priority over housing activism, which tends to work in a fluctuating web of relationships, threads, dormant and re-emerging groups, projects and reactions to the people's housing situations and the wider political landscape. And so, the fire emerged onto an international media stage, in a context of violent state abandonment that confounded people with poor, flawed and inadequate information, little clarity and threadbare, contradictory and sloppy support. This scene began to characterise what many had to contend with in the year following the fire.

The Radical Housing Network

A network of over 30 housing groups and campaigns, the Radical Housing Network was formed in 2013. It emerged from a number of meetings on housing activism focused on strategies of resistance as the increasingly harsh housing and welfare policies implemented as part of the coalition government's austerity agenda began to impact those they targeted. The growing number of diverse and very active housing groups and campaigns in the city at the time was remarkable. Because of the way housing policy and individual housing decisions are made in the UK, local groups will often take their local authority or landlord as the key target in their fight against an eviction, demolition, on disrepair issues or for any number of housing concerns. A cornucopia of tactics and efforts to pressure councils into making beneficial housing decisions abound.

It was in this context that a number of these local campaigns, representing a range of residents in different tenures and circumstances, from across London, decided that the Radical Housing Network should be formed in order that groups could share information, tactics, resources and ideas. The hope, too, was that the city's movement for housing justice could be strengthened and amplified beyond the sum of its parts; that RHN might work together and on a larger scale.

Across London, the Network as a whole has a wide range of skills and expertise developed amongst its members. Eviction resistance networks were set up with tactics on how to prevent someone from being forced from their home. These included council agitation including letter writing, sit-ins and creative protest. Occupations had been held by several members as well as by the Network. Events, workshops, toolkits, guides, meetings and socials that were held by and amongst members helped to spread this breadth of cross-tenure organising efforts, news and ideas across the growing member list. The Network itself also took action as a whole: running occupied residences, organising conferences, and twice shutting down MIPIM (Le marché international des professionnels de l'immobilier), the international property fair, where councils could be found making deals with developers, when the fair came to London.

This Landscape and Grenfell Fire

Many members of RHN were (and still are) facing extreme housing stress. Estate regeneration in London in particular has been an acute problem that razed entire communities. The scars of the loss of the Heygate Estate, the ongoing battle over the Aylesbury, success on the Carpenter's Estate in Newham, and continuing campaigns across the city, have marked the way in which housing pressure, its exploitation by property developers and the local resistances to this dispossession, shaped London. In West London, a slew of regeneration and privatisation was taking place. Local groups such as Save Our Silchester and Westway23 resisted attacks on housing and communal facilities. The Grenfell Action Group (GAG), a local resistance effort, joined the Radical Housing Network in 2014. Formed in Grenfell Tower, the group was focused particularly on issues of outsourcing, disrepair, corruption, safety and other complaints against their landlord, KCTMO, and the local authority, RBKC, who had been treating local residents, particularly in the poorer northern part of the borough, with increasingly reckless and brutal disdain. Much of GAG's public-facing work was done on their blog where, to this day, forensic accounts of misconduct by the council and their landlord can be found. One post, which went 'viral' in the fire's immediate aftermath, described how Group members had indeed seen from their ongoing experiences with both the council and the TMO that only a disaster, and potentially a large loss of life, might bring to light their landlord's contempt and failure to their residents.

On joining RHN, the Grenfell Action Group upped its campaigning in the local area. The Network worked with GAG to support the campaign against the diversion of council funding away from poorer residents towards services benefiting the area's wealthiest residents, such as the allocation of large sums to Holland Park Opera while cutting millions from social services budgets. One RHN member worked intensively with GAG during 2015 helping to organise tower residents and their campaign to challenge aspects of the refurbishment programme during which the flammable cladding was installed on the tower. Alongside GAG, RHN supported other local protests aimed at challenging local regeneration and dispossession processes that were impacting local residents. It was in this context, of both increasing pressure from austerity and a deepening push to privatise and monetise the land on which social tenants lived, that the fire at Grenfell Tower took place. The fire was also born into the resistance of those pressures: the active, dispersed and fluctuating network of community groups, local connections, activists, and national campaigns that some tower residents had been involved with before the fire happened.

Lancaster West Estate Residents

Of most urgent importance following the fire, and, sadly, still remaining unmet two years on, were people's immediate needs. For this chapter, we focus on the voices of Lancaster West Estate residents with whom the network worked in the days and weeks following the fire, and with whom members are still working today. Although it should go without saying, it is important to mention that the work of RHN was just one corner of a huge interconnected body of organising, community work, care, campaigning, legal support and many other projects and contributions that were undertaken and are still being run by many different people in that part of West London. We do not hope to be exhaustive in documenting even our own work over this period, but to give a snapshot of the kinds of activities we were engaged in – as well as setting out the context in which these activities took place. Much of the work described below happened 'behind the scenes' – the ethos of RHN being to work as much as possible in support of local organising activity, building capacity of those who are authentically representing their own communities. In the months following the fire, the intensity of RHNs work in the area subsided, and strong, genuinely local, campaigning groups have taken root. It is these groups, firmly based in the local area, that play the most part in seeking justice and reparations for those affected by the fire.

Away from the media and political focus on the surviving (and bereaved) residents of Grenfell Tower, hundreds of residents who lived in the blocks of low-rise flats immediately adjacent to the tower ('the Walkways') on the Lancaster West Estate, in which Grenfell Tower was situated, were also unable to return to their homes. Emergency services had evacuated these residents, both for the residents' safety, and also so that the rescue could be carried out. These residents, like those that had been in Grenfell Tower, had been forced to sleep in churches and community centres, where makeshift communal shelters had been established in the area.

As the days and then weeks went on, ongoing problems with the walkways blocks continued to make homes uninhabitable. The flats' external areas were covered in toxic debris from the fire, internal communal areas and stairwells were flooded, and security systems were not working. Inside their flats, residents had no gas or hot water. Although the local tube station standing next to the estate had been closed for public safety reasons, the residents themselves received little information from RBKC on the safety of their homes, and that which they did receive they didn't trust to be accurate. Many were worried about air quality in the immediate area. Residents were told by RBKC that they could return to their homes at their own risk. In addition to these practical problems with their flats, most of these residents were also experiencing severe shock and trauma. They had been evacuated from their flats during the fire and so had stood, many with their children, watching as the tower burned.

The low turnover of residents on the estate meant that there were strong and close relationships between tower residents and residents in these adjacent blocks, which were built in the same phase as Grenfell Tower, in the early 1970s, with a number of residents inhabiting their homes on the estate for over four decades. These people had witnessed close friends, family members, school friends, immediate neighbours trapped in their homes as the fire burned, with many never escaping.

Media Work

The Network's first steps, arriving in the chaos and grief of West London over those first few days, was to attempt to make contact with those we knew from our work before the fire and assist in organising meetings with these residents. Taking advice from INQUEST, a charity providing expertise on state-related deaths and their investigation, we made the initial steps to support those survivors to access legal advice, while those survivors themselves attempted to establish contact with one another, and began the very first steps of organising themselves into the group of survivors and bereaved that became Grenfell United. In these first days, we made a number of new contacts with residents from the wider Lancaster West Estate. Again, we supported these walkways residents in accessing legal advice, and started work helping to facilitate and advise on residents' meetings. It was clear there were also huge needs for housing, financial and justice support for them – and we sought to support them in getting their voices heard and their interests recognised, by those with the power to address them.

The continual frenzied media pressure meant Grenfell's official story was being written at a dizzying pace, with residents feeling strongly that their concerns and experiences were not being presented fully or accurately. In that context, the support and coordination of residents' potential media appearances was of central importance. Together with residents, we established key messages they wanted to communicate and worked to draft press releases. Media training was one first port of call. In conjunction with the New Economy

Organisers' Network, one of many organisations that offered facilities, expertise and support in the days after the fire, we arranged for basic media training to be delivered to estate residents and other community members who were compelled to campaign and were being continually asked for comment by media organisations.

Residents with whom the Network worked have said they found support for organising and media very useful. As one resident explained,

> When it started it was spontaneous, a group of residents that formed around us and built organically. We built some order from chaos and those meetings and trainings helped us to formulate what we felt into 'media language'. Helping us through that process, and coordinating the logistics of those meetings and trainings were critical.[1]

For these residents in particular, being able to clearly articulate and stake a claim in the wider effects of what was happening around the tower and the community was crucial. 'We understood the system rather than being used and manipulated [working with RHN]', another resident told us, 'We took hold of the narrative – and I only now see what that means. [...] We [the wider estate residents] were only recognised because of the work we did.'

Another local, Melvyn, agreed that learning the game of media language provided a foundation that has gone on to help residents over the past year.

> I've done lots of media stuff and [that early work] really helped me to stay on topic in what I need to say. From that media training, I'm now directing and coordinating our position as residents' voices. It taught me to stay focused in interviews, that even when the interviewer or other guests try to deviate that you can manage to reinforce the topic we want to get across.

Rehousing

In the months following the fire, RHN members continued to work with residents, particularly those in the walkways, in their attempts to ensure that their temporary accommodation provision remained in place until they were able to return, and their efforts to secure adequate permanent accommodation were successful. The walkways blocks are a distance of only metres from the tower itself; the view from the windows of many of these flats looked directly onto the enormous burned out remains of the tower. Something RHN members heard from a number of these residents, when they attempted to return to their homes, was 'I still see their faces at the windows'. Many, particularly those with young children, found living in such proximity to the remains of the tower simply too traumatic.

Throughout and beyond the year that followed the fire, the council issued deadlines and ultimatums for those who had been evacuated from the walkways to return. Residents organised in response to defend their position and extend their temporary accommodation. At the same time, particular right-wing journalists and papers turned from their initial support of residents to a strategy of undermining their calls for social and legal justice. Differences between groups within the local community were exploited, tensions exacerbated and a cleavage between legitimate and illegitimate voices was deepened. Residents were portrayed as undeserving or aggressive, and the needs they were articulating as unreasonably demanding. Such attacks had real consequences for relationships and organising on the ground. Many of these media attack pieces appeared timed to coincide with key events and dates where public focus would return to the subject of the fire and those affected by it, for example, at the six-month anniversary of the fire, or the formal opening of the Public Inquiry. Much time was also therefore spent on defensive media rebuttal work, ensuring that certain 'attack' pieces were counterbalanced with more accurate portrayals of local residents and their campaigns.[2]

And so the need for residents to strategise and coordinate to ensure their voices are heard, and heard well, has been unrelenting. The tower was finally completely wrapped to hide its huge and hideous charred exterior from public view, just a couple of days before the first anniversary of the fire. The fact that the tower was no longer visible has enabled many walkways residents to return home. However, at time of writing, there remain in temporary accommodation a significant number of residents who will never be able to return to their old homes in the walkways. Invariably, their temporary accommodation is totally unsuitable – often small, unfurnished, up to 12 miles from where they conduct their normal lives, and almost always very precarious. At least two families had to move from one temporary place into another in the first year after the fire, as their landlords decided to return or sell up. Some have not returned for psychological reasons, while for others returning is a physical impossibility, as since the fire their health has degenerated to such an extent that their old homes are no longer physically accessible to them. The council is currently in the process of removing the financial support that has allowed those former residents to afford their stay in temporary accommodation, and is telling them that they must now relinquish their old secure tenancies, with no offer of secure permanent alternative homes. For many residents, the fire is thus being used to force them out of secure council properties and into precarious and expensive temporary accommodation on a permanent basis. RHN continues to work alongside residents campaigning against this.

Let us also say that this does not cover the extent of work undertaken by RHN, or projects by its individual members. Network members worked with charities and local legal support groups to campaign for undocumented survivors of the fire to be granted the right to remain in the UK, for example. More recently, Fuel Poverty Action has worked with residents of a building wrapped in flammable cladding in Salford and have added these residents' voices to Grenfell United's call for all 'Grenfell style' flammable cladding to be removed and banned. Many more connections, relationships and contributions have been made and, as aforementioned, all of RHN's work comprises just a tiny corner of the mammoth, interconnected and ongoing community and campaign work undertaken since the fire.

Divisions and Coordination

Those involved in community-based organising campaigns will always encounter varying degrees of differences and divisions amongst and within different sections of the community they are working in. The community around Grenfell is no exception, and the extremely stressful and traumatic context after the fire, not to mention the low level of trust that local people have towards the public authorities, provided fertile ground for conflict and divisions. Considering this, it is worth noting the relatively limited nature of internal conflict within the community and amongst the campaigns focused on different aspects of the fire and its consequences.

Those impacted by the Grenfell fire can be categorised, and often self-organised, into different groups. This was sometimes according to their varying situations in relation to the fire: survivor, bereaved, walkways resident, wider Lancaster West Estate resident, wider community member, for instance; or according to their focus on housing, on the public inquiry, on the humanitarian response, or on mental and physical health issues; or on their chosen tactics, for example, those who favoured direct political opposition, or those choosing a less direct conciliatory approach to the relevant public authorities.

Of course, these categories change and overlap, but they inevitably mean that sections of the local community have perceived varied interests and assumed different positions across time. The residents we spoke to said that while these differences have at points acted to hinder coordinated action, they have learned the importance of trying to work around them, to develop strategies to ensure that as much as possible their campaigns are coordinated, acting to strengthen rather than impede their struggle for justice. 'At the beginning we were naive, looking back,' one said, describing the difficulties of coordinating across the community. 'To be most effective we need class action, but where that hasn't been possible I've seen the value of just acting to improve the situation of just some groups within the community.'

There has been valuable learning; an unwelcome yet cruelly necessary education in politics and political and administrative processes has been gained. One resident described their familiarity with the lengthy but worthwhile process of ensuring that as much as possible their organised efforts were representative, 'reflecting what the community is feeling, developing a culture of trying to sing from same hymn sheet'.

Current Landscape

In the public diagnosis and discussion after the Grenfell fire, the decades of privatisation, disinvestment and slashing of 'red tape' that had once protected ordinary people, were openly shown as society-wide issues, key factors that contributed to the production of such an atrocity in the world's most wealthy borough.

Beginning with Thatcher's deliberate destruction of social housing under Right to Buy, homes have been increasingly treated as assets rather than as a public good. Rather than local and national state bodies being wholly responsible for the welfare and benefit of their tenants, homes increasingly became housing – empty vessels for private investment and the production of profit.

The Radical Housing Network, along with many other residents and housing campaigning groups, implored the public and government to ensure that Grenfell be the last atrocity of its kind: that safe, decent and affordable homes be provided to all who needed them – and that space always be made for residents' voices to be heard in the management of their own homes, voices to which public and private bodies were to be unequivocally responsive and accountable.

Unfortunately, despite the widespread shock from across the world at the horror of Grenfell, sufficient action to reverse these decades of criminal neglect has not been taken. For the survivors of Grenfell, wider Lancaster West Estate residents and the local community – as well as for council and private tenants across the UK – the necessary changes that such an atrocity might have triggered in housing policy, such as better local authority oversight, justice for victims of state and corporate negligence, and improved safety regulations and practice are far from being realized.

This is not to mention that many of those affected by the fire are still fighting for their basic needs to be met. At time of writing, survivors from the tower and residents of the Lancaster West Estate remain in inadequate accommodation. Aggressive regeneration projects, including those that threaten residents' safety, continue across London. Many buildings – from homes to schools and hospitals – are still coated with flammable cladding. As exposed by the work of groups such as Fuel Poverty Action and campaigning residents on estates in Salford and other parts of the UK, there are still many council tenants who are experiencing, with chilling similarity, the contempt and attempts to thwart and divide organising by the community from their council of the kind meted out by RBKC and

KCTMO to their residents. As Edward Daffarn, Grenfell Action Group member told the Channel 4 journalist Jon Snow in his first broadcast interview, a year on from the fire, the lack of action from national and local government on issues for which we have already seen an intolerable human cost, leads him to believe that 'Grenfell two is in the post'.

For many social housing tenants and wider housing campaigners, Grenfell was the realization of their worst fears, the inevitable result of dangerous policies and practices they had fought against for decades, that they continue to fight. Grenfell United, the official organisation of tower survivors, continues to campaign tirelessly on both the public inquiry into the tragedy and alongside other housing tenants on issues of safety, particularly around flammable and toxic cladding. Threaded through this ongoing assault on social housing, many community groups and organisations are building those tactics, networks and movements towards small victories that can turn the tide of housing policy and practice in this country, a country whose authorities, despite seeing the unconscionable cost of their actions in broad daylight, has condemned thousands of people to displacement, and precarious or unsafe homes.

Notes

1. Some residents asked not to be named out of concern it could be used against them in future by the local authority.
2. Media responses to the local community over time would be a very useful and interesting area of further focused study.

Ghosts of Grenfell

Lowkey

The night our eyes changed
Rooms where, love was made and un-made in a flash of the night
Rooms where, memories drowned in fumes of poison
Rooms where, futures were planned and the imagination of children
    built castles in the sky
Rooms where, both the extraordinary and the mundane were lived
Become forever tortured graves of ash
Oh you political class, so servile to corporate power

Did they die, or us?
Did they die, or us?
Did they die, for us?
Ghosts of Grenfell still calling for justice
Now hear 'em, now hear 'em scream
Did they die, or us?
Did they die, or us?
Did they die, for us?
This corporate manslaughter will haunt you
Now hear 'em scream

Words can not express
Please allow me to begin though
1:30am heard the shouting from my window
People crying in the street
Watchin' the burning of their kinfolk
Grenfell Tower, now historically a symbol
People reaching, from their windows
Screaming, for their lives
Pleading, with the cries
Tryna reason with the skies

Dale youth birthed champions
Comparison is clear though
That every single person in the building was a hero
So don't judge our tired eyes in these trying times
'Cause we be breathing in cyanide, the entire night
They say Yasin saw the fire and he ran inside
Who'd thought that would be the site where he and his family died
The street is like a graveyard, tombstones lurching over us
Those shouting out to their windows, now wish they never woke
   them up
Wouldn't hope your worst enemy to go in this position
Now it's flowers for the dead and printed posters for the missing,
   come home

Did they die, or us?
Did they die, or us?
Did they die, for us?
Ghosts of Grenfell still calling for justice
Now hear 'em, now hear 'em scream
Did they die, or us?
Did they die, or us?
Did they die, for us?
This corporate manslaughter will haunt you
Now hear 'em scream

I see trauma in the faces of all those that witnessed this
Innocence in the faces of all those on the missing list
See hopes unfulfilled
Ambitions never achieved
No I'm not the only one that sees the dead in my dreams
Strive for the bravery of Yasin, artistic gift of Khadija
Every person, a unique blessing to never be repeated
Strive for the loyalty of siblings that stayed behind with their parents
Pray that every loved one lost can somehow make an appearance
We are, calling like the last conversations with their dearest
Until we face, what they face we will never know what fear is
We are, calling for survivors rehoused in the best place

Not to be left sleeping in the West Way for 10 days
We're, calling for arrests made and debts paid
In true numbers known for the families that kept faith
We're, calling for safety in homes of love
They are immortalised forever, the only ghosts are us
I wonder

Did they die, or us?
Did they die, or us?
Did they die, for us?
Ghosts of Grenfell still calling for justice
Now hear 'em, now hear 'em scream
Did they die, or us?
Did they die, or us?
Did they die, for us?
This corporate manslaughter will haunt you
Now hear 'em scream

قولولي وين اروح
ناس عم تحترق في ساعة سحور
أحس إني بألم تاني
أحس إني بألم تاني
قولولي وين اروح
ناس عم تحترق في ساعة سحور

To whom it may concern, at the Queen's royal borough of Kensington in Chelsea. Where is Yasin El-Wahabi? Where is his brother Mehdi? Where is his sister Nur Huda? Where is their mother and where is their father? Where is Nura Jamal and her husband Hashim? Where is their children, Yahya, Firdaus and Yaqoob? Where is Nadia Loureda? Where is Steve Power? Where is Dennis Murphy? Where is Marco Gottardi? Where is Gloria Trevisian? Where is Amal and her daughter Amaya? Where is Mohammed Neda? Where is Ali Yawar Jafari? Where is Khadija Saye? Where is Mary Mendy? Where is Mariem Elgwahry? Where is her mother Suhar?

Tell us, where is Rania Ibrahim and her two daughters? Where is Jessica Urbano Ramirez? Where is Deborah Lamprell? Where is Mohammed Alhajali? Where is Nadia? Where is her husband Bassem? Where are her daughters, Mirna, Fatima, Zaina and their grandmother? Where is Zainab Dean and her son Jeremiah? Where is Ligaya Moore? Where is Sheila Smith? Where is Mohammed-nour Tuccu? Where is Tony Disson? Where is Maria Burton? Where is Fathaya Alsanousi? Where is her son Abu Feras and her daughter Esra Ibrahim? Where is Lucas James? Where is Farah Hamdan? Where is Omar Belkadi? Where is their daughter Leena? Where is Hamid Kani? Where is Esham Rahman? Where is Raymond Bernard? Where is Isaac Paulos? Where is Marjorie Vital? Where's her son Ernie? Where is Komru Miah? Where is his wife Razia? Where are their children Abdul Hanif, Abdul Hamid, Hosna? Where are Sakineh and Fatima Afraseiabi? Where is Berkti Haftom and her son Biruk?

Tells us, where is Stefan Anthony Mills? Where is Abdul Salam? Where is Khadija Khalloufi? Where is Karen Bernard? Where are these people? Where are these people? Where is Gary Maunders? Where is Rohima Ali? Where is her six-year-old daughter Maryam, her five-year-old daughter Hafizah and her three-year-old son Mohammed? God bless you all! Where are all these people?

Where are all these people?
The blood is on your hands
There will be ashes on your graves
Like a Phoenix we will rise
The blood is on your hands
There will be ashes on your graves
Like a Phoenix we will rise

5

A Border in Every Street
Grenfell and the Hostile Environment
Sarah Keenan

During summer 2015, the British government announced that it would pass laws requiring landlords to evict tenants who do not hold valid visas. As part of her efforts to convince African migrants that 'our streets are not paved with gold', the then Home Secretary Theresa May planned to make it a criminal offence for landlords to rent to irregular migrants (May and Cazeneuve, 2015). This plan, which has since been implemented by the Immigration Act 2016,[1] was part of May's professed intention of intensifying the 'hostile environment' for irregular migrants that her government had begun creating with the Immigration Act 2014 (Travis, 2013). As the Church of England put it, the so-called 'right to rent' requirement creates a border in every street (Robinson, 2014).

How do we understand such borders, which are at once invisible and real, intermittent and permanent; borders that operate by attaching to individual subjects wherever they go rather than bounding off a defined physical area; borders that are internal to the nation that has already been entered. In particular, how do we understand internal borders in Britain, a political entity that as Kojo Koram has argued, 'has never really existed as a nation, it has only really functioned as an empire' (Koram, 2016); an empire which once sought to extend its borders to encompass as much of the world as possible? As the empire crumbled, patterns of migration shifted from white British subjects moving out to colonise the world, to brown and black British subjects moving from home countries depleted of resources by the colonisers to the island motherland, seeking work and a better life (Bhambra, 2016). The British state responded to this arrival of non-white subjects with increasingly restrictive immigration laws, which have the maintenance of white supremacy[2] at their core. Immigration law has then combined with other areas of law to increasingly and literally restrict the physical space in which non-white subjects are able to safely exist on this island. Examining the hostile environment produced by the internal borders of the 2014 and 2016 Immigration Acts helps us to make sense of the means through which law produces racist landscapes in which material spatial boundaries exist for particular subjects and not others. I offer this theorisation of Britain's racist landscape as a way of explaining some of the broader context in which the Grenfell Tower fire occurred, an atrocity which disproportionately claimed the lives of non-white subjects, with inherited histories of colonisation, migration and the negotiation of hostile spaces. Beginning with a brief discussion of how legal geography, critical race theory and critical disability studies assist in understanding the relationship between law, space and the human subject, I put forward the concept of 'taking space with you' as a way to understand the racist British landscape in which we live today.

'We Don't Cross Borders, Borders Cross Us'

The liberal democratic state, and the law it creates, are underpinned and legitimised by notions of universality and neutrality – theoretically, law delivers justice to all subjects on an equal basis. Critical race and feminist theorists have long noted the flaws in this theorisation, demonstrating ways in which law operates unevenly depending on who you are (see Bell, 1970; MacKinnon, 1983). More recently, legal geography has also demonstrated ways in which law operates unevenly depending on *where* you are (see Blomley, Delaney and Ford, 2001). Legal geography, critical race and feminist theorists have argued that law falsely constructs spaces as being politically neutral, uniform and fixed. They instead argue that space in fact consists of multiple, dynamic realities – realities which affect different people in different ways. Here I always find geographer Doreen Massey's work useful. Instead of thinking of places as bounded areas, Massey imagines them as 'articulated moments in networks of social relations and understandings' (Massey, 1993). Because the same moment will be experienced and articulated differently by different people, this understanding accounts for the same place having mismatched and even contrasting meanings for different people. The place that is 'the British Border' at Heathrow Terminal 4 airport on any given day, for example, is a familiar workplace for UK border guards, a congested but still fast-moving queue for EU-passport holders, and a very physical barrier – a place of potential violence and humiliation – for a bearded Muslim man who may be detained and subject to a Schedule 7 search.[3] Before the fire, the place that was Grenfell Tower was a home to those who lived there, an eyesore to be managed until it could be 'regenerated' as cheaply as possible for Kensington and Chelsea Borough Council,[4] and an irritant to quite literally be covered up – in cheap, flammable cladding – for Kensington and Chelsea Tenant Management Organisation, the landlord which for many years ignored the repeated pleas of residents to improve the building's fire safety mechanisms (Grenfell Action Group, 2017). Places mean different things to different people depending on how they are socially and physically located.

Thinking about space as multiple in meaning and constantly in motion also allows for spatial entities such as nation-states to be understood beyond their bounded physical landmass. Nation-state borders are not simple lines of demarcation, but complex institutions (Balibar, 2002). As Anderson, Sharma and Wright argued (over a decade before 'hostile environment' became government policy), 'borders follow people and surround them as they try to access paid labour, welfare benefits, health, labour protections, education, civil associations and justice' (2009). Another way of saying this is, as Sydney activist group Cross Border Collective put it, 'we don't cross borders, borders cross us'.[5]

The Space You Take With You

One way to understand the complicated connection between human subjects and the places we live in and move through is the idea of 'taking space with you': that we take a particular space with us when we move. This idea requires that we take seriously the meanings and consequences which attach to particular spaces and to those constructed as belonging to them. Within the contemporary English landscape, for example, the space of council-owned 'the tower block' has become stigmatised and discriminated against (Hastings, 2004). As Lindsey Hanley writes, 'there is one phrase in the English language that has come to be larded with even more negative meaning than "council estate", and that is "tower block"' (2007: 97). Hanley traces how, over the past 30 years, tower blocks came to be seen by outsiders as 'slums in the sky' primarily housing poor, racialised people. As individual flats within tower blocks were sold into private ownership and the responsibility for maintaining the building became more difficult to manage, the blocks physically deteriorated (Carr, 2017). Stigmatisation of tower blocks was accompanied by government and corporate policies of containment and malicious neglect, particularly as these spaces are seen as blights on a rapidly gentrifying landscape, bringing down property prices and getting in the way of 'regeneration'. Belonging to the space of the tower block means having an identity that will not be listened to or taken seriously by those in power, even when – as the Grenfell Action Group blog shows us – it is a matter of life and death. Belonging to a tower block means you are likely to be racialised. As Danny Dorling's research shows, most children who live above the 4th floor of tower blocks in England are black or Asian (Dorling, 2011). All human subjects are intimately connected to, and to some extent defined by, the spaces where we live. Who we are, what is within our reach, and our vulnerability to violence is constantly (re)determined by where we have been and what has happened around us. As Donna Haraway suggested in the early 1990s, our bodies do not end at the skin (Haraway, 1991). The critical disability scholar Margaret Shildrick argues that in fact we humans are all hybrids – combining with, separating from and being both enabled and obstructed by physical environments in different ways (Shildrick, 2015). There is no purely organic, bounded embodied human subject who lives in isolation from others and from space.

So space attaches to us all, we combine with it and it defines who we are and what we can access (Keenan, 2015). Race, gender, ability and other categories of belonging materialise, on an individual level, through intimate interactions between space and the body. There is no doubt that coming from a particular part of the world operates as a signifier of racial difference. So too can living in a particular part of London. Wearing particular kinds of clothing or consuming particular kinds of food can operate as signifiers of racial difference, even though clothes, food and places are not part of the body, but exist in the space beyond it (Lentin, 2012). Sara Ahmed argues that racism can operate as a 'brick wall' that has been built up by history, a wall that can appear in different places and times, but only in front of particular subjects, preventing them from accessing resources or simply continuing their journeys (Ahmed, 2012). The brick wall of racism is a space that many subjects take with them as they move, whether the journey is across the world or across the road. Race is a social construct originating in European colonialism, but it is reproduced on a pervasive and daily basis by laws and norms that restrict the physical space particular subjects can safely occupy, thus obstructing their life paths. The category of race and the racist landscapes that maintain it are produced through the repeated operation of 'brick walls', which obstruct particular journeys and let subjects know they do not belong.

The Immigration Acts 2014 and 2016: Building Internal Borders

The Immigration Acts of 2014 and 2016 introduced a scheme of regulation which creates a landscape in which a subject's immigration status acts as a physical barrier to basic needs including housing. The Acts produce a landscape of bespoke hostility to migrants and those seen as non-British by regulating the behaviour of landlords. While a subject's visa status has traditionally been checked at the territorial entrance point, the Act introduces a range of 'in-country' immigration status checks, meaning that those who provide not only housing but also banking services, drivers' licences and marriage certificates are required to check the immigration status of applicants before providing them with the relevant service/access. While British universities have been acting as Home Office proxies since at least 2012 (Abdelrahman et al., 2014), the new Acts extend the internal border regime well beyond higher education to everyday services necessary for human survival. Those who tend to come up against the 'brick wall' of passport and visa checks at the territorial entrance point, must now expect to come up against that brick wall wherever they attempt to rent a home in England.

Using spatial metaphors, human rights group Liberty describes the new immigration checks as 'gateway requirements' for access to basic services (Robinson, 2014). The Asylum Support Appeals Project described them as 'hurdles' (ASAP, 2017). And it was the Church of England, which predicted that the Act would create 'a border in every street' (Robinson, 2014). But the in-country 'gateways' and 'borders' that these groups refer to are, like Sara Ahmed's 'brick walls', not only metaphorical. For subjects who have had their claims for asylum rejected, who have overstayed their visas or who for other reasons do not have either EU citizenship or a valid British visa, these regulations constitute material barriers to physical spaces. Bureaucratic 'brick walls' serve the same exclusive purpose as physical ones.

But which subjects exactly will be met with a border on every street? How does the Act build a specifically racist landscape? British immigration law has a long history of operating as a 'brick wall' for particular subjects, and producing categories of race in the process. As Nadine El-Enany explains, in an attempt to keep the crumbling empire together, the British Nationality Act was passed in 1948 (El-Enany, 2019). It granted all nationals of Commonwealth countries and colonial British subjects, some 600 million people, rights of entry to Britain itself. When non-white British citizens began arriving in Britain throughout the 1950s and 1960s, increasingly restrictive immigration legislation was passed to limit their presence. The Immigration Act 1971 restricted the right to enter and remain in Britain to those whose parents or grandparents were born in Britain. While not framed in explicitly racist language, the law had explicitly racist motives. Coming on the heels of white supremacist Enoch Powell's rivers of blood speech and growing racist and xenophobic sentiment among British voters, the Act made it more difficult for non-white British subjects to come to Britain. Unless they had the requisite bloodline to Britain stretching back to a time when the motherland was overwhelmingly white and migration of non-white subjects to Britain was very rare, citizens of Britain's remaining colonies and those of Commonwealth countries had to apply for permission to be cleared to enter Britain. The 1971 Act

thus constructed an initial 'brick wall' for some British subjects, con-
stituting them as a racial category in the process. This wall operated
at or before the point of entry into the actual British landmass.

Entry clearance requirements impose an administrative border
on subjects born in particular places, a border that extends all the
way into their home states and areas they might pass through on the
journey to Britain. The extension of the border well outside Britain's
physical boundaries has been referred to as the 'external border' (Van
Houtum, 2010), and might also be understood as Ahmed's brick wall
of racism, a wall that appears in the path of particular subjects before
they have even left their homes. The operation of the British external
border in Calais,[6] for example, enables British border officers to
prevent people from coming to Britain well before they reach British
territory. The external borders of Britain and other EU countries
are policed by FRONTEX, the EU's border force, which effectively
enforces EU borders in locations across the world but most notably
in the Mediterranean and along the northern and western African
coast, where boats might attempt to enter EU territorial waters. Tens
of thousands of people have died trying to cross the EU's external
borders (Ward, 2015; UNITED, 2018).

While provisions from the 1971 Immigration Act to FRONTEX
produce an external British border, the new Immigration Act 2016
produces internal borders. The internal and external British borders
are driven by racist colonial anxieties, and are reproductive of racial
categories. Race, as Stuart Hall argued, is a moving signifier – who
is 'white' and who is racially other is not natural or permanent but
shifts over time (the altered status of EU migrants in Britain, Poles
in particular, post-Brexit referendum, is one example of a recent
shift away from whiteness [Krupa, 2016]). Categories of race are
reproduced through material structures of racism, from the extreme
impoverishment of former British colonies to the everyday acts of discrimination endured by individuals designated as belonging to those
colonies. A young Igbo woman having spent her life in Nigeria may
not see herself as 'black' (see Nadura, 2014), but she likely will once
she encounters the British border. If she is fortunate enough to pass
the external border, she will then encounter the internal one every
time she tries to rent a flat (or open a bank account or get a driver's

licence). Every interaction with the internal border is productive of her understanding of herself as foreign, and of the British landscape as a white supremacist environment.

The space that the irregular migrant takes with her as she travels both towards and within Britain is a process of constant negotiation with borders. This process not only determines the subject's identity but also literally restricts the physical spaces in which she can safely exist. Her body does not end at the skin because a border appears before her at every turn. She becomes an embodied hybrid of human and border control. She takes the space of racist colonial exclusion with her wherever she moves.

The widespread fear, amongst non-white communities living in Britain today, of coming up against this wall and potentially facing deportation is one reason why, in the wake of the Grenfell fire, the Radical Housing Network and other community groups signed an open letter calling for full immigration amnesty to all survivors of the fire who did not have regularised immigration statuses (Radical Housing Network, 2017). As they point out in that letter,

> migrant survivors are concerned they will be later detained and/or deported. This is confirmed by advisors on the ground who report that individuals continue to sleep rough, rather than receive the vital support they need to rebuild their lives.
>
> (Radical Housing Network, 2017)

And that space of racist colonial exclusion does not move only with the irregular migrant. Many predicted that landlords will simply opt to rent to tenants with English-sounding names, so as to avoid the risk of contravention and the need to do extra paperwork, and a 2017 report by the Joint Council for the Welfare of Immigrants confirmed this to be the reality (JCWI, 2017). As well as creating a 'hostile space' for irregular migrants, the combining of private property and border controls produces a national space in which all non-white subjects (or at least those who lack the enormous wealth required to buy their own property and thus escape the rental market) are likely to be spatialised as aliens, taking a space of exclusion and vulnerability with them wherever they go.

As Jon Burnett argues, the aim of the Immigration Act is to make life intolerable for undocumented migrants so as to force them to leave – their destitution is used as a government tool of deportation (Burnett, 2016). The internalisation of the border through right to rent requirements thus bolsters the white supremacist landscape of contemporary Britain, creating a physical environment in which racialised subjects take the violence of colonial anxieties and brick walls with them, in every street.

Looking Forward in the Wake of Grenfell

In the faces of the Grenfell dead and missing, we can see that the internal border was in operation in London's richest borough. The burnt out remains of the block and the haunting screams of those who perished surely function for Theresa May as an unmistakably clear communication of her message to African migrants that 'our streets are not paved with gold'. Not for them. The right to rent requirements of the 2014 and 2016 Immigration Acts serve to bolster the hostile environment that 40 years of housing policy and close to a century of exclusionary citizenship policy have already produced for poor, non-white migrants and their children (Carr, 2017; El-Enany, 2019). The first confirmed victim of the fire was Mohammad Alhajali, a 23-year-old Syrian refugee and engineering student. He lived in the tower with his 25-year-old brother, who survived. As Alhajali's friend told *The Telegraph*, 'He survived Assad, the war in Syria, only to die in a tower block in London' (Ensor and Horton, 2017). The images of Grenfell on fire are reminiscent of the many burnt out building shells in Syria that we are shown by the media. What happened to Mohammed Alhajali was for me the most horrific demonstration of the taking space with you idea: a space of disproportionate vulnerability to the most extreme forms of violence, which Alhajali took with him all the way from Syria to Kensington.

The British landscape we live in today is not fixed in time. The publicisation in 2018 of the violence and destitution enforced on members of the Windrush generation caught by the hostile environment led to the resignation of Home Secretary Amber Rudd and a renaming of the policy. Of course, these are superficial changes, but the public sentiment that brought them about suggests the possibility of more meaningful change in the longer term. We need a multiplicity of campaigns and tactics to tackle the multiplicity of racist spaces which law and history have produced: because we are hybrids, and because law racially excludes not only through immigration law but also through property and administrative law, it is this endemic and structural racism embedded everywhere that we need to fight. Campaigns for human rights (framed as if our bodies end at the skin) are not enough. We need to also fight for housing, universal health care and education, transparency and accountability in university management and other government institutions, in order to not only empower individual human subjects but to reshape the environment that surrounds and defines them, and to build a version of Britain that allows the subjects of empire and their children to finally leave the heinously resilient and sticky space of white supremacist violence behind.

Notes

1. Section 39 of the Immigration Act 2016 amends the Immigration Act 2014, inserting s33A, which creates the offence.
2. Following Cheryl Harris, I am using Frances Lee Ansley's definition of white supremacy:

> By 'white supremacy' I do not mean to allude only to the self-conscious racism of white supremacist hate groups. I refer instead to a political, economic and cultural system in which whites overwhelmingly control power and material resources, conscious and unconscious ideas of white superiority and entitlement are widespread, and relations of white dominance and non-white subordination are daily re-enacted across a broad array of institutions and social settings.
>
> (Ansley 1989 cited in Harris, 1993: 1714)

> White supremacy has its roots in British and European colonialism, projects orchestrated and maintained by the ruling classes of those societies. White supremacy does not benefit all white people equally and is itself instrumental in the maintenance of a power structure which oppresses working people of all racial categories (see Allen, [1994] 2012; James, [1974] 2012).

3. Under Schedule 7 of the Terrorism Act 2000, police, immigration officers or customs officials have the power to stop, search and hold individuals at airports, without the need for any grounds of suspecting the person has any involvement in terrorism or any other criminal activity.

4. A record of Rydon's application to demolish Grenfell, lodged in 2014, can be found at this Royal Borough of Kensington and Chelsea's Planning and Building Control page: www.rbkc.gov.uk/bconline/buildingControlDetails. do?activeTab=summary&keyVal=_RBKC_BCAPR_123520 (accessed 3 October 2018).

5. The notion of 'We didn't cross the border, the border crossed us' has long been present in Chicana feminist historiography (including Anzaluda, 1987; Hernandez, 2012: 245).

6. Under the Sangatte Protocol agreed in 1991 between Britain and France.

References

Abdelrahman, M. et al. (2014) 'Checks on Students Undermine Trust'. *The Guardian*, 2 March. www.theguardian.com/education/2014/mar/02/checks-on-students-undermine-trust (all websites in this list last accessed November 2018).

Ahmed, S. (2012) *On Being Included: Racism and Diversity in Institutional Life.* Durham, NC: Duke University Press.

Allen, T. W. ([1994] 2012) *The Invention of the White Race, Volume 1.* London: Verso.

Anderson, B., N. Sharma and C. Wright (2009) 'Editorial: Why No Borders?' *Refuge*, 26(2): 5–18.

Anzaldua, G. (1987) *Borderlands/La Frontera: The New Mestiza.* San Francisco, CA: Aunt Lute Books.

Asylum Support Appeals Project (ASAP) (2017) 'Briefing Note: The Right to Rent Scheme and Asylum Support'. June. www.asaproject.org/uploads/June_2017_-_Briefing_note_-_The_right_to_rent.pdf.

Balibar, E. (2002) *Politics and the Other Scene.* London: Verso.

Bell, D. (1970) *Race, Racism, and American Law.* New York: Aspen Publishers.

Bhambra, G. (2016) 'Brexit, the Commonwealth, and Exclusionary Citizenship'. *Open Democracy*, 16 December. www.opendemocracy.net/gurminder-k-bhambra/brexit-commonwealth-and-exclusionary-citizenship.

Blomley, N., D. Delaney and R. T. Ford (2001) *The Legal Geographies Reader: Law, Power and Space.* Oxford: Blackwell.

Burnett, J. (2016) Institute of Race Relations 'An IRR discussion paper on the Housing and Planning and Immigration Bills 2015–16'.

Carr, H. (2017) 'Grenfell Tower and the Unravelling of Forty Years of Housing Ideology'. *SLSA Blog.* http://slsablog.co.uk/blog/blog-posts/grenfell-tower-and-the-unravelling-of-forty-years-of-housing-ideology/.

Dorling, D. (2011) *So You Think You Know About Britain?* London: Constable.

El-Enany, N. (2019) *(B)Ordering Britain: Law, Race, Empire.* Oxford: Hart.

Ensor, J. and H. Horton (2017) '"He Survived Assad Only to be Killed in a Tower Block in London": First Victim of Grenfell Fire is Syrian Refugee Mohammed al-Haj Ali'. *The Telegraph*, 15 June. www.telegraph.co.uk/news/2017/06/15/came-better-life-first-victim-grenfell-fire-syrian-refugeemohammad/.

Grenfell Action Group (2017) 'Grenfell Tower Fire'. 14 June. https://grenfellactiongroup.wordpress.com/2017/06/14/grenfell-tower-fire/.

Hanley, L. (2007) *Estates: An Intimate History.* London: Granta.

Haraway, D. (1991) 'A Cyborg Manifesto: Science, Technology, and Socialist-Feminism in the Late Twentieth Century', in D. Haraway, *Simians, Cyborgs and Women: The Reinvention of Nature.* New York: Routledge, 149–181.

Harris, C. I. (1993) 'Whiteness as Property'. *Harvard Law Review*, 106(8): 1701–1791.

Hastings, A. (2004) 'Stigma and Social Housing Estates: Beyond Pathological Explanations'. *Journal of Housing and the Built Environment*, 19(3): 233–254.

Hernandez, R. D. (2012), 'Sonic Geographies and Anti-Border Musics: "We Didn't Cross the Border, The Border Crossed Us"', in Arturo J. Aldama, Chela Sandoval and Peter J. García (eds), *Performing the US Latina and Latino Borderlands.* Bloomington, IN: Indiana University Press, 235–257.

James, S. ([1974] 2012) *Sex, Race and Class.* Oakland, CA: PM Press.

Joint Council for the Welfare of Immigrants (2017) 'Passport Please: The Impact of the Right to Rent Checks on Migrants and Ethnic Minorities in England'. February. www.jcwi.org.uk/news-and-policy/passport-please.

Keenan, S. (2015) *Subversive Property: Law and the Production of Spaces of Belonging.* Abingdon: Routledge.

Koram, K. (2016) '"I'm not looking for a new England": On the Limitations of Radical Nationalism'. *Novara Media,* 9 October. https://novaramedia.com/2016/10/09/im-not-looking-for-a-new-england-on-the-limitations-of-a-radical-nationalism/.

Krupa, J. (2016) 'The Killing of a Polish Man Exposes the Reality of Post-Referendum Racism'. *The Guardian*, 5 September. www.theguardian.com/commentisfree/2016/sep/05/death-arkadiusz-jozwik-post-referendum-racism-xenophobes-brexit-vote.

Lentin, A. (2012) *Racism: A Beginner's Guide.* London: Oneworld Publications.

MacKinnon, C. A. (1983) 'Feminism, Marxism, Method, and the State: Toward Feminist Jurisprudence'. *Signs: Journal of Women in Culture and Society*, 8(4): 635–658.

Massey, D. (1993) 'Politics and Space/Time', in M. Keith and S. Pile (eds), *Place and the Politics of Identity.* London: Routledge, 141–160.

May, T. and B. Cazeneuve (2015), 'Migrants Think Our Streets are Paved with Gold'. *The Telegraph*, 1 August. www.telegraph.co.uk/news/uknews/immigration/11778396/Migrants-think-our-streets-are-paved-with-gold.html.

Nadura, C. (2014) 'Nigerian Author Chimamanda Ngozi Adichie: "I Became Black in America"'. *Moyers*, 16 December. https://billmoyers.com/2014/12/16/nigerian-author-chimananda-ngozi-adichie-identity/.

Radical Housing Network (2017) 'Migrant Rights Groups Call for Full Amnesty for Survivors of the Grenfell Tower Fire'. 19 July. https://radicalhousingnetwork.org/migrant-rights-groups-call-for-full-amnesty-for-survivors-of-the-grenfell-tower-fire/.

Robinson, R. (2014) 'A Border in Every Street'. *Liberty*, 3 April. www.
libertyhumanrights.org.uk/news/blog/border-every-street.

Shildrick, M. (2015) 'Why Should Our Bodies End at the Skin?: Embodiment,
Boundaries, and Somatechnics'. *Hypatia*, 30(1): 13–29.

Travis, A. (2013) 'Immigration Bill: Theresa May Defends Plans to Create
"Hostile Environment"'. *The Guardian*, 10 October. www.theguardian.com/
politics/2013/oct/10/immigration-bill-theresa-may-hostile-environment.

Van Houtum, H. (2010) 'Human Blacklisting: The Global Apartheid of the
EU's External Border Regime'. *Environment and Planning D: Society and
Space*, 28(6): 957–976.

UNITED (2018) 'UNITED Updated List of 34,361 Refugee Deaths Published
in The Guardian'. 20 June. www.unitedagainstracism.org/blog/2018/06/20/
press-release-united-list-of-34361-refugee-deaths-published-in-the-
guardian/.

Ward, B. (2015) 'The EU Stands By as Thousands of Migrants Drown in
the Mediterranean'. *Human Rights Watch*, 25 February. www.hrw.org/
news/2015/02/25/eu-stands-thousands-migrants-drown-mediterranean.

Photo Essay
Parveen Ali

I wanted to focus on something positive and maybe it will give somebody some hope because the community was amazing – it came together beautifully, and differences were put aside.

In the afternoon of 14 June 2017, close to the tower, a neighbouring resident plays with a dog on the grass; he then kisses the dog. Despite the tower burning behind him, he continues to stay calm.

Late in the afternoon 14 June 2017, close to St Clements church. I spoke with local residents who were having a drink. I asked why they were drinking and they replied, 'we are drinking in remembrance of those who have lost their life.'

Outside St Clements church, volunteers help move hundreds of boxes. I met volunteers from all over the UK from different nationalities and different religions. People forgot their differences and helped each other. This is my favourite photo because this represents British values and British diversity.

A group of young Muslim women outside St Clements church help with the donation boxes. It was Ramadan, so they were fasting. It didn't matter where you were from or what religion you followed. We were all as one, helping for the sake of humanity.

Close to Latimer Road station, both local and non-local people gather and set up a table bringing donations of food. Whilst on the ground, I witnessed this each night, Sikhs, Muslims, Christians, atheists, everyone: the community spirit was beautiful.

Outside the Westway Sports Centre, two young boys look at the missing persons board.

A food van parked close to the tower provides free food for local residents and volunteers. A Muslim lady from the van came out and gave me food to open my fast because it was Ramadan.

Afternoon 14 June 2017. I lifted my camera to take a photo of the men sitting on the grass. Behind them the tower. A man trying to stay calm in the worst situation possible lifts his arm showing his muscle then smiles. I take the photo and smile back.

On 14 June 2017, a young boy finishes school, oblivious to what's going on. His mother looks up at the tower horrified. He plays with one of the four dogs.

6

Grenfell on Screen

Anna Viola Sborgi

A television news programme is on in the living room and shows a tower block ablaze. The violence of the image on the screen is duplicated as the camera moves to capture the actual tower out of the apartment's window, showing that we are not watching a disaster movie, rather an atrocity taking place under our eyes in twenty-first-century London.[1] The sequence, which appears to be mobile phone footage, is reproduced in the BBC1 documentary *Grenfell* (2018) and powerfully evokes the crucial role of screen mediations of the Grenfell Tower Fire.[2] One of the most shocking aspects of what happened, the horror of watching without being able to intervene, often comes up in the testimonies of survivors and witnesses. The proliferation of videos, Snapchats and Facebook live streams, relayed by media outlets in London and across the world, made the scale of the disaster instantly apparent to those who were outside, who, in turn, did not know whether those images – or at least some of them – were being seen by those inside.

More than one year after Grenfell, the videos of the fire, remediated in several news programmes and documentaries still embody collective trauma and, at the same time, still seem surreal and difficult to grasp: how could this happen? The endless reproduction of the fire is harrowing to watch: survivors and residents avoid the footage and the Grenfell Public Inquiry has instituted trigger warnings before any images of the blaze are shown after bereaved and survivors' understandably distressed reactions when footage was shown earlier in the proceedings (Bowden, 2018).

At a further level, however, the footage provides a visual record and important information on how the fire spread. The independent research agency Forensic Architecture, based at Goldsmiths,

University of London, started a project aimed at collating footage from Londoners' cameras and smartphones in order to assemble them within a 3D model of the tower, merging them with footage from Sky News. As a statement on the project website details: 'Every one of those videos is a unique piece of evidence, containing unique information.'[3] Differently from other projects carried out by the agency 'the Grenfell project is unique for its open-ended timescale and undetermined outcomes, and could ultimately be put to a number of uses,' says Bob Trafford, one of the researchers in the group in an interview (Kafka, 2018). What it is certain, though, is that this effort is informed by a public-input, open-access logic that aims at a providing a visual archive of the fire from the widest variety of points of view possible. This aspect becomes relevant not only because the images provide both evidence for a civic investigation of the fire – in line with the agency's scope – and as historical testimony but because the act of weaving together in one composite image a myriad of perspectives evokes one of the crucial questions in the story of Grenfell, the question of representation: before and after the fire; mobilised across a series of point of views, corresponding to different systems of power and agency within the city; across a series of different media circuits, from grass-roots productions to more institutional broadcasting outlets. In this chapter, I will trace how the screen media representation of Grenfell has evolved in the year and a half since the fire, and how the narratives from the ground have gradually started to inform the mainstream media production.

The large media coverage at the time of the event catalysed an unprecedented wave of attention towards the conditions of British social housing, an issue that, until the fire, had been debated consistently only among dedicated, established commentators and an active community of campaigners. At the time, many wondered whether this could be a radical turning point, both in terms of representation and policies of social housing, aspects that are, crucially, tightly connected. Since June 2017, Grenfell has never been out of the news completely, but, predictably, attention was raised again significantly only in conjunction with the one-year anniversary.

A Representation Mismatch?

As all this media attention poured into the community, the moment was characterised by a friction between the journalists – regardless of their political orientation – and some of the residents, a reaction to the long-standing neglect the residents had experienced. This reaction can also be understood within a wider distrust of conservative mainstream media (Harrison, 2017). Ten days after the fire, an Al Jazeera English report in the programme *The Listening Post* investigated the hostility the media experienced on arriving at the scene. The Al Jazeera reporters interviewed members of the local community asking whether they felt they had been fairly represented by mainstream media. Many of the interviewees expressed profound frustration at having been placed at the centre of attention by journalists looking for 'juicy stories', after being ignored for years when they were complaining about the fire safety of the building.[4] At the same time, they also expressed distrust of mainstream media, admitting they only relied on social media for news. Social media on this occasion provided an effective space for communication from the ground. 'Grenfell Speaks', created in the aftermath of the fire, operates as an independent local news channel and uses social media to share news and information daily, both keeping track of political and judicial developments and recording solidarity initiatives at the local level.[5]

The report was the first to assess the way the fire had been covered in UK media. The distinctive structure and profile of Al Jazeera English as part of a global network worked well to establish the focus on the international dimension. Specifically, *The Listening Post*, a commentary programme that each week explores the media agenda, is broadcast from London and introduced by Canadian presenter Richard Gizbert (2017). Although it was produced close to Grenfell, the international branding of both network and programme, together with Al Jazeera's remit of producing independent news provided an internal and an external standpoint at the same time, which allowed the reporters to provide a more critical look on the ongoing news production on Grenfell.[6]

The programme introduced some of the key questions that would later be picked up by Channel 4's Jon Snow, who had been faced by angry reactions on the site. On 23 August 2017, Snow admitted the failings of the media in a public lecture, where he claimed that 'reporting on Grenfell' had made him 'feel on the wrong side of social divide', and he admitted the responsibilities of journalists in not picking up the numerous health and safety concerns raised prior to the fire by local groups (Ruddick, 2017; Snow, 2017).[7] Snow recognised a failing in the press and a mismatch between the media and larger sectors of society. At the same time, he expressed concern for the disappearance of the local press and the role of the growing monopoly of tech giants in managing access to news and information. He also admitted, however, that as journalists, they found themselves increasingly dependent on social media for monitoring the situation on the ground.

Both the Al Jazeera programme and Snow's intervention signposted the importance of going beyond the sensationalism of the emergency in the reporting, but also the necessity of a long-term, in-depth media response. In a way, the Grenfell community went from being completely outside the radar of the media to an extraordinary visibility. Whether this attention will transform into an in-depth long-term investment in representing the most vulnerable in society, however, is still to be seen in the future.

Wider Media Production

At the same time, since the fire, a great number of documentaries, news programmes and videos have emerged. Some are grass-roots productions, such as the documentaries *On the Ground at Grenfell* (Nendie Pinto-Duschinsky and Stowe Films, 2017) and *Failed by the State* (Daniel Renwick and Ish, in collaboration with Redfish, a Berlin-based independent journalists' organisation, 2017), or the moving music tribute videos by Lowkey and Mai Khalil's *Ghosts of Grenfell* (2018) and *Fire in Grenfell* (2018), a cover of R&B artist Emili Sande's song *Read All About It* by teenage girls Yousra Cherbika and Johara Menacar, a tribute (directed by Brooke Colman) to their young friend Nur Huda el-Wahabi, who perished in the fire.[8]

At the same time, the main television networks have devoted hours of screen time to the tragedy in the form of news programmes, like the several instalments of BBC *Newsnight* and *Channel 4 News*, or ITV's report *Grenfell the First 24 Hours* (2017). In addition to the main news coverage, both the BBC and Channel 4 have commissioned specific documentaries: *Searching for Grenfell's Lost Lives*, presented by Reggie Yates, broadcast on BBC2 on 27 March 2018 and *Grenfell*, directed by Ben Anthony and broadcast on BBC1 on 11 June 2018. Channel 4 commissioned a 15-minute virtual reality documentary, *Grenfell Our Home* (2018), where a series of residents are invited to recall what their apartments looked like and their memories of life in the tower as the VR technology recreates animations from their words around them, as if they were still sitting in the flats. The film won the Audience Award at Sheffield Doc/Fest's Alternative Realities exhibition and aims to challenge the stereotyped assumptions about the experience of living in the tower.[9]

In September 2018, even BBC1 television series *DIY SOS* produced a two-part episode on Grenfell. In the first episode, Nick Knowles and his team rebuilt a gym for the Dale Youth boxing club that was previously hosted in the tower and in the second they built a new community centre for local groups, both under the Westway. The members of the team are aware that this is the most important task they have faced, and they are anxious to 'get it right', they want 'to rebuild with community and for the community', Nick says. They showcase the best materials and repeatedly ensure that the new constructions are built not only according to, but 'above' building regulations, meaning they want to give the residents the highest standard of construction possible. In both episodes, the crew is also joined by Prince William, who had already appeared in previous episodes of the programme. William talks to the builders and the fire fighters and carefully listens to survivors, confirming the more successful media presence that has, since the early days after the fire, characterised the Royals in contrast to the government. A *Daily Mirror* cover on 17 June 2017, with the headline *A Tale of Two Leaders* crystallised the two different photos of the Queen meeting the survivors and Theresa May escorted by the police, trying to avoid them. A further programme, *Before Grenfell*, broadcast on BBC2 on the occasion of the one-year anniversary, provided a much-needed contextualisation of the events within the history of the area. Through archive material and interviews, the documentary shows the historical origins of the extremely polarised social make-up of North Kensington with regards to wealth distribution; this is an area where the ultra-rich live next door to some of the least wealthy communities in the country.

Significantly, too, the Public Inquiry has been streamed online since its formal opening in September 2017. It effectively opened in May 2018 with a series of hearings where the survivors and bereaved were given a chance to commemorate their loved ones lost in the fire. This can be seen as a response to the initial protests following the lack of consultation with residents about the composition of the inquiry panel and the decision to appoint Sir Martin Moore-Bick as its head, choices that appeared to demonstrate disregard for the community.

This corpus of screen representations, which is still being produced at the time of writing, requires further examination. What are the production histories, their positioning, their multiple ways of framing a story the scale of which makes it almost impossible to apprehend and narrate? Is screen media a privileged medium to narrate this particular trauma both in terms of circuits of production and circulation, and what are the possible shortfalls? As these productions are still being shaped at the time of writing, the definitive answer to these questions can only be found within a long time-frame that provides historical distance from the facts. However, I will start answering these questions by focusing on three main case studies exemplifying different documentary styles and production history: *On the Ground at Grenfell*, *Searching for Grenfell Lost Lives*, and *Grenfell*. The power of these three productions resides, in different ways and to different degrees, in their claim to a narration from the ground and the pursuit of a plurality of voices in the discourse on Grenfell, in order to articulate a more nuanced perspective on the community. The representation of the disaster is structured around different key moments and on selected aspects in depth. However, a few specific themes emerge across the three of them: the interrogation of what community means, the role of the youth, and the intercultural and global ramifications. I will show how these aspects, initially emerged in grass-roots productions, have been gradually taken on board by network television documentary production.

On the Ground at Grenfell

An immediate response to the fire, *On the Ground at Grenfell* was directed by the film-maker Nendie Pinto-Duschinsky and 'a group of 9 young people: survivors, local residents, and volunteers'. The film-makers involved in the project were at the site when the fire broke out, working on a documentary on the closure of the Stowe Youth Club (Labour Westminster, 2017). When the fire happened nearby and directly affected members of the team, they decided to film what was happening and the local people's testimonies. The collaborative nature of the project is reinforced both by the absence of a narrative voice-over and by the closing titles, listing all the names of the people involved, and is part of an overall attempt to single out survivors and residents as human beings with their individual life stories and different ways of coping, rather than portraying the community as an indistinct whole.

The film was presented in London for the first time in August 2017 at the Frontline Club and eventually won the Best Film Award at the Portobello Film Festival. It has been screened in a variety of venues, from community centres – including the Maxilla Social Club, which is right under the Westway, very close to the tower, and was used as a volunteer organisation centre right after the fire – to universities (Goldsmiths, LSE, Birkbeck). The film also reached political venues such as at The World Transformed, a festival of ideas and politics that took place in conjunction with the Labour Party Annual Conference in Brighton (24–27 September 2017), where participants in the film were also invited to speak. On 13 December 2017, it was screened in Parliament. Finally, in conjunction with the one-year anniversary of the fire, the documentary was made available online.[10]

The film merges together different materials to give the viewer the immediacy of the moment: direct interviews with survivors, footage of the fire from inside the tower (both CCTV footage and videos made by people who were trapped inside, such as Rania Ibrahim, who was killed in her 24th floor flat with her two children), videos and stills from the news and a mix of noises including screams, heart rate monitors, and the actual sound of the burning fire. These, together with people's voices, are the only sounds in the score; there is no emotional use of music in the film. The result is an immersive, often touching viewing experience, which has, at the same time, a kind of sobriety and rawness – most of the interviews are conducted in bright daylight and alternate with other images with the tower looming in the background – reminding us very effectively of the double condition of survivors, who are on the one hand expected to resume their everyday lives and on the other hand deal with the enormity, the almost surreal nature of what hit them. The impact on the mental health of both survivors and witnesses is one of the main themes touched on by the documentary. The shocking experience of the fire obviously affects the whole community, but puts further strain on those who are already suffering from mental health problems.

The awareness of difference at various levels is also a prominent element in the film: the diverse composition of the community in terms of race, ethnicity and religion, the plurality of point of views, and even, sometimes, the division within the community itself. Adrienne, one of the film-makers involved, recalls that three days after the fire,

> no one was looking at each other's colour [...] I know this area can be very divided in terms of race, in terms of whether you're from Ladbroke Grove or Westbourne Park, but there was no animosity, it was kind of overwhelming how many people came out in abundance to help.

Another local resident, Reem, points out how this is a place where social and racial segregation has been fuelled and the residents of the tower were, in fact, a 'mixture of minorities'. In many ways, Grenfell embodied the crisis in the myth of London as a cosmopolitan, open city, welcoming people from all over the world, who could rebuild their lives (safely). It highlights how this myth is questioned by a deeply rooted inequality that often results in social segregation. Michael, a local community worker for over 33 years, points out:

that block is the prime example that, you know, English wasn't their first language, and they were just chucked into this place and just left there, like, we're doing you a favour. Many of them have seen things that none of us have endured, they've seen war, they've seen family members murdered in front of them, they've endured famine, you know, all sorts of things, and then, we bring them to the West where we are meant to be bright and shiny and fantastic and we then don't look after them.

At the same time, the film shows the dignity of the people who lived in the tower and their awareness of their contribution to society. Mahad, one of the survivors from the 4th floor, describes the residents' growing physical and mental exhaustion after the fire and points out that, before, in spite of all the difficulties, 'we were living a happy life, we were businessmen, businesswomen, workers, taxpayers, you know, contributors to the society.'

The film also makes the role of the youth emerge powerfully. This especially comes up in the discussion of the anger and the frustration of the residents in the first days after the fire. Local resident Reem talks about how the proportions of this accident can be augmented by the misconceived assumption that 'because people come from some areas [they] might bring anti-social behaviour.' She adds, 'These people are raw. Their emotions are raw. And it comes across more so from the youth, I think.' The voice off camera asks her: 'Do you think people are afraid of the youth?' and she answers, opening up in a big smile: 'They shouldn't be. Because ... I think the youth are just ... They're wise .... They're knowledgeable.' Swarzy, a young volunteer from Ilford, East London, who has been helping out since the day after the blaze, recalls having just finished reading Martin Luther King Jr.'s autobiography and thinking how that text represented 'almost like a manual, a tool guide on how you deal with community, how you love and serve people, and how you don't reject anger but you love people through it.' The film ends with the powerful image of a drawing created by children living in and around the area with the help of artist Constantine Gras, on Grenfell Tower Fun Day, 14 May 2015, and children's voices reading some of their writing.

Searching for Grenfell's Lost Lives

In *Searching for Grenfell's Lost Lives,* acting in both the role of presenter and journalist, Reggie Yates starts with a visit to the Memorial Wall, where he asks himself a question: who were the people who died 'before they became names on a wall'? Reggie embarks on a journey in the local community to tell the stories of a group of victims: young British Moroccan Yasin El-Wahabi, who ran back into the tower to save his family; a Filipino woman, Ligaya Moore, whose niece arrives in London to get answers about how her aunt died; Mohammad Al-Haj Ali, the first named victim of the fire, who escaped war in Syria with his brother only to lose his life in the fire; Tony Disson, a well-known local figure who was active in the Dale Youth Boxing Club; and 12-year-old Jessica Urbano Ramirez, one of 18 children to lose their lives. The faces and names of these victims are now sadly familiar from the mainstream media coverage, but the documentary takes a step back to trace their stories before the fire.

As a well-known radio host and television presenter, Yates proves a good choice as a relatable interviewer, being both a Londoner of Ghanaian descent and having grown up on a council estate himself: people receive him well and open up to tell him their stories, both in their houses and in the street.[11] At one point early in the documentary, Reggie joins the community in the silent vigil; he looks around and reflects on the fact that these are people that he could have grown up with and, ultimately, he says, 'this is something that could have happened to someone like me.' This feeling of a shared background is reiterated at many points in the documentary; it enables a connection with the interviewees and seems to be able to make people talk effortlessly to him. Asked in one interview about his feelings in covering 'a tragedy that was so recent and close to home', Yates responds:

> It was so different to documentaries I've made in other parts of the world. People opened up to me straight away. A lot of them had seen me on TV. There was a level of trust. People were saying, 'We're not talking to the press, but we'll talk to you'.
>
> (Walker-Arnott, 2018)

The presenting style works well in the combination of extended personal voice-over – that shows us how Reggie is invested in finding out about the stories of the victims – and the pregnant pauses when he listens to the survivors and witnesses.

Again, one of the main aspects developed in the documentary is the international dimension. As the individual stories unfold, it is clear that it is not just a large community in London mourning the victims, but that the grief spreads across the globe. Ligaya Moore's niece flies from the Philippines to come to terms with her aunt's death and Reggie himself travels to Morocco when he finds out that many of the victims come from the same small town in the north of the country, Larache. A whole town in Morocco mourns Yasin and his family. As Abdul, a local journalist who covered the story points out:

This accident wasn't like our usual news stories. Larache is used to stories of bodies washing up on the shore. Young people losing their lives in the sea. Illegal migration happens almost every day because of the lack of opportunities in the city. What had a big impact is that it wasn't just a father, or a mother, or a son. The family lost the father and the mother and the children. It was the whole family that was lost in this tragedy.

Like other documentaries, *Searching for Grenfell's Lost Lives* remediates the footage from social media, but, similarly to *On The Ground*, it concentrates on the different ways of coping with what happened and, at the same time, asks us to take one step back in time to trace the story of those 'images on a memorial wall'. The opening sequence brings us back to 2013 and it is, in fact, a montage of photographs of Mohammed from the time after he escaped Syria and started a new life in London with his brother Omar. In the documentary, Omar talks about the painful experience of having to rebuild a new life from scratch again.

The theme of youth seems crucial in this film too, in the attention it devotes to the young victims and to the young friends who mourn them and who cope through the means of their generation: Jessica is still there on her friends' phone, fixed forever in a Snapchat animation as much as in a mural in the streets, and her friends tell Reggie they still send messages to her. Yasin's heroism – he had escaped but came back to try and save his family members – is marked by a series of graffiti, murals and a portrait in the Dale Youth Club.

As we see the stories unfold, we also see, repeatedly, crucial moments around which grief is articulated: the count of the victims, the Memorial Wall, and the Silent Vigil, which open and close the film. The film ends, therefore, with the announcement of the final list of victims by the coroner. We see Reggie going back to the silent vigil and his first-person voice-over concludes his search:

I'd got to know just a handful of those who'd died. But returning to the silent vigil, I realised their stories weren't just the stories of individuals ... they were the story of a community. A word we all use. But which I now felt I truly understood.

This final commentary frames the whole film as a way of understanding the meaning of the term itself by listening to the stories that come from the ground.

Grenfell

This same attitude to listening characterises Ben Anthony's *Grenfell*, which, like the other two documentaries, is structured around interviews of members of the community: survivors from the tower; not only relatives of the victims, volunteers and faith leaders, but also members of the current local council narrate their experiences. In one of the first sequences, we see the interviewees getting ready and adjusting their microphones. They seem eager to start the conversation, but at the same time, in their micro-gestures and expressions, there is a moving sense of shyness in front of the camera. This *making of* sequence delicately establishes how intimate and complicated the process of talking through the horrific memories of the fire in front of a camera is and the dignity and courage of witnesses and survivors. This attitude to listening is reinforced by the absence of voice-over, which enables all the persons involved to tell their stories without evident mediation. At the same time, as in *Searching for Grenfell's Lost*

Lives and differently from *On the Ground at Grenfell*, music is used to reinforce particularly emotionally intense moments. Ben Anthony is previously known for his award-winning documentary on the London 2005 terrorist attacks, *7/7: One Day in London* (BBC2, 2012), which was constructed on the testimonies of people who were directly affected.

Both because it comprises footage filmed and collected in the course of one year – as the crew were on the site from the early days, filming in very difficult conditions – and because its broadcast on the occasion of the first anniversary closed a first cycle, the scope of the documentary clearly is more comprehensive than the previous two films considered. The structure unfolds around the different aspects of the tragedy: the trauma of the fire itself; the following disorientation and lack of coordination on the part of the council; the spontaneous organisation of the volunteers; the anger and the initiative of the Silent Walk as a way to clear the air and help the community to process their grief; the harrowing wait for the identification of victims; the consequences on mental health; the quest for truth; and the institutional shortcomings at local and national level.

In this film, the aspect of the fire as an international crisis is not only highlighted in terms of the diverse ethnic background of the victims, but also in the comparison with international disaster zones. In relation to this, a particularly interesting moment in the documentary is when Bhupinder Singh, leader of the Sikh community and volunteer, uses his international crisis volunteer experience to discuss the chaos and lack of coordination from the institutions in aid provision in the early days of the tragedy, a situation that made members of the community step in. He also points out how members from all communities, no matter their race or religion, all came down to help.

Like the other documentaries, the film remediates footage from social media, often collated in a three-framed structure, which evokes the idea of creating a visual archive with multiple points of view. The role of social media is further highlighted by one of the interviews, where Faisal Metalsi, who set up Grenfell Speaks, shows us the simple equipment that he put together:

Grenfell Speaks is a social news channel. I don't edit anything, I just put stuff up raw. It feels personal to me. The lapel mic that a friend donated. [...] An iPhone. The reach is about 5 million since the channel started. There are people that watch the streams from Queensland in Australia to Brazil.

One of the initial sequences crucially sets the question of the repetition of the images of the tower as a ghastly spectacle still haunting the survivors, both in their memories and in the permanence of its burnt shell. We see several bird's eye views of the area from different angles and at different times of the day – presumably from a drone – and we hear an off-screen voice saying:

I have been filming every other day for the last nine months. I know I'm not supposed to fly the drone ... but I film different angles to try and show any other image than what it normally looks like. Although they do not condone it, my psychologists believe that it's some way that I've been self-medicating to get over what I witnessed.

The film does not give out any form of judgement on the practice itself, rather, it highlights the complexity of the act of looking both at the videos of the fire and of the haunting presence of the burnt shell of the tower. Everyone reacts differently: some would prefer not to see them anymore, some keep being drawn to them, almost obsessively, trying to make sense of this horrific spectacle.

Like other materials analysed so far, this scene foregrounds the crucial question of the tragedy as horrific spectacle.[12] It could be argued that the shocking images of the tower, in endless circulation, bring a form of desensitisation – something that leads to excesses, such as the ghastly phenomenon of 'grief-tourists' taking selfies with the tower as a backdrop – and that removing all these images would be a more productive visual strategy. In fact, one of the documentaries mentioned, *Failed by the State*, explicitly avoids images of the tower. As the presenter Ish explains at the beginning of the film: 'You won't see any shots of the fateful night in this film. We never want to see it again' (Oppenheim, 2017). There is not just an easy answer to these questions, which seem to characterise many modern disasters, where the mediatisation of suffering has become an inevitable part of contemporary experience, the other (darker) side of the proliferation of accessible media platforms.[13] In her last book, *Regarding the Pain of Others* (2003), Susan Sontag used documentation of atrocities by war photography as a case study to question the ambivalences in the process of looking at images of suffering, their mediation and spectacularisation and how we engage with them – and our positioning in relation to them. One of the arguments she makes is that there is no evidence that the repetition of images desensitises the viewer and their real impact is not just measured by the process of looking at them, but in the way it prompts a sustained engagement with thinking and eventually, action.[14]

Conclusion

One year on, the approach to the narration of Grenfell seems to have developed even in media outlets from a sensationalist one, where the emotional tones prevailed, to a more careful attempt to portray the individuals and the stories behind them and, at the same time, to connect them with a reconstruction of events from multiple points of view.[15] At the same time, they provide more space to the important role the community has played in managing the emergency itself. In a way, television documentary seems to have adopted an approach that has learned from the documentaries and videos produced on the ground. In very different ways, the three documentaries I have considered mobilise the question of point of view in an attempt to make a portrait from within the community emerge. Either they do that by avoiding a narrative voice-over to provide a plurality of voices – such as in the case of *On the Ground at Grenfell* and *Grenfell* – or, in the opposite way, by making the role of interviewer explicit, as in the case of *Searching for Grenfell's Lost Lives*, where the television host's recognisability and likeability facilitates establishing a dialogue with the residents.

Media representations seem to have developed a wider attitude to listening to the different voices of the community and, in many ways, the films are an extended reflection on the word community itself.

In his 1976 *Keywords*, Raymond Williams discusses the ambivalent uses of the term:

> Community can be the warmly persuasive word to describe an existing set of relationships, or the warmly persuasive word to describe an alternative set of relationships. What is most important, perhaps, is that unlike all other terms of social organization (state, nation, society, etc.) it seems never to be used unfavourably, and never to be given any positive opposing or distinguishing term.
>
> (Williams, 1976: 76)

The productions analysed here share an attitude to listening and make a point of going beyond a taken for granted use of 'community'. They offer an account of both its richness and its shortfalls. While in the early hours, the Grenfell community was somehow perceived as an indistinct whole, it gradually emerges in these later representations in a more complex way that attempts to portray more accurately the racial, ethnic, religious diversity of the area and the individual stories, an aspect that was present from the start in the many grass-roots productions that have been circulated online and through activists' networks. All these media productions, indeed, exist in a dimension of circularity, in a communication flow where the grammars originated by the media merge with the bottom up imaginaries built everyday by city dwellers. As Myria Georgiou notes the 'responses to the challenges that the urban world presents to humanity are as much negotiated in the media as they are in the street' (Georgiou, 2013: 1). This seems particularly true in the case of Grenfell where, in a circulation process that is still being shaped at the time of writing, the representations of mainstream media are eventually combined with those coming from the ground.

Although the shock of Grenfell will never be forgotten, it can become a turning point for the wider perception of social housing, but it can only become so if a longer-term response goes beyond the commotion and memorialisation of the first period and takes on board different, intertwined problems: the in-depth and long-term aspects of Grenfell and the wider commitment to keep in the news agenda not just the fire itself, but the larger conditions of deprivation and neglect that remain a reality for many social housing developments and could contribute to other disasters in the future.[16] Representing Grenfell, it is necessary to devote attention to the systemic aspects of this paradigmatic event. It is necessary to acknowledge first of all the violence – which also passes through those endlessly repeated images of the fire – of Grenfell as the destruction of home as shelter (in a Bachelardian sense). Moreover, as David Madden and Peter Marcuse suggest in their recent book *In Defense of Housing*:

> Housing is more than shelter; it can provide personal safety and ontological security. While the domestic environment can be the site of oppression and injustice, it also has the potential to serve as a confirmation of one's agency, cultural identity, individuality, and creative powers. The built form of housing has always been seen as a tangible, visual reflection of the organisation of society.
>
> (Madden and Marcuse 2016: 12)

These words resonate powerfully with Grenfell, in many ways a site of oppression and injustice. The visual reflection that bounces back at us from the media reproductions of the tragedy is that of a society that devalues the protection of the home. The present historical moment has reached a tipping point in the exacerbation of an endemic and long-standing housing crisis. As a reaction to this process, low-budget, activist-driven documentary, in particular, has in recent years emerged as a particularly productive form of social critique from the widely circulated *Dispossession* (Paul Sng, 2017), a densely informative exposé of the housing crisis at the national level, to *Estate: A Reverie* (Andrea Luka Zimmerman, 2015), an essay film blending participant observation with experimentalism deriving from a seven-year engagement with the community of the Haggerston Estate, a now demolished social housing complex in East London. These are just two of the many films that are 'setting the story right' against the stereotyping and sensationalism associated with representations of social housing tenants and, more generally, working-class people. In doing so, they respond to a failure in representation that has been perceived as coming not just from the most populist mainstream media, but also from public networks like the

BBC and even Channel 4, which seem to have lost their original social critique documentary vocation in favour of productions that can often sustain stigmatising attitudes towards council tenants, blending factual documentation with reality show, contest-like spectacularisation (*How to Get a Council House*, Channel 4, 2013–2016; *Swap My Council House*, BBC, 2014; *Britain's Weirdest Council Homes*, Channel 4, 2016). These productions participate in a wider tendency in the rise of what has been called Factual Welfare Television (FWT), in the line of programmes like *Benefits Street* (2014).

The television documentaries I have analysed in this chapter, therefore, might be the first markers of an inversion of that tendency, where a 'Grenfell effect' can make mainstream media become receptive to emerging tendencies in activist-film-making and influence the kind of programmes they decide to commission. In February 2018, campaigners from *Justice for Grenfell* put up three billboards on three vans travelling around London, resembling those used in the Academy award-winning film, *Three Billboards Outside Ebbing, Missouri* (Martin McDonagh, 2017). The billboards contained slogans asking for justice for the victims of the fire and represented another example of how campaigning and screen productions can borrow each other's language and tactics to keep the pressing issues of Grenfell and social housing in the public eye.

Screen Productions Cited

Benefits Street (Channel 4, 2014).
Britain's Weirdest Council Homes (Channel 4, 2016).
Before Grenfell: A Hidden History (BBC2, 2018).
Cracks in the System (Hannan Majid and Richard York with Rainbow Collective, 2018).
Dispossession (Paul Sng, 2017).
Estate: A Reverie (Andrea Luka Zimmerman, 2015).
Failed by the State (Daniel Renwick and Ish, in collaboration with Redfish, 2017).
The Fires that Foretold Grenfell (Jamie Roberts, BBC2, 2018).
Fire in Grenfell (Yousra Cherbika and Johara, directed by Brooke Colman, 2018).

Genova 11.36 (42° Parallelo, forthcoming in spring 2019).
Ghosts of Grenfell (Lowkey and Mai Khalil, 2018).
Grenfell (Ben Anthony, BBC1, 2018).
Grenfell Our Home: VR Documentary (Channel 4, 2018).
Grenfell Public Inquiry streaming (Enquiry YouTube Channel, 2017–2018).
Grenfell the First 24 Hours (ITV, 2017).
How to Get a Council House (Channel 4, 2013–2016).
The Listening Post: 'Covering the Grenfell Fire: UK Media in the Spotlight' (pres. Richard Gizbert, Al Jazeera English, 2017).
On the Ground at Grenfell (Nendie Pinto-Duschinsky and Stowe Films, 2017).
Three Billboards Outside Ebbing, Missouri (Martin McDonagh, 2017).
Swap My Council House (BBC 2014).
Searching for Grenfell's Lost Lives (BBC2, Reggie Yates, 2018).
7/7: One Day in London (Ben Anthony, BBC2, 2012).
DIY SOS: Grenfell, two episodes (BBC1, 2018).

Notes

1. In her last book *Regarding the Pain of Others* (2003), Susan Sontag pointed out how the recurrence of the expression 'like a movie' – substituting the previously more common 'like a dream' – used by survivors of 9/11 as a way to describe the 'short-term unassimilability' of the experience they had just been through.
2. This chapter develops and expands from two earlier short articles I published at the end of summer 2017 (Sborgi, 2017a; 2017b).
3. See Forensic Architecture cases, www.forensic-architecture.org/case/ (all websites in the notes last accessed November 2018).
4. Community blogs were pointing out the fire safety risk in the building as early as 2013.
5. 'Grenfell Speaks', https://twitter.com/grenfellspeaks.
6. Al Jazeera's remit as an independent news source has often been questioned in relation to its global corporate structure, but it certainly works in terms of branding and expressing the network's targets.
7. The Grenfell Action Group blog pointed out health and safety risks in multiple occasions, with the now widely known post:

> It is a truly terrifying thought but the Grenfell Action Group firmly believe that only a catastrophic event will expose the ineptitude and incompetence of our landlord, the KCTMO, and bring an end to the dangerous living conditions and neglect of health and safety legislation that they

inflict upon their tenants and leaseholders ... their sordid collusion with the RBKC Council is a recipe for a future major disaster.

(Grenfell Action Group 2016)

One of the posts on health and safety risks dates back to 2013 (Grenfell Action Group, 2013).

8. *On the Ground at Grenfell*, www.onthegroundatgrenfell.com/; *Failed by the State*, www.youtube.com/watch?v=9tFPCUgjbfA; *Ghosts of Grenfell*, www.youtube.com/watch?v=ztUamrChczQ; *Fire in Grenfell*, www.youtube.com/watch?v=DiZ589GAn4E.

9. *Grenfell Our Home: VR Documentary* (Channel 4, 2018), www.channel4.com/collection/grenfell-our-home.

10. 'Swarzy Macaly Speaks at the Labour Party Conference 2017', www.youtube.com/watch?v=iqwof2aE8Rc&feature=youtu.be.

11. Yates' screen presence stands its test, notwithstanding some previous controversies for an 'offensive' comment about Jewish music managers for which he apologised. When asked about this in an interview, he responds:

It's changed me. The main thing I've taken from it is that there is no justifiable context when you've hurt people. I'm privileged to have the career I have. There's a responsibility that comes with that. It's easy to forget how far your voice will go.

(Walker-Arnott, 2018)

12. The Sky News cameraman Keith Hopkins recalled how having to film the tragedy for hours was itself a deeply challenging emotional experience (2018).

13. Little more than one year after Grenfell, and, coincidentally, on 14 August 2018 – I find myself again watching images in the news that seem to belong to a disaster film but are, indeed, real. This time the images come from back home in Genoa, Italy, where the colossal Morandi motorway bridge – built in reinforced concrete in the 1960s – collapses, cutting the city and the wider region in two: 43 people lose their lives. The analogies with Grenfell are many: the disregard for public safety, the neglect and lack of maintenance of ageing public infrastructure, the disastrous interaction between public and private interests, the preventability of the tragedy, people's displacement from their houses. Images of the severed bridge travel across the world and, even in this case, sadly, grief-tourists make their appearance, among the vehement protests of the residents. A documentary, *Genova 11.36* (the time code of the collapse) produced by the group of journalists 42° Parallelo, will be released in spring 2019 and, like in the case of the Grenfell documentary, aims, first of all, at giving back the dignity and memory of the individual victims (Genova Today Editorial Board, 2018).

14. Interestingly, in her book, Sontag points out how 'being a spectator of calamities taking place in another country is a quintessential modern experience' (Sontag, 2003: 18) and this acquires further resonance in relation to Grenfell, which happened in a radically reconfigured media landscape –

and the process of this transformation was only starting to take place as the book was published. Moreover, Grenfell did not happen in a faraway country, but close to home; at the same time, it is the clear expression of a colonial logic, as demonstrated elsewhere in this book.

15. As I was closing this chapter, a new BBC2 documentary was broadcast on 30 October 2018, *The Fires that Foretold Grenfell* (Jamie Roberts, BBC2, 2018), which contextualises Grenfell within the wider history of previous fires in post-war Britain and traces the failings in fire safety regulations and policies showing how, 'had lessons been learnt' – probably the most repeated refrain from politicians and media alike in the days after the fire – Grenfell could have been avoided. The documentary is harrowing to watch both for the repeated use of the footage of the fires and the painstaking reconstruction of emergency scenes. However, it might suggest a further turn in network television representation of the fire, with a shift from testimony to a more sustained engagement with the causes of the fire.

16. At the East End Film Festival in May 2018, a whole day was dedicated to housing movements and film (East End Film Festival, 2018). One of the most shocking documentaries shown on the day was a film titled *Cracks in the System*, filmed by the resident Hannan Majid, with Richard York of Rainbow Collective, on the alarming state of the Ledbury Estate in Peckham, where tenants live in flats with cracks so big that they can pass a whole arm or a book from one flat to the other. The residents were particularly worried after Grenfell happened because these gaps and cracks could compromise the fire safety of each flat. A preview of the film is available at www.youtube.com/watch?v=QT3hJE7boMw.

References

Bowden, G. (2018) 'Survivors Flee Grenfell Tower Inquiry as Video of Blaze Played Without Warning'. *The Huffington Post*, UK Edition, 22 May. www. huffingtonpost.co.uk/entry/grenfell-tower-inquiry-video-played-warning_uk_5b043400e4b003dc7e46b8f2 (all websites in this list last accessed November 2018).

East End Film Festival (2018) *Building a Movement*. May. www.eastendfilm festival.com/programme-archive/action-housing-talks-screenings/.

Genova Today Editorial Board (2018) '*Genova 11.36*, il trailer del documentario sul ponte Morandi'. *Genova Today*, 23 October. www.genovatoday.it/video/genova-1136-documentario.html.

Georgiou, M. (2013) *Media and the City: Cosmopolitanism and Difference*. London: Polity.

Grenfell Action Group (2013) 'Fire Safety Scandal at Lancaster West'. 28 January. https://grenfellactiongroup.wordpress.com/2013/01/28/fire-safety-scandal-at-lancaster-west/.

Grenfell Action Group (2016) 'KCTMO – Playing with Fire!'. 20 November. https://grenfellactiongroup.wordpress.com/2016/11/20/kctmo-playing-with-fire/.

Harrison, A. (2017) 'Can You Trust the Mainstream Media?'. *The Observer*, 6 August. www.theguardian.com/media/2017/aug/06/can-you-trust-mainstream-media.

Hopkins, K. (2018) 'The Horror of Filming the Grenfell Tower Fire'. *Sky News*, 14 June. https://news.sky.com/story/the-horror-of-filming-the-grenfell-tower-fire-11404089.

Kafka, G. (2018) 'How Forensic Architecture is Harnessing the Power of the Public to Investigate the Grenfell Tower Disaster'. *Metropolis*, 27 March. www.metropolismag.com/ideas/forensic-architecture-grenfell-tower-fire/.

Labour Westminster (2017) 'Labour Anger as Tory Cuts Gut the Historic Stowe Youth Club'. *Labour Westminster Blog*, 4 February. https://labourwestminster. wordpress.com/2017/02/04/labour-anger-as-tory-cuts-gut-the-historic-stowe-youth-club/.

Madden, D. and P. Marcuse (2016) *In Defense of Housing*. London: Verso.

Oppenheim, M. (2017) 'Grenfell Tower Residents Urge Visitors to Stop Taking Selfies: "You Want to Slap the Phones out of Their Hands"'. *The Independent*, 20 June. www.independent.co.uk/news/uk/home-news/grenfell-tower-residents-selfies-angry-grief-tourism-party-a7799591.html.

Ruddick, G. (2017) 'Jon Snow: Reporting on Grenfell Made Me Feel on Wrong Side of Social Divide'. *The Guardian*, 23 August. www.theguardian.com/media/2017/aug/23/jon-snow-grenfell-mactaggart-media-diversity.

Sborgi, A. V. (2017a) 'The Day Social Housing Hit Mainstream Media'. *Mediapolis – A Journal of Cities and Culture*, 3(2), 27 September. www.mediapolisjournal.com/2017/09/the-day-social-housing-hit-mainstream-media/.

Sborgi, A. V. (2017b) 'An Update on Grenfell'. *Mediapolis – A Journal of Cities and Culture*, 3(2), 30 September. www.mediapolisjournal.com/2017/09/an-update-on-grenfell/.

Snow, J. (2017) 'Grenfell Proved It: The British Media are Part of a Disconnected Elite'. *The Guardian*, 23 August. www.theguardian.com/commentisfree/2017/aug/23/grenfell-british-media-divide.

Sontag, S. (2003) *Regarding the Pain of Others*. London: Penguin.

Walker-Arnott, E. (2018) 'Reggie Yates: 'People said: "We're not Talking to the Press, but We'll Talk to You"'. *Time Out*, 19 March. www.timeout.com/london/film/reggie-yates-people-said-were-not-talking-to-the-press-but-well-talk-to-you.

Williams, R. (1988) *Keywords: A Vocabulary of Culture and Society*. London: Fontana Press.

7

Law, Justice and the Public Inquiry into the Grenfell Tower Fire

Patricia Tuitt

Public inquiries are chief among the various means by which the state seeks to direct away from the courts individuals who have suffered preventable physical and/or psychological harm, or loss of home and property. The inquiry into the Grenfell Tower fire is no exception. The inquiry was established just days after the numbers who died or were injured in the fire had begun to emerge. This chapter does not reject the idea that public inquiries may provide an effective alternative to a conventional court action. However, it argues that the conditions that will make such alternatives feasible are absent from the Grenfell situation. Until the inquiry reflects the diversity of the Grenfell Tower community, the legal claims which began with the judicial review application challenging the prime minister's decision to appoint Sir Martin Moore-Bick to sit alone when conducting the inquiry will proliferate. The chapter explores the decision in *R (on the application of) Daniels* v. *May* [2018] (the Grenfell Judicial Review decision) in order to show how the dissonance between law and justice is emphasised whenever the question of justice is raised in the face of racism and other forms of exclusion. Through their insistence on access to the courts, the victims of the Grenfell Tower fire are resisting the forces which would seek to divest them of legal capacity, and the importance of such resistance cannot be understated. However, it is doubtful that recourse to the courts will bring them closer to the justice they seek.

Law, Justice and 'Justiciability'

The majority of the victims of the Grenfell Tower fire, which raged for approximately 60 hours from just after midnight on 14 June

2017, are from racial and religious communities whose day-to-day life experiences give expression to those questions that raise matters which, for one reason or another, would not give rise to a legal claim upon which a court could adjudicate. Other victims share similar experiences. The law deems certain claims to be 'non-justiciable' – the technical term used to categorise questions that cannot be settled in court. If 'justiciability' is lacking, an issue cannot be determined through a legal process.

A question which has long preoccupied human rights scholars and practitioners concerns the 'justiciability' of claims against the state for injury or other losses arising from an alleged systematic failure of the state to appropriately manage its resources so as to cater for those in need of basic amenities, including safe and affordable housing; or, in other words, whether such claims can be heard in a court of law. The question has become a very salient one in the wake of the Grenfell Tower fire. Writing of the fire in the context of Britain's social welfare landscape, Robbie Shilliam argued that the 'fatal mal-management' of the Grenfell estate building, which contributed to the deaths, physical and psychological injuries and homelessness of the residents, was traceable to 'longer-term processes of gentrification and social cleansing' (Shilliam, 2018: 166).

According to Shilliam, the processes of 'social cleansing' were, in turn, authorised by decisions on the allocation of public housing based on a 'racialized distinction between deserving and undeserving' (Shilliam, 2018: 159). For Nadine El-Enany, the fire demonstrates how impossible it is for such communities to 'escape their condition of coloniality' (El-Enany, 2017). In the event of a claim brought against the British state (as represented by the Royal Borough of Kensington and Chelsea) upon the terms suggested by El-Enany and Shilliam's analysis of the underlying causes of the Grenfell catastrophe, the weight of academic opinion suggests that it would very likely fall within the category of 'non-justiciable' claims (see also Langloise-Therien, 2012: 213–232).

So, when Sir Martin Moore-Bick, Chair of the public inquiry into the Grenfell Tower fire, refused requests to expand the terms of reference of the inquiry so as to enable scrutiny of the Grenfell Tower fire within the broader historical context of Britain's social housing policy (*Daniels* [2018], para. 11), those familiar with the law, and with the culture of judicial decision-making, were not surprised to see the 'justiciability' notion invoked. According to Moore-Bick:

> The inclusion of such broad questions within the scope of the Inquiry would raise questions of a social, economic and political nature which in my view are not suitable for a judge-led inquiry. They are questions which could more appropriately be examined by a different kind of process or body, one which could include persons who have experience of the provision and management of social housing, local government finances and disaster relief planning. It could operate in parallel with the Inquiry and would be welcomed by many.
>
> (*Daniels* [2018], para. 11)

The reaction to the decision to structure the inquiry according to significantly more narrow terms of reference than suggested in the advice Moore-Bick had solicited and received during his consultation meetings with various interested parties has been well documented elsewhere. For example, BMELawyers4Grenfell were reported to have expressed the conviction that a 'colonial' style inquiry was now inevitable (Baksi, 2017). I do not intend to rehearse these criticisms and concerns in this chapter. What needs to be said is that Moore-Bick's position introduced a new and unwelcome dimension to the Grenfell residents' always fraught interactions and negotiations with the British state. His position was later endorsed by the High Court in the judicial review permission application in the case of *Daniels* [2018].

Grenfell Tower residents have become inured to the spectacle of British judges holding just beyond their reach the powerful weapons of the law. A particularly striking illustration of their disenfranchisement is to be found in Didi Herman's analysis of how and why civil restraint orders, which have the effect of preventing an individual from pursuing a legal case without the consent of the court, are disproportionately deployed against 'non-white' litigants (Herman, 2012: 27–46). Thus, no undue faith was placed in the legal system by the Grenfell residents and their representatives. However, by

invoking the idea of 'justiciability' in the context of the inquiry's terms
of reference, Moore-Bick posed 'justiciability' in direct opposition to
the 'justice' which the inquiry process was supposed to deliver. In so
doing, Moore-Bick revealed the unpalatable truth that, in relation to
certain communities – racialised minorities in particular – 'justice' is
no more nor less than the law as dispensed by the courts.

Very swiftly after the Grenfell Tower fire came the announcement that there would be a judicial inquiry into the causes of the fire.
The British Prime Minister, Theresa May, promised an inquiry that
would 'provide justice for the victims and their families who suffered
so terribly' (*Daniels* [2018], para. 3). Since then, there has been
intense public debate over the meaning of justice, in the context of
the Grenfell Tower fire and its aftermath. Not least of the questions
framing the debate is whether the source of the meaning of justice
can be discovered from within the organs of the state or from within
the wider public, especially those most affected by the fire and its
devastating consequences.

As a legal academic (once practitioner), I have become used to the
equation of justice with law, but I am by no means reconciled to the
idea that the 'victims' of Grenfell and the wider public must be pressed
towards the conclusion that law – or more precisely, legal concepts
like 'justiciability' – should be allowed to determine everywhere, and
at all times, the place of justice, and its limits.

The Judicial Review Permission Application

Inevitably, in light of the foregoing, I must call into question the
strategy of the lawyers and campaigning groups who have chosen to
pursue the residents' quest for justice from within the courts. Further,
they are beginning to insist on the increasing deployment of court-
style processes within the inquiry. As regards the latter point of
criticism, recent attempts by the 'campaign and community groups
Inquest, Grenfell United, Justice4Grenfell and Relative Justice
Humanity for Grenfell' to introduce into the inquiry an adversarial
process (Fouzder, 2018), are to be regretted. Whether it is actually
believed that there is no justice outside of law, or whether it is simply
that some have become used to *acting* as if such a belief were held, the

strategy has proved to be injurious to the Grenfell survivors, bereaved and general residents' quest for justice. The outcome of the judicial review permission application, analysed below, provides some support for my conclusion that an idea of justice, which, in the interests of the Grenfell Tower community, should be a negotiated one, is rapidly being reduced to a narrow legal conception.

For communities who have been at the receiving end of social welfare laws, which have been purposely designed to withhold vital state support (especially public housing) from black and minority ethnic people and others categorised as undeserving (see Shilliam, 2018), justice for Grenfell demands that racial, religious and class diversity is introduced in the inquiry's fact-finding and decision-making process, since such exercises are far from neutral. Thus, absence of diversity from the inquiry's decision-making is synonymous (in and of itself) with an absence of justice. Contrary to the conclusion of the High Court, in the judicial review permission decision, to the effect that arguments about the need for diversity 'are not all one way' (*Daniels* [2018], para. 45), the diversity argument must be sovereign, if justice for Grenfell is to be attained. However, such a conception of justice, although necessary for the Grenfell bereaved, survivors and wider constituency of residents, cannot be understood by a court.

Instead, the more historically situated the abuse or disadvantage (see El-Enany, 2017), the more that abuse or disadvantage is liable to be deemed 'non-justiciable'. So determined, there is no live question the answer to which cannot be found by a judge, who possesses a wealth of experience in the sifting of evidence and the reaching of objectively determined conclusions. For the court, diversity is just one among a number of legitimate factors that a decision maker may take into account in ensuring that the constitution of a public inquiry conforms with the requirements of the Inquiries Act 2005. It was almost inevitable, therefore, that in response to the question of whether an arguable case for judicial review arose as a result of the decision not to appoint a more diverse panel of decision makers, the court would conclude that:

The wishes of the survivors and the bereaved, however tragic the case, as to who should constitute a tribunal to investigate how the tragedy occurred cannot be conclusive. For my part I do not think it can even arguably be said that the decision of the Prime Minister to appoint Sir Martin without other members being appointed to the Inquiry panel was outside the range of rational decisions in the circumstances of this case.

(Daniels [2018], para. 35)

There is evidence also of a growing distance between the Grenfell residents and the courts and state representatives over questions concerning the *timeliness* of justice. From the moment the inquiry was proposed, it was made known that time is of the essence in the state's conception of justice. The prime minister was 'clear that we cannot wait for ages to learn the immediate lessons' *(Daniels* [2018], para. 4). For Moore-Bick, the 'need for my Inquiry to complete its work as quickly as possible' *(Daniels* [2018], para. 13) was self-evident – not least because of the possible/probable existence of other unsafe housing estates. Endorsing these views, the court concluded that 'the Prime Minister was entitled to take into account, as an important consideration, the need for the Inquiry to complete its initial report as quickly as reasonably practicable' *(Daniels* [2018], para. 47).

Is justice as immediately graspable as these statements about the 'obvious' need for a speedy determination of phase one of the inquiry would suggest? For many, justice is instantiated in the slow and sometimes cumbersome processes which reveal that time and money are not prioritised above human dignity. It has not yet been found as conclusive fact that the decision to save money by compromising the quality and durability of the cladding to the Grenfell Tower exterior was causally relevant to the fire and its still unfolding consequences, but the trauma that knowledge of this paltry saving has caused to survivors, the bereaved and the community immediately within the vicinity of the Grenfell Tower cannot be underestimated. It is in the interests of costs and the convenience of the inquiry chair, his team and the legal representatives that the decision was taken not to hold inquiry hearings closer to North Kensington where most of the Grenfell survivors reside. A recent *Guardian* newspaper report detailed the widespread unhappiness felt by non-state core participants, witnesses and their families over the decision. Chief among their concerns was the fact that the current venue, located in Holborn, was not accommodating of victims and was 'cramped and full of lawyers' (Booth, 2018).

The Case for Non-Legally Qualified Chairs of Public Inquiries

If it is to be 'justice' and not 'justiciability' that directs the inquiry towards its conclusions, then some attempt must be made to overcome the attachment to the legal form of those whose actions most influence how an inquiry process develops. In January 2015, the Centre for Dispute Resolution produced a report titled *Setting Up and Running a Public Inquiry: Guidance for Chairs and Commissioning Bodies* (Mackie and Way, 2015). The report contained an early promise of a reimagined inquiry process. Commenting on the development of the public inquiry framework, the report observed that insufficient consideration has been given to:

> testing more innovative approaches to achieving the core purposes of inquiries – investigation; fact-gathering and truth-finding; recognition for 'victims'; healing of wounds caused by social incidents; and engagement with practical methods of implementation of recommendations.
>
> (Mackie and Way, 2015: 9)

Ultimately, however, the report addressed few of the matters of dispute which have been the source of tension in the Grenfell Tower fire inquiry. Indeed, it is notable that despite the inclusion in the report of sections on how to handle 'emotions' (Mackie and Way, 2015: 38–40), addressing 'difficult' questions (42–44) and dealing with different 'groups' (44–47), it is silent on the challenges and opportunities presented when issues of diversity are factored into the design and operating processes of a public inquiry.

The report neglected another important opportunity to initiate radical reform when it problematised, but failed to indicate how to overcome, the expectations that a judge or other legally qualified person is most suited to the role of chair of a public inquiry (Mackie and Way, 2015: 8). However, credit must be given to the report authors for at least raising the issue of what kind of professional expertise is required of a chair, and, in doing so, pointing to a way in which inquiries may be reimagined. Whilst any change will come too late for Grenfell, reform of the current public inquiry model might prove to be one of Grenfell's more positive and enduring legacies.

If, as I suggest, the inquiry process must be wrested from the legal process, then change must come at the level of the chair. In the last few decades, there have been less than a handful of inquiry chairs who were not within one or two years of retiring from the ranks of the senior judiciary. Such individuals will inevitably carry with them into the inquiry forum fairly entrenched notions as to the futility of looking for a justice that exists beyond the strict rule of law and the decisions of the courts.

A great deal of careful argument was presented by the lawyers representing the government in the judicial review permission action as to why it was evident that the prime minister had not departed from the terms of the Inquiries Act 2005 when acting on her conviction that any gap in Moore-Bick's knowledge and expertise could be supplemented by expert assessors and, potentially, an advisory panel. Their arguments were ultimately accepted by the High Court as being within the range of reasonable considerations which the prime minister might have in mind when concluding that Moore-Bick would be the sole decision maker in relation to the fact-finding stage of the inquiry. Surely, this very logic can be inverted in a way which accommodates a shift towards non-legally qualified chairs, with the result, one would expect, of a greater chance that chairs would be drawn from more diverse communities? I accept that some expertise in the handling of evidence is an important resource, to which every inquiry must have access. However, a public inquiry process would work well if arranged so as to ensure that a non-legally qualified chair is able to draw upon the knowledge and skill of a judge who will have been appointed to assist the inquiry in the role of expert adviser on the law of evidence, and on other relevant areas of substantive law and procedure.

No Diversity, No Sympathy

It is a telling fact that the 2015 report by Mackie and Way, referenced in the preceding subparagraph, was commissioned by an organisation committed to exploring and promoting alternative dispute resolution mechanisms. As indicated in the synopsis to this chapter, it is important that we see in the objectives of the inquiry into the Grenfell Tower fire an attempt to divert the bereaved and the survivors of Grenfell away from the ordinary courts in their pursuit of redress for the deaths of family and friends and for the physical and psychological injuries, displacement from home and economic losses which they have suffered in such appalling large numbers. It is also important that we understand that it is against a decimated legal aid landscape that many of those affected by the Grenfell fire find they have little choice other than to place their faith in the public inquiry as a means towards achieving some form of closure.

Whereas twentieth-century legal systems were preoccupied with directing individuals away from the resort to private violence and towards the law for the resolution of disputes, the predominant objective of contemporary legal systems, no less the English legal system, is to deprive certain individuals of legal capacity. It is beyond the scope of this chapter to examine the criteria according to which it is determined which individuals should be directed away from the legal system, however, my reference to Didi Herman's article on the racially discriminatory use of civil restraint orders was intended to signal that the criteria are demonstrably, albeit not exclusively, racial in character (2012: 27–46). This chapter does not argue that for an inquiry to operate as an alternative dispute forum is *per se* objectionable. However, it does argue that the Grenfell inquiry cannot be effective in this regard as long as its decision not to appoint a diverse panel to share decision-making powers with Moore-Bick remains unchanged.

If we were to follow the philosopher, Walter Benjamin, we would conclude that alternatives to the deployment of legal power in the ordinary courts are possible and effective, but not through the conditions under which the inquiry into the Grenfell Tower fire is taking place, for 'courtesy, sympathy, peaceableness, trust' are the 'subjective preconditions' of such alternatives (Benjamin, 1995: 289). What this means for the Grenfell inquiry is that – at the very least – those who have suffered the violence of Grenfell should be recognised as being entitled to engage in the official process of making findings about the causes of the fire and reaching decisions that will impact on the futures of those who depend upon public housing.

The structure of the UK public inquiry contains an implied promise that these 'preconditions' will be present in its arrangements and operating practices. It assumes a collection of individuals, usually chaired by a legally qualified person, often a retired judge, all working together to arrive at the 'truth' behind the events in question. However, what the Grenfell inquiry has revealed is that, for many, the absence of Benjamin's 'preconditions', and therefore the absence of the conditions that make the inquiry objectives achievable, is signalled by an absence of diversity in the decision-making body and/or a suspicion that the decision maker/decision-making body exemplifies the legal system's traditional hostility to difference.

In the context of a catastrophe that claimed the lives and well-being of so many residents, the absence of such 'preconditions' cannot be disentangled from the absence of racial diversity. How many vulnerable individuals have been induced to take part in the inquiry process, as core participants, because of an expressed or implied promise that the terms of her or his involvement would be determined by the rules of civility which Benjamin correctly saw as an indispensable requirement of an effective alternative dispute mechanism?

From my observations, non-state core participants in the Grenfell inquiry began their involvement from a genuine desire to help create the conditions under which, per Benjamin, indirect solutions might offer a reasonable alternative to recourse to an adversarial process. Faced with the realisation that their marginality is the very circumstance which will ensure that his 'preconditions' are permanently withheld, they then become vulnerable to being persuaded to turn to the court system in the ultimately vain hope that the British judiciary might understand why attention to their histories of oppression must precede any attempt to deliver justice.

Conclusion

Grenfell Tower must not be valorised as a site within which content can be given to the idea of justice, and/or where the idea of justice might receive a decisive break from its association with the law as practised in the courts, and as overseen by judges. It is not the first forum of this kind to offer such a valuable opportunity to build a collective sense of what is just or unjust, and it will not be the last. However, the scale of the suffering produced through the Grenfell Tower fire marks Grenfell out as one of the most important sites of contestation over the meaning and scope of justice. It is for this reason that the question of justice for Grenfell must not be conflated with the question of law.

References

Baksi, C. (2017) 'Judicial Review over Grenfell Tower Inquiry Team Refused'. *Legal Voice*, 13. September. http://legalvoice.org.uk/judicial-review-grenfell-tower-inquiry-team-refused/ (all websites in this list last accessed November 2018).

Benjamin, W. (1995) 'Critique of Violence', in *Walter Benjamin: Reflections, Essays, Aphorisms, Autobiographical Writings*. New York: Schocken Books.

Booth, R. (2018) 'They Want me to Relive Grenfell Then Get on a Rush-Hour Tube Home'. *The Guardian*, 24 September. www.theguardian.com/uk-news/2018/sep/24/they-want-me-to-relive-grenfell-then-get-on-a-rush-hour-tube-home.

El-Enany, N. (2017) 'The Colonial Logic of Grenfell'. *Verso Blog*, 3 July. www.versobooks.com/blogs/3306-the-colonial-logic-of-grenfell.

Fouzder, M. (2018) 'No Place for Court-Lie Cross Examination in Public Inquiries, Grenfell Team Says'. *Law Society Gazette*, 17 September. www.lawgazette.co.uk/no-place-for-court-like-cross-examination-in-public-inquiries-grenfell-team-says/5067566.article.

Herman, D. (2012) 'Hopeless Cases: Race, Racism and the "Vexatious Litigant"'. *International Journal of Law in Context*, 8(1): 27–46.

Inquiries Act 2005 (UK).

Langloise-Therien, L. (2012) 'The Justiciability of Housing Rights: From Argument to Practice'. *Journal of Human Rights Practice*, 4(2): 213–232.

Mackie, K. and R. Way (2015) *Setting Up and Running a Public Inquiry: Guidance for Chairs and Commissioning Bodies*, Centre for Effective Dispute Resolution.

Shilliam, R. (2018) *Race and the Undeserving Poor*. Newcastle: Agenda Publishing.

R (on the application of Daniels) v. *Prime Minister & Anor* [2018] EWHC (Admin).

The Interloper

Jenny Edkins

From the platform at Latimer Road I can see it clearly: more clearly than at any other point during my visit. I try not to look, to appear as though I am not a stranger, a visitor, a tourist. Definitely not a voyeur, though that's what I feel like. A train comes and goes. I sit waiting, head lowered. But it's there, solid, in front of me. Eyeless windows, charred black. Screams long since silent, flames extinguished.

On the way down, just a few hours earlier but much longer ago, I'd been sitting on the tube with my back to that view. Boarding at King's Cross, I knew I was on the wrong side – facing north rather than south as the train travelled west – but the carriage was full and there were no seats opposite. It emptied as we passed Edgware Road then Paddington, and emerged into the light. But I was rooted to my seat. After Westbourne Park, the line turns south, and as we drew out of Ladbroke Grove I caught a glimpse from the window.

I'd not been intending to go, at least not yet. I didn't want to. It was both too personal and nothing to do with me. Residents resented people taking photographs as if on some sightseeing trip, and rightly so. The media had descended before it was even over, seeking out the worst stories and disappearing to write them up, speaking to camera in tones perfected in distant tragedies. But it wasn't a tragedy. It was an impossibility, a horror, an atrocity.

In the lounge at the Crescent Hotel late the previous night, Will had insisted.

'You should go,' he said. 'It'll make use of your journey here.'

I'd had to travel down to London unexpectedly, but I knew he meant more than that. We'd spoken about Grenfell. He sensed my reluctance.

'OK. I'll see how I feel in the morning.'

I made a bargain with myself. If I was up early enough, and if I could work out how to get there, and if I felt up to it, I would go. I was meeting Rachel at Paddington to catch the twelve thirty to Temple Meads, so it was only a minor detour.

Around nine in the morning, I found myself boarding the Hammersmith and City line to Latimer Road.

Down the steps, card on reader, out of the exit, I turn left. I don't have a smart phone and I've not brought a map with me. But I studied one beforehand. I know if I head south, the tower will be on my left. Feigning familiarity, I set off.

Ordinary suburban streets, haunted only in my imagination. Passers by: mothers with pushchairs squeezing past me between bus stop and wall. Were they there that night? What did they see? A smartly dressed woman, heels clicking briskly, walks alongside a tall man in a suit. Out of place – like me.

'So when's the exhibition on until?' he asks.

'Well, it's going to be extended,' comes the reply.

Something to do with what happened, surely? And further along, railings carrying small remnants of ribbons, posters, mementoes. Notices saying where to go for help.

I need to turn left at some point; I'm getting further away. Past a small triangle where a road joins on the right. Cafés, shops. I could stop, sit, pause, but I don't. I carry on.

Finally I turn left at random down a long street, the white fences of flats on one side, red-brick on the other. At the end I go left again, past smart Victorian terraces with tiny front gardens. I am basically lost, but I carry on to a T-junction and turn left again. It is increasingly hard to give the impression I know what I'm doing. The network of small streets is impenetrable, and I don't recognise anything. I make out a spire in the distance, and head for that. Shortly after it happened there were gatherings of people outside the nearest church, and tributes piled up against the railings. When I get there, I recognise it from the media coverage.

I remember when I first heard about what happened. I was in the kitchen, making breakfast. Something prompted me to turn on the radio. It was about nine, maybe later. I can't remember what they said, but I remember listening in horror. I didn't go and turn on the television; I just carried on listening. It was only later I saw the images, watched survivors speaking to reporters, saw the video fire-fighters took as they approached along Westway, incredulous. I watched and watched, all through that day and the next. And for weeks I could think of little else.

When the planes hit the twin towers in New York, I was in London with a friend, at the British Museum. A guide gave us directions to a particular Roman mosaic.

'They've hijacked four planes and crashed two into a skyscraper in Manhattan and two into the Pentagon,' he added, urgently. 'There's a fifth plane flying around with six hundred people on board.'

We looked at each other. Was it a joke? Was he crazy? We left anyway. Snatches of conversations heard outside confirmed what had happened, but it wasn't until I got home that I saw the pictures.

I visited that site, six months afterwards. Like here, it was difficult to navigate: to reconcile the images I'd seen with what was there. But I never felt like an intruder.

I cross the road past the church and take another random turning. I can feel I'm closing in now. Suddenly, I'm looking at a phone box I recognise, the one that was covered in missing person posters. Scraps remain: corners sellotaped to the glass.

For weeks, I thought I would remember my visit clearly. Now, writing this, I pause to search for pictures of the phone box to remind me what it looked like. I realise that what I've just written can't be right. The street name in the photos is Blechynden Street. But on the map that street is the other side of the tube station. I must have passed it on the way back, not on the way out. My memory is hazy at best, then: distorted, even. Checking Google, I plot my route. I must have gone south along Bramley and St Anns, left into Stoneleigh Place, left again down Sirdar, then down Grenfell Road to where it's blocked off, past the leisure centre, then somehow, but I can't work out how, through to Notting Hill Methodist Church on Lancaster Road. I resume my writing.

I continue past the church, and eventually find myself outside the Maxilla Social Club, relieved but exhausted. Not just from carrying a heavy backpack, but from taking it all in. This is as far as I will go, but this is also a hub. I know it well, although I don't know it at all. People were interviewed here. People gathered to support each other, to provide food, to talk. The club stayed open all through that dreadful night.

Odds and ends of inhabitation are abandoned now: chairs and plastic covered tables, candles, boxes, a piano, incongruous under the concrete arches of the Westway flyover. 'The People's Public Inquest: First Hand Accounts. Facts. Testimonies', announce strong capitals painted on the wall behind. In a zigzag formation, A4 sheets carry statements or messages of support. I read through them one by one. They are heartbreaking. I weep. Fumbling in my bag for a piece of paper, I copy some down. 'Politics is the difference between life and death,' signed Anthony Anaxagorou. Another, 'Horror must be when your eyes show something you cannot process,' is just signed RIP.

I sit for a time. Then I go through the arches and turn towards the tube station again. In this direction there are large banners demanding justice, posters fastened to trees, and, of course, the phone box. I stand in front of it for a while. From here the tower is visible. Many of the photos of the missing posters took pains to include it. I turn away, walk on to the tube station.

I check the departure board for the next service and sit down to wait for the train back, averting my eyes from the tower. There is a cold wind, and the punched metal seats are freezing.

'Passengers are requested not to take photographs from this station,' comes an announcement.

I don't have a camera with me anyhow: I am not a tourist. On one of the hoardings in New York after 9/11, someone called Mariette had written 'We all lost you all, and mourn together. We are not "sightseers".'

Looking back as I waited for Rachel in the café on Paddington station, I felt as though the images in my head had gained a landscape to inhabit. If I wrote about what happened, my writing would be more grounded.

I'm not so sure now. I've put a tentative hand on the backdrop, nothing more. I have seen the tower with my own eyes: seen a grey ribbon of fabric hanging from a high window flapping in the wind. But the landscape cannot speak. Maybe it lies. Or maybe things are just more complicated. Maybe it was not a visit anyway, but a pilgrimage. I wish I'd taken flowers, a card, a candle, anything: an offering to leave behind.

8

From Grenfell to Windrush

Gracie Mae Bradley

Racism is above all a technology aimed at permitting the exercise of biopower, 'that old sovereign right of death'.

(Mbembe, 2003: 17)

A year after the devastating fire at Grenfell Tower in June 2017, as the inquiry unfolded, the survivors, local community and wider society continued to reel from the loss of 72 lives and the institutional indifference that followed and preceded it. Emails from the Royal Borough of Kensington and Chelsea (RBKC) council released through Freedom of Information revealed one unnamed worker's racialised view of the tower's residents: 'language problems, lack of education and understanding how anything works', with parts of the community characterised as '*territorial*' in nature and apparently comparable to 'gangs' (Booth, 2018b).

By contrast, residents knew enough about 'how things work' to have chosen fire resistant cladding during a 2012 consultation on the tower's refurbishment. The fire-resistant version of the cladding that was ultimately installed would have cost just £5,000 more, according to *The Times* (Mostrous, O'Neill and Joiner, 2017). The smoke ventilation system failed eight days before the fire, with a proposal to fix it for £1,800 reportedly unanswered, and no maintenance contract in place (Booth, 2018a). A year after the fire, two-thirds of affected households from Grenfell Tower and Grenfell Walk were without a permanent home (Grenfell Support, 2018).

Grenfell Tower was home to families from countries all over the world, including many from North Africa. It takes its name from nearby Grenfell Walk, itself named after Francis Wallace Grenfell, who fought numerous colonial wars there on behalf of the Crown ount, 2017). While many residents were British, or had secure immigration status, some did not. In the immediate aftermath of the fire, an impromptu campaign for an immigration amnesty gathered pace. Health workers and legal representatives found that some people were too afraid to seek support from the emergency services or other officials, fearing that any contact with the state would be used as a pretext to detain and deport them under the auspices of the government's 'hostile environment' (Quinn, 2017).

The government eventually set out a tortuous route to settlement, but it was no amnesty. People would face three rounds of applications over five years and the state reserved its right to refuse and deport them on the basis of their perceived 'character, criminality or associations' (Home Office, 2017–2018). In the meantime, family members wishing to attend the inquiry from overseas to ascertain precisely what happened to their loved ones were unable to obtain visas (*National* Newsdesk, 2018).

One year after Grenfell, a further state-enabled cruelty made its way into the light: what has come to be called the Windrush scandal. People who had travelled to the UK as British subjects, or, more technically, 'Citizens of the United Kingdom and Colonies' after the Second World War had, in a context of target-driven deportations, been informed in their hundreds by the government that they were suspected of being in the UK unlawfully, and would have to prove that they were not, or face deportation.

When the 1971 Immigration Act came into force it regularised everyone in the UK who had settled there from the colonies up to that point, while simultaneously ending the ability of others to do so without proving close and effectively white family ties to the metropole, in a bid to stem the flow of black and brown arrivals. The 1981 Nationality Act further did away with birthright citizenship, leaving those Windrush citizens who had not applied for citizenship with recourse only to a lesser right of abode, and their children and grandchildren at risk of statelessness and deportation. Thus, it was that as internal immigration controls tightened in the 2000s, first under New Labour and then under the auspices of the 'hostile environment', people who had lived essentially their entire lives in the UK were forced to attempt to prove their immigration status to an administration that had adopted a rigid, box-checking culture of refusal, even when they furnished extensive proof of long residence.

While Windrush is less immediately fatal than the fire that over-whelmed Grenfell Tower, the effects of a 'hostile environment', intentionally devoid of everything a person needs to live (as Theresa May proudly described it as Home Secretary – see Kirkup and Winnett, 2012) cannot be ignored. Windrush citizens were denied or charged for health care, and lost their jobs, accommodation and access to welfare benefits. People were unable to buy presents for their grandchildren; unable to visit dying mothers or attend loved ones' weddings and funerals, and in some cases left the UK for holidays only to be told that they could not return home. They were un-documented by the state; their proof of long residence suddenly inadequate, landing cards destroyed, and protection from deportation quietly repealed.

While scientists have suggested that racism may damage us at the deepest cellular level, accelerating the ageing process (University of Maryland, 2014), the health effects of destitution are more prosaic: Windrush citizens who were stripped of their homes and livelihoods can only have been made poorer and sicker as a result. At least three people wrongly deported died in exile (Gentleman, 2018c). Sarah O'Connor, a formidable campaigner for the rights of the Windrush generation, died in September 2018 at 57 years old, a naturalised British citizen at last, but still staring down the barrel of homeless-ness (Gentleman, 2018d). The mother of Dexter Bristol, a second Windrush citizen who died in 2018, attributed his death to the stress he experienced in trying to prove that he was entitled to an immi-gration status that had always rightfully been his, and which should never have determined how he lived and died. 'This is racism,' she said, 'he was a victim of their policies' (Gentleman, 2018a).

At a time when racism is increasingly flattened into a container marked 'individual racially discriminatory acts or unpleasant views', 'hate crime', or, indeed, 'free speech', it is right that we make a renewed effort to abandon 'the habit of considering racism as a mental quirk, as a psychological flaw' (Fanon, 1967: 38). This is not an abandon-ment that I find difficult: I am the granddaughter of the migrations that followed the Second World War, and the English working class. Two of my grandparents were Windrush citizens, and my other grandfather was an African-American stationed in England during the Cold War. Racism is what undergirded the teacher who suppressed my infant mother's school grades, closing off who knows what possible futures; it is the logic of the police who let skinheads roam free to harass my grandfather, and who saw fit to burst into his home and trample the clean washing (but picked it up with deference when my white grandmother came into view). It is what left him with little financial option for survival but Vietnam, and only drugs to blank out what he saw there. It is what stops and searches my young cousins three times each day in our hometown, and leaves them with nowhere to turn when they fear falling victim to violence themselves.

Racism foreshortens the possibilities of people and peoples. At its most intense, it is, like poverty, condemnation to a life and death of drudgery, exploitation, illness and want. Racism forecloses any meaningful sense of security: the security of knowing that we will not be ripped from our homes and families and die alone in an unknown land or in a Kafkaesque battle with an implacable bureaucracy; that we will not die by fire in our sleep or terrified waking. Of course, racism does not do all of these things by itself; it is 'only one element of a vaster whole: that of the systematized oppression of a people' (Fanon, 1967: 33). And this in turn is how race as the modality in which class is lived comes into relief; because of course, not everyone who lived in Grenfell Tower was a migrant, and some who have been dispossessed in a similar vein to the Windrush generation are, in fact, white.

The responses of the state to Grenfell and Windrush mark similar tracks. First came the careful demarcation of the victims: the Home Office took great care to define Windrush citizens with a criminal record out of the numbers of people wrongly deported (Gentleman, 2018b). Next came the state's regret and apology at the most narrow and extreme manifestations of the harm that it had caused or allowed, but no acknowledgement of or remorse at the systems that enabled that harm – be that the widespread managed decline of social housing and rampant property speculation across the UK, the hostile environment, or, more broadly, a political consensus that disavows Britain's imperial past and for the most part, is prepared to tolerate the lawful entry of only the richest and the whitest would-be immigrants, meting out the violence of destitution, detention and deportation to the rest. In each instance, the institution of some kind of formal redress – a public inquiry; a euphemistic 'lessons learned review' – in effect functions for calls for immediate or radical policy change to be labelled premature. Victims are encouraged to come forward, compensation schemes and faux-amnesties are promised, and the media furore dies down.

And of course, all of this happens in such a way as to reinscribe the logic that enabled those initial catastrophes, and the responses of the well-meaning outraged all too often reinscribe that logic too. Some parliamentary Windrush campaigners were quick to aver that Windrush was about cherished, law-abiding citizens who had been wrongly treated as 'illegal immigrants', with little mention of why excluding undocumented people from health care, housing, or work might be cruel and unjust in and of itself; or indeed the practice of forcing anyone to apply for citizenship at all. In discussions that I observed, some residents and charities responding to the Grenfell Tower fire were quick to label mention of undocumented residents 'unhelpful', or to reiterate that *they* weren't here illegally. Thus, Windrush citizens who have braved making applications to the Home Office, in the absence of any legal aid or avenue of appeal, are still liable to be refused leave on grounds of criminality, insufficient evidence or bad character (Bulman, 2018) – the same grounds on which undocumented Grenfell applicants may be denied settlement, and the same grounds on which hundreds of children – the majority of them black – are routinely refused citizenship (Mohdin, 2018). Up and down the country, thousands of people sleep each night in buildings still clad in material very similar to that which turned Grenfell Tower into a 'death trap' (Tobin, 2018).

Grenfell and Windrush represent an unremitting reminder (to those with the luxury of forgetting) that racism is 'the state-sanctioned or extralegal production and exploitation of group-differentiated vulnerability to premature death' (Gilmore, 2007: 28). Each of these catastrophic events lays bare the sometimes lethal intersections of race and class while at the same time demanding that we rigorously interrogate them. Those of us who respond to that call must commit to doing so with sufficient care, attention and humility as to avoid reinforcing the institutions and practices that allowed Windrush and Grenfell to happen in the first instance. We cannot be content to divide the dead and dispossessed into those who are worthy of popular anger, and those who are not. Nor can we satisfy ourselves with partial demands for amnesty, compensation or citizenship. We should do the work of building solidarity across struggles against racial, economic and all forms of oppression; and we should not be constrained by national borders as we do so, because the 'systematized oppression of a people' calls for a systematic and intersectional response. As Barbara Smith reminds us in her reflections on the 40th anniversary of the Combahee River Collective statement, coalitions are 'how we win [...] and how we survive in the meantime' (Smith, 2017: 64). So our horizon of justice must be broad and brave enough to contemplate not only retrospective reparation, but also the opening up of foreshortened and foreclosed futures, and the simultaneous possibility of 'never again'. And even then, far from the end, that will be only the beginning.

References

Booth, R. (2018a) 'Grenfell Tower's Smoke Ventilation System "Failed Days Before Fire"'. *The Guardian*, 5 June. www.theguardian.com/uk-news/2018/jun/05/grenfell-towers-smoke-ventilation-system-failed-days-before-fire (all websites in this list last accessed November 2018).

Booth, R. (2018b) 'Grenfell Emails Reveal Turmoil at Council in Aftermath of Fire'. *The Guardian*, 8 June. www.theguardian.com/uk-news/2018/jun/08/grenfell-emails-reveal-turmoil-at-council-in-aftermath-of-fire.

Bulman, M. (2018) 'Windrush Generation Members to be Refused UK Citizenship, Government Announces'. *The Independent*, 21 September. www.independent.co.uk/news/uk/home-news/windrush-citizens-latest-citizenship-refused-home-office-sajid-javid-a8549101.html.

Fanon, F. (1967), *Toward the African Revolution: Political Essays*, translated by H. Chevalier. New York: Grove Press.

Gentleman, A. (2018a) 'Mother of Windrush Citizen Blames Passport Problems for his Death'. *The Guardian*, 18 April. www.theguardian.com/uk-news/2018/apr/18/mother-of-windrush-citizen-blames-passport-problems-for-his-death.

Gentleman, A. (2018b) 'Windrush Row: Javid's Apology Overshadowed by New Removal Figures'. *The Guardian*, 21 August. www.theguardian.com/

uk-news/2018/aug/21/sajid-javid-says-sorry-for-18-windrush-removals-or-detentions.

Gentleman, A. (2018c) 'Windrush: Three People Wrongly Deported from UK Have Died, Says Official'. *The Guardian*, 30 August. www.theguardian.com/uk-news/2018/aug/30/windrush-people-deported-from-uk-died-jamaica-foreign-minister.

Gentleman, A. (2018d) 'Windrush Victim and Campaigner Sarah O'Connor Dies Aged 57'. *The Guardian*, 19 September. www.theguardian.com/uk-news/2018/sep/19/windrush-victim-campaigner-sarah-oconnor-dies-aged-57.

Gilmore, R. W. (2007) *Golden Gulag: Prisons, Surplus, Crisis, and Opposition in Globalizing California*. Berkeley, CA: University of California Press.

Grenfell Support (2018) 'Commemorating Grenfell One Year On'. *Grenfell Support News*, Issue 25, 1 June. https://grenfellsupport.org.uk/wp-content/uploads/2018/06/Grenfell-Newsletter-1-June-2018.pdf.

Home Office (2017–2018) 'Guidance. Grenfell Tower Fire: Handling Immigration Cases'. 5 July–6 April. www.gov.uk/government/publications/grenfell-tower-fire-handling-immigration-cases.

Kirkup, J. and R. Winnett (2012) 'Theresa May Interview: "We're Going to Give Illegal Migrants a Really Hostile Reception"'. *The Telegraph*, 25 May. www.telegraph.co.uk/news/uknews/immigration/9291483/Theresa-May-interview-Were-going-to-give-illegal-migrants-a-really-hostile-reception.html.

Mbembe, A. (2003) 'Necropolitics', translated by L. Meintjes, *Public Culture*, 15(1): 11–40.

Mohdin, A. (2018) 'Children as Young as 10 Denied UK Citizenship for Failing "Good Character" Test'. *The Guardian*, 21 September. www.theguardian.com/uk-news/2018/sep/21/children-as-young-as-10-denied-uk-citizenship-for-failing-good-character-test.

Mostrous, A., S. O'Neill and S. Joiner (2017) 'Grenfell Tower: Fire-Resistant Cladding is just £5,000 More Expensive'. *The Times*, 16 June. www.thetimes.co.uk/article/grenfell-tower-fire-resistant-cladding-is-just-5-000-more-expensive-6gjqkg98g.

Mount, H. (2017) 'My Great-Grandfather, a Victorian Den of Poverty – and the New Slums'. *The Daily Telegraph*, 17 June. www.pressreader.com/uk/the-daily-telegraph/20170617/281603830457050.

National Newsdesk (2018) 'Grenfell Tower Victims' Family Members Speak Up over Visa Issues'. 30 May. www.thenational.scot/news/16259353.grenfell-tower-victims-family-members-speak-up-over-visa-issues/.

Quinn, B. (2017) 'Grenfell Tower Survivors "must have Total Immigration Amnesty"'. *The Observer*, 15 July. www.theguardian.com/uk-news/2017/jul/15/grenfell-immigrant-survivors-permanent-residency-motion.

Smith, B. (2017) Interview in K-Y. Taylor (ed.), *How We Get Free: Black Feminism and the Combahee River*. Chicago, IL: Haymarket Books.

Tobin, O. (2018) 'Almost 500 Buildings in the UK have Same Cladding as Grenfell Tower, Government Report Reveals'. *The Evening Standard*, 30 June.

www.standard.co.uk/news/london/almost-500-buildings-in-the-uk-are-using-the-same-cladding-as-grenfell-tower-government-report-a3875396.html

University of Maryland (2014) 'Racism may Accelerate Aging in African American Men'. *UMD Right Now*, 7 January. https://umdrightnow.umd.edu/news/racism-may-accelerate-aging-african-american-men.

9

Housing Policy in the Shadow of Grenfell

Nigel de Noronha

This chapter explores the historical roots of housing policy in the UK, the contradictions that were exposed and the struggles for improvement. The Grenfell Tower fire challenged the government, council and housing sector disregard for the victims and those living in similar properties. This contempt is not new but reflects a return to the open hostility that the British ruling classes have felt towards the working classes and colonial subjects that they ruled over. Whilst the UK has recognised the right to adequate housing since 1976, the historical evidence suggests that some groups have been excluded by policy changes and financialisation of housing (UN, 1966; Farha, 2017). The opportunity to change housing policy should recognise housing as a fundamental right and ensure it is accessible to all.

The initial response to the disaster included large-scale individual support for the survivors as well as an outpouring of anger at those seen to be responsible. The monthly commemoration of the event in the silent march continues to highlight the solidarity felt with the victims and survivors. The shameful images of those seen to be responsible for the fire, the council and tenants' management organisation were juxtaposed with the emerging stories of those who had died. Evidence presented to the Inquiry has suggested that the spread of the fire was caused by inadequate safety features, that the response was inadequate and failed to protect the lives of the 72 who died and to deal with the trauma that affected the remaining survivors and neighbours. As Matt Wrack, General Secretary of the Fire Brigades Union, notes:

> A point that tends to be forgotten in the reporting around Grenfell is that every aspect of fire safety in the tower – the safety measures

designed and built into the fabric of the block in 1974 – all spectacularly failed. The fire lifts did not work. The fire doors were not
of the correct standard. The smoke extraction did not work. The
windows failed. The water supply was inadequate.

(Wrack, 2018)

The chapter uses the concepts of social stigmatisation and racialisation. Social stigmatisation is applied to people, places and to people
who live in those places (Tyler and Slater, 2018; Slater, 2018). I use
racialisation to explain how racialised groups and places are categorised as different and then receive unequal treatment (Garner,
2017). The genesis of this chapter was involvement with activists and
barristers making a submission to the Public Inquiry. The submission
argued the need to examine the structural factors that led to the fire
and the subsequent response.

The Historical Context

This chapter shows that decisions about housing policy have reflected
the interests of those in power in response to major contradictions at
different times and places in the UK. This historical analysis is partial
as the structure of the state and local contexts create the conditions
for local variations. Government housing policy created a framework
for interpretation by the local state. Councils, social reformers and,
in some cases, local residents have been the major players in the
planning and delivery of housing. The roots of state investment in
social housing for the working classes are in the campaign to build
'homes fit for heroes' after the First World War (Harloe, 1995;
Boughton, 2018). At the time, the majority of households lived in
the private rented sector (PRS), many in poor conditions. Nationally,
the freezing of rents in 1915 and the commitment to build 'homes fit
for heroes' were a response to often militant working-class demands.
The Act freezing private sector rents was forced by the rent strikes in
Glasgow that highlighted the profiteering of landlords in urban areas
(Gray, 2018). After the war, the use of tanks to break the dockyard,
transport and manufacturing strikes in Glasgow in 1919 reflected
the level of government concern about workers' insurrections (Foster,

1990). These strikes and industrial militancy were happening across the UK, as workers demanded improved pay and conditions, whilst employers sought to reduce costs.

From Homes Fit for Heroes to Slum Clearance

The Housing Act 1919 provided subsidies and gave responsibility to local councils to deliver housing for working people (Harloe, 1995). These could include homes built privately with the grant made to the builder acting as an effective subsidy for the tenants or built by the council themselves using loans. The new town programme provided a model that was to be followed by many councils building garden estates to rehouse residents away from the polluted inner city. The rent needed to cover both the repayment on the loan and the cost of maintenance. Due to the high price of land, this meant that council housing tended to be more expensive and though larger and built to better living standards, it was often an option unavailable to those in insecure or poorly paid employment. Progress in meeting local housing needs was variable reflecting the difficulties in assembling land, planning and developing the large estates that councils aspired to. Other barriers to the new council housing that was available included the desires of those who wanted to stay close to family and friends, or their workplace.

The Housing Act 1930 extended the obligations of local councils to provide housing as a social service and clear remaining slums. The legislation required councils to submit a housing needs assessment for the working classes in their local area every five years, to define slum housing for clearance and develop plans to rehouse families affected (Henderson and Maddocks, 1930). This programme was the responsibility of individual councils leading to significant variation in the pace of delivery due to local land availability, levels of housing need and political commitment. Between the First and Second World War, local councils built over 1 million homes with some areas investing largely in the PRS and others in the social housing sector.

Local variations in the implementation of housing strategies during this period reveal the difficulties that the slum clearance programme caused. In Leeds, the local subsidy provided to incentivise people to move into the new council estates on the periphery of the city became unaffordable as a result of the investment required to meet their slum clearance obligations (Bradley, 1999). In Manchester, the lengthy clearance process involved assessment of individual houses, compilation and consultation of neighbourhood plans and the provision of accommodation to rehouse residents in slum clearance areas. This slowed down the development of the garden estates programme and, in the view of reformers in the city, meant that those in the greatest need were not eligible for the council housing that was built (Simon and Inman, 1935). The advent of the Second World War interrupted these clearance plans in most areas.

The Rise and Fall of Social Housing: From State Provision to Residualisation

The Beveridge report summarised the findings of a committee established by the coalition government in 1941 to investigate social insurance and allied services (Parliament, 1942). The report highlighted the five great evils of squalor, ignorance, want, idleness and disease and is often cited as the foundation of the British Welfare State as it proposed universal social insurance and a comprehensive welfare system to address want (IPPR, 2014; Dorling, 2010). Beveridge's other great evils were addressed through social policies, which extended universal secondary education, planned for full employment, introduced universal health care and invested in house building. Squalor was associated with inadequate housing and the consequent poor health of its residents. The post-war government of Clement Attlee addressed housing needs by building over 1 million homes, 80 per cent of which were let by councils. The affordability of housing was addressed through the 1948 National Assistance Act which repealed the poor law, provided a safety net for those who could not make insurance contributions, placed a requirement on local authorities to provide residential accommodation for vulnerable and homeless households, and, provided a means tested provision for those who could not afford the prescribed rent (parliament.uk, 2015). This provision was the first time that a state subsidy of housing was provided to the tenant rather than the property owner. This meant that social housing became affordable for many more households.

The Town and Country Planning Act in 1947 moved the responsibility for planning decisions from parliament to councils. Planning provides the framework for developing and maintaining the housing stock. Planning processes stipulate how and where new properties can be built, existing properties can be altered and the conditions to ensure that the increase in value from planning permission (planning gain) is used to improve the infrastructure, amenity and accessibility of these properties. The planning authorities were required to complete a local plan, setting out detailed policies and specific proposals for the development and use of land in their area. This legislation was introduced at a time of major public investment in infrastructure, housing and the development of 13 new towns across the UK.

These enabling laws provided the framework for a common acceptance of the right to good quality housing for British citizens. The experiences of migrants from the New Commonwealth suggest this was not extended to them. The provision of housing for those arriving to contribute to the reconstruction of post-war Britain was a responsibility that some councils did not take up. The introduction of a qualifying period of five years to get a place on the council housing waiting list in Birmingham is an example of the way that the new arrivals were forced to either buy property or to live in the PRS (Rex and Moore, 1967). The infamous 'No Blacks, No Irish, No Dogs' notices provide a visual reminder of the hostility experienced in some areas and created the patterns of concentration in a number of inner-city areas that have characterised racialised groups and migrant residential choices. It also led to many buying properties in poor condition as they could not access the rental market. For some of the new migrants their ownership was short-lived as the properties they had been encouraged to buy were compulsorily purchased to make way for redevelopment; for example, West Indian settlers in Manchester were encouraged to buy properties in a part of Moss Side which was subsequently designated the site of a brewery and their homes were compulsorily purchased.

With the election of a Conservative government in 1951 came a commitment to a property owning democracy. This manifesto promise was difficult to achieve at first as the incentive for private development failed to deliver the required number of houses and council house building contributed around 75 per cent of the 300,000 homes a year target. The government argued that the continuing rent freeze at 1939 levels meant that there was little incentive for landlords to invest in the maintenance or improvement of their properties. It was also difficult to sell them to people who wanted to own them as existing tenants had security of tenure. The government introduced the 1957 Rent Act, which reduced these restrictions by allowing landlords to increase the rent for new tenants. This encouraged the growth of practices to get rid of sitting tenants. 'Rachmanism' entered the English language to explain the phenomena. Perec Rachman bought up housing around North West London and then used 'intimidation and other illegal or antisocial practices' in order to increase rents or to 'remove rent-controlled tenants' so that properties could be sold (Davis, 2001).

The resulting London 'housing crisis' of the 1950s and early 1960s led to the appointment of a Royal Commission by the Minister for Housing and Local Government. Their report was published in 1965 with many conclusions incorporated in the Rent Act of that year (Davis, 2001). The Act 'introduced regulated tenancies (with long-term security of tenure) and fair rents assessed by independent rent officers' (Heath, 2013: 6).

The need for new housing to replace slums was acute in many cities and further outward urban spread was constrained by green belt policies. Technological advances enabled the development of prefabricated components speeding up construction times, and increasingly social housing was sited in large housing estates that included tower blocks alongside lower rise housing. Whilst there were many problems with the quality of some of this construction, it offered a solution for city politicians and planners that promised to address the housing needs of their residents. The role of the PRS fell significantly as both ownership and social housing became the dominant tenures.

The extent to which citizens from the New Commonwealth had access to this social housing is difficult to assess as ethnic monitoring was not included in administrative or census data for the period. Race Relations legislation, which outlawed discrimination, was extended to housing in 1976 and investigations by the Commission for Racial Equality from around that time suggest that there were endemic problems in some council housing allocation policies. The 2001 census suggests significant variation between the proportion of racialised groups in social housing with only 10 per cent of Indian and 16 per cent of Pakistani households compared to around half of Bangladeshi, black African and Caribbean households. This might reflect the exercise of the right to buy by more Indian and Pakistani households. The proportion living in social housing varied significantly between local authorities, with around 80 per cent of Bangladeshis in social housing in Tower Hamlets, Camden and Southwark. In Kensington and Chelsea, the borough where Grenfell Tower is sited, around 70 per cent of the 4,500 black African and Caribbean population were living in social housing in 2001 (ONS, 2011). The evidence available suggests that many of those who had come to Britain to help with post-war reconstruction in major cities were housed on social housing estates, much of which was high rise.

From Residualisation to Stigmatisation

The election of a Conservative government with a radical agenda for change in 1979 has been cited by many as the start of an attack on public provision of housing through the introduction of the right to buy council houses at substantial discounts and the removal of rent controls and security of tenure for those in the PRS. The 1980 Housing Act reflected a new commitment to the ideal of a property-owning democracy by giving social housing tenants the right to buy at a subsidised rate, which led to the purchase of around 2 million homes between 1980 and 2012. The Housing Act 1988 introduced short-term assured tenancies. These tenancies provide the base for the current PRS. Landlords only need to provide six month tenancies, can remove their tenants through a court process that can be completed within two months, and can increase rents without regulation. Although the provisions allowed for longer tenancy periods, most contracts were for either six or twelve months, often a condition of buy-to-let mortgages, creating the insecurity of tenure associated with the PRS. They were based on political assumptions that these were 'essential preconditions for a financially viable and vibrant private rental housing market' (Kemp and Kofner, 2010: 380). The consolidation of rent rebates into Housing Benefit in 1988 contradicted the commitment to a free market espoused by the government providing state subsidy to landlords at the same time as allowing them freedom to set market rents. By the 1990s, home ownership, albeit with a mortgage, became the dominant tenure with both private renting and social housing meeting the needs of a minority of households (Gurney, 1999).

There has been a political and academic failure to identify the racial dimensions of these and other policy changes. Whilst housing in the garden estates built by councils since the 1930s was attractive to those who had been given the right to buy, flats in tower blocks and maisonettes often were not. Alongside the fire sale of the social housing stock, housing budgets were cut back, leading to the reduction in maintenance programmes that allowed the remaining social housing stock to deteriorate. The differential impact of this neglect on the housing conditions of those who had come from the New Commonwealth and their children was exacerbated by policies on immigration, the economy and policing.

The 1981 Nationality Act introduced citizenship categories that limited the rights of newer arrivals and to children born after 1984. Citizenship status excluded some from the right to live in the UK and to access public services including housing. The anti-immigration rhetoric of politicians such as Margaret Thatcher led to more pernicious forms of discrimination (Lukes, de Noronha and Finney, 2018). Direct and indirect discrimination in accessing housing and other services was legitimised by a popular discourse that characterised immigrants as unwelcome.

The development of the new financial industry, the transfer of state industries into the private sector and de-industrialisation decimated communities who had relied on the manufacturing and mining industries and impacted differentially in other areas by the changes to the public sector through privatisation and budget cuts. These impacts were mitigated for the existing workforce by reducing the levels of recruitment but led to a rise in youth unemployment that varied spatially and contributed to a growing North–South divide in economic well-being and political allegiance. The 1980–1981 rioters were represented as racialised groups. The Scarman inquiry into the riots confirmed that police discrimination in the use of stop and search laws to target young black men, which, combined with structural youth unemployment and racism contributed to the riots. The state response set the scene for neighbourhood-level interventions to address the problems of the inner cities. In hindsight, this focus on 'problem places' has many precedents and has been used as a lever to justify their transformation through population change. The 'social question' of the nineteenth century, 'race' problems of the 1950s and 1960s, the riots and later the 'sink estates' of the 1980s all reflected the stigmatisation of certain residential areas and their populations (Harloe, 1995; Wacquant, 2008). Addressing the perceived problem through Area Based Initiatives (ABIs) reflected dominant political discourses. In the 1980s, the Conservative government sought to extend social control over the 'dangerous classes', premised on theories of the underclass (Murray, 1990). At the same time, they silenced voices of dissent through the media and state policies. Alongside a general attack on the 'political correctness' of those engaged with anti-racism campaigns, the Greater London Council was first portrayed as the 'loony left', in part because of the support for these campaigns and then subsequently abolished. This ideological attack shifted the grounds of political debate by moving from structural explanations to a focus on individual responsibility. State responsibilities to address housing needs and the racism and discrimination in society were abandoned in favour of discourses that blamed the individual and abandoned the commitment to the public good.

Civil wars in Ethiopia, former Yugoslavia and Sri Lanka and the first Gulf War led to periodic inflows of refugees and migrants, some of whom were provided with social housing. Over time, this led to increasing racial diversity in housing estates in major urban centres. Structural unemployment and the growth of low-paid jobs created conditions that were used to stigmatise these estates (McKenzie,

2015). Within this discourse of deprivation ABIs were designed to change neighbourhoods by changing the social mix, encouraging gentrification, extending home ownership and promoting active citizenship (Taylor, 1998; Somerville, 1998; Rowlands, Murie and Tice, 2006; Glennester et al., 1999; Amin, 2005).

From Residualisation to Clearance

To the strains of 'Things can only get better', the New Labour government promised to deliver a caring society and redress the neglect of previous years. Their initial analysis identified the problem as social exclusion and disadvantage. Their solutions drew from ideas of social capital and neighbourhood effects (Putnam, 2000; Sampson, Morenoff and Gannon-Rowley, 2002). Both approaches have been criticised for their failure to engage with the structural forces that create and locate poverty in particular places and to adequately allow for the agency of the subjects of the intervention (Wilson, 1987; Wacquant, 2008; Slater, 2013; Dorling and Pritchard, 2010). The New Labour approach at different times associated crime, anti-social behaviour, worklessness, radical extremism and troubled families with 'problem' places (Atkinson and Helms, 2007; Johnstone and Mooney, 2007; Wacquant, 2008; DCLG, 2014). Sink estates, inner city ghettoes and slums were identified as sites for new interventions. The growth in the number of households of around 2 million between 2001 and 2011 compounded the housing crisis. It was accommodated by the growth of a largely unregulated PRS.

The promise of solutions to address the long-term neglect of the remaining social housing was eagerly anticipated by those working in the field. A number of state investments in high-profile estates were planned as pathfinders (Boughton, 2018). The policies associated with the investment enforced mixed tenure housing for new development by reducing 'problematic' social housing to a maximum of 40 per cent of the mix (Boughton, 2018). They also included a range of partnership projects to address crime, worklessness and the environment. There were no parallel initiatives to challenge the 'ghettoes' of house owners by introducing a percentage of social housing.

The murder of Stephen Lawrence and subsequent MacPherson Report identified institutional racism in the police and contributed to the passing of the Race Relations Amendment Act 2000, which gave public authorities duties to address discrimination and promote good relations between racialised groups. Importantly, immigration and nationality functions were excluded from the scope of the Act, which sustained the conditions under which racial discrimination could be legitimised (Lukes, de Noronha and Finney, 2018). The recognition of institutional racism within public services was undermined by the report on the disturbances in Bradford, Burnley and Oldham, which defined the problem as community cohesion and claimed that different racialised groups led 'parallel lives' (Cantle, 2001). This analysis failed to recognise the structural racism which had led to the residential settlement patterns and continued to negatively affect people, and failed to recognise the diversity within the communities of the towns or to recognise that most places did not have such spatially distinct settlement patterns.

The introduction of regional spatial planning frameworks in 2004 promised integration of planning at a regional level to meet demographic and economic needs. Morphet has argued that the spatial turn in 2004 in England represented a 'significant shift in planning's role within the local governance structure shifting from a set of regulatory policies to being a delivery mechanism' (2011: 1). The ambiguity of the term 'spatial planning' meant that academic analysis has interpreted it as both a progressive mechanism to meet housing needs and a mechanism to support private sector investment and increasing control of the housing market (Morphet, 2011; Lord and Tewdwr-Jones, 2014). Regional planning reflected an increasingly place-based model of development with an intermediate state function engaged with planning land use and development for commercial and residential purposes. The move to spatial planning introduced place-shaping as a responsibility for local government and property-led economic development (Lord and Tewdwr-Jones, 2014). New Labour combined the introduction of regional planning processes and local authority place-shaping to get to grips with what they described as the 'wicked' issues in UK policy. These issues were described as cross-cutting because they need to be addressed across the organisational, departmental and funding silos of national government and local public services. They provided funding linked to area deprivation to enable investment in programmes to address these issues. The legal framework for cross-cutting approaches was put in place in 2000 and extended across all council areas in England through national Public Service Agreements linked to local area performance targets. Within their remit, they encouraged local planning authorities to identify target neighbourhoods for regeneration and develop proposals for ABIs to compete for development funding. These proposals continued to be informed by a commitment to mixed tenure housing, the acceptance of the housing market and the role of private developers in the delivery of the regeneration proposals. At a local level, the legal framework led to councils taking a leading role in developing local partnerships of public, voluntary and private sector organisations to produce and implement a Sustainable Community Strategy for their areas. For many areas, affordable housing was a major issue and the S106 provision within the Town and Country Planning Act 1990 supported the use of 'planning gain' to require private sector developers to make provisions within their schemes.

The introduction of the Local Housing Allowance in 2008 capped the housing benefit available to tenants in the PRS to 50 per cent of the market rent with the effect that parts of the city were no longer available to people. This meant that households both in and out of work who were eligible for housing benefit could no longer afford to live in many neighbourhoods.

People with a social housing tenancy were protected from the increasing cost of housing to some extent but the demand was far more than was available. In 2002, a major programme of investment to improve social housing to the Decent Homes standard was introduced. This investment was dependent on transferring the housing stock from the council to housing associations in order to move the debt from the public sector balance sheet. This programme of investment was designed to address the poor conditions arising from the neglect of previous decades. For larger projects, the requirement to provide mixed tenure sites meant that some demolition was required. Some local authorities decided to carry out wholesale demolition with a resulting loss of homes that were not replaced. The increased complexity of designing new housing, managing the move of existing tenants and commissioning the delivery of elements of the contract meant that schemes were not completed before the budget available for the improvements was cut after the 2008 financial crash.

Tightening the Screw

The election of a coalition Conservative–Liberal Democrat government in 2010 saw the regional planning framework dismantled and the performance regime that identified a range of quality of life outcomes replaced with localism (Clarke and Cochrane, 2013). The conditions were created for spatial liberalism: the freedom for local authorities to behave '"responsibly" and meet the expectation of Ministers regarding conduct' (Clarke and Cochrane, 2013: 13). Localism has been differently interpreted by the past three Westminster administrations. For New Labour, it meant meeting minimum national standards for public service delivery with regulatory mechanisms in place to assess compliance. For the Coalition government, and continuing into the Conservative administration from 2015, there was more tolerance of local variation. In housing policy, both of these approaches were problematic as 'local housing systems have an identifiable functional coherence at different geographic scales' (MacLennan and O'Sullivan, 2013: 605). Housing systems operated in neighbourhoods within and across local authority boundaries, often reflecting spatial patterns of segregation based on income and wealth. Despite the requirement to produce a Sustainable Community Strategy being repealed in 2010, many areas continued with similar approaches to local area planning, and some groups of councils, such as Greater Manchester, have worked together to produce plans encompassing aspirations for economic development, transport and housing.

The Conservative Housing Strategy of 2011 focused on individual investment through loans to support housing ownership. There were no plans to invest in social housing. The 1990 Town and Country Planning Act had enabled planning authorities to specify how some of the increase in land value arising from their decisions on its future usage would mean 'that local communities better share in the benefits that growth can bring' (Barker, 2006: 36). The right for developers to appeal S106 provisions was introduced in 2013, with the consequence that the levels of affordable housing required in many approved developments were reduced and new plans had little or no requirements (Early, 2014; Brownhill et al., 2015).

The government also watered down the approach to race equality, which had been enshrined in the Equality Act 2010, by removing the requirement to carry out and publish equality impact assessments of their decisions. This enabled social housing providers to ignore the effect of their clearance and redevelopment plans on different racialised groups. Whilst some housing associations and councils continued with the practice, many did not. The development of the hostile environment policy extended border control to the provision of public and private services including both social and private rented housing. The reform of the welfare system had significant effects on access to housing. The Local Housing Allowance was reduced to the 30th percentile of market rents, single people under 35 received funding for a room in shared accommodation, support was limited to a maximum of four bedrooms and the overall annual benefit payable to a household was capped (Powell, 2015). The introduction of affordable rented properties based on 80 per cent of the market rent for social housing increased the rent levels for new tenants in these properties. The 'bedroom tax' meant that existing social housing tenants who under-occupied their property needed to find more money to stay in their homes or move out. However, there were insufficient smaller properties to accommodate those who needed to downsize within the sector. Other measures that have affected tenants in both the PRS and social housing include the withdrawal of part of the council tax subsidy, the imposition of a benefit cap and the roll-out of universal credit with its single monthly payment.

The Home Office continues to manage contracts with private landlords for those waiting for a decision about their application for refugee status (Perry, 2012). In 2012, the regulations that allowed a local authority to carry out its homelessness duty by placing households in the PRS were enacted. Policy shifted from providing social housing to schemes designed to increase ownership. Both the Conservative and Labour party promised to build new towns in the south east of England with homes for ownership at least some of which would be built for private landlords. Whilst house price inflation exceeds the returns available from other investments, it is also likely that landlords will be active in these new housing markets. The state role in assessing overall housing needs and providing investment to promote building and improvement plans continued through the Home and Communities Agency including investment in the private rental market with the stated intention of developing an institutional commitment to the sector and longer-term tenancies.

The devolution agenda of the 2015 Conservative government promised to extend their version of localism across England. The social elements of these agreements were often limited; the Greater Manchester Strategy focused largely on long-term economic growth through increasing gross value added (GVA), an area-based measure of GDP. The strategy recognised the need to attract new people to live in Greater Manchester by 'creating clean, green, healthy and safe neighbourhoods' and promoting 'independent and resilient communities' (GMCA, 2013: 7). The housing focus was on addressing the increasing shortfall in housing supply through new build and fuel poverty by retrofitting energy efficiency measures for existing housing stock. Migration confounded demographic forecasts that informed spatial planning; migration from EU accession countries from 2004 onwards undermined the assumptions that had led to a significant investment in Housing Market Renewal programmes. These migrants are now reflected in housing needs assessments. If they choose to move on rather than settle and form families, plans for future housing requirements will be unreliable.

The Housing and Planning Bill 2015/2016 proposed removing the right to lifetime tenancies for social housing and extending the right to buy to Housing Association tenants. The first proposal has now been withdrawn but housing authorities are still able to use this approach. The right to buy is being piloted in the West Midlands and, if implemented nationally, is likely to see the removal of a significant tranche of remaining social housing. The Bill also includes changes to planning regulations that allow permission in principle where the land use was designated for development and introduces competition into the planning system. If these changes are enacted, property developers will have more power to shape housing developments in the future.

The United Nations rapporteur highlighted the failure to deliver adequate housing, saying that 'the United Kingdom faces a critical situation in terms of availability, affordability and access to adequate housing, particularly in some geographical areas' (Rolnik, 2013: 7). She concluded that:

> For many, private tenancy is the only option. However, there are significant problems, such as insecurity of tenure, poor management practices and discrimination against specific population groups by landlords and letting agents. In areas of high demand, like London, these problems can be severe.
>
> (Rolnik, 2013: 9)

Grenfell: From Denial to Acceptance?

The initial police investigation provided a definitive identification of the victims of the fire and concluded that a criminal investigation into the events was justified. The government ordered urgent fire tests on high-rise social housing across the country. The results showed that most properties failed the test. The prime minister announced an inquiry into the fire, which would look at 'the necessary action to prevent a similar tragedy from happening again' and seek to learn 'the wider lessons from both this catastrophe, and the inspections of other buildings around the country that followed it' (May, 2017). Submissions to the inquiry argued that terms of reference needed to pay attention to the discrimination and marginalisation experienced by the victims and potential victims identified through the fire safety tests of tower blocks across the country. The joint submission by Race on the Agenda, voluntary and community organisations and local tenants' groups argued that the inquiry needed to consider a range of issues, including the following:

- the history of contempt and neglect that has enabled building regulation failures, including, in particular, governmental indifference to the issue of the safety of public sector tenants in high-rise blocks as evident from the several missed opportunities to take action through legislation and other measures

- the culture of institutionalised discrimination against the low-paid, the vulnerable and those of BME and migrant communities, within the public housing sector
- the consequential marginalisation of the safety concerns of tenants
- the legislative gaps and the administrative practices employed by local authorities and others in charge, which prevent the realization of safety standards and which stifle and discourage take-up of tenants' safety concerns
- the non-existence of effective and legally enforceable protection systems which ensure that the voices of tenants and of affected communities are heard and taken seriously, including the inability of tenants to take up effective legal action themselves
- the systemic failure to secure, without discrimination, the meaningful protection of the fundamental rights of tenants to life, freedom from degrading conditions and treatment, respect for one's home, adequate housing and peaceful enjoyment of possessions without arbitrary interference
- the right to be able to take effective legal action themselves with legal aid (which currently is often unavailable in any practical sense), rather than being forced to rely on those in power (who have no interest in doing so).

(ROTA, 2017)

These proposals were rejected by the inquiry and the coalition of interest groups was not recognised as a core participant meaning that it would not have access to the evidence presented to the committee. It is particularly concerning that both the Equality and Human Rights Commission and the United Nations rapporteur on adequate housing were not granted core participant status. It seemed that the government wanted an inquiry into the technical aspects of the fire without considering the wider social implications. In response to the protests that this approach generated, the government has promised that a second stage will consider broader issues.

We are living through a social crisis in which access to housing symbolises inequalities between poor and rich, young and old, black and white. Resistance to these inequalities is evident in the conflict over the right to housing articulated by residents of London housing estates. Regeneration plans that include clearances have been challenged by residents who object to the way that state and commercial actors have stigmatised the places in which they live and the use of this stigma as a justification for displacing them from their homes. Residents know that these processes are designed to free up valuable land for others who can pay more and recognise that this will create places in which they and their families do not belong. The violence that this approach to regeneration represents should be seen as a result of the failure by successive governments to adequately invest in meeting housing needs. Governments have not delivered on their responsibilities, giving power and control to the market where supply is provided by property developers and construction companies, and access is regulated by estate and letting agents.

The recent Green Paper on social housing may provide an opportunity to change housing policy. It promises to build new homes, to make homes safe and decent, to empower residents and make sure their voices are heard and to tackle the stigma associated with social housing (gov.uk, 2018). However, the promises are unfunded and loosely described, the new social housing will still be subject to the right to buy and the interpretation of stigma used is individually rather than structurally focused. The response of the government to the consultation will need to address these issues if the proposed social housing Act is to deliver improvement. The broader issues of financialisation of housing and legal exclusion from housing will require further attention.

This chapter has shown that the history of housing in Britain has been a history of struggle, that reforms have been fought for and won but that these have only ever been partial. It has also shown that with each positive reform there have been categories of exclusion built in. In the investment in 'homes fit for heroes' and slum clearance programmes of the 1920s and 1930s, poorer tenants were excluded through higher rents charged for new social housing. During major reconstruction after the Second World War, exclusion was based on racialisation of those who had come from parts of the British Empire to contribute to the programme. The growth of high-rise housing created spatial divisions within the city and provided the conditions for the stigmatisation of social housing estates and the people who lived in them. This stigmatisation was based on the racialised groups associated with many places. The restriction of legal rights to housing in national legislation and the local application of length of residence restrictions added a further dimension of exclusion and created a climate in which discrimination could thrive. The promise of regeneration offered by New Labour proved to be illusory as their plans too often favoured the developers' interest in the new market for ownership rather than meeting the needs of existing residents. The existence of social housing in UK cities was put under threat through these programmes. In the shadow of Grenfell, the nature of the debate may be shifting. The evidence from this historical analysis suggests that achieving the right to adequate housing for all requires struggle and resistance, that it will not be given freely by the neoliberal state and that activists need to guard against in-built exclusionary mechanisms.

References

Amin, A. (2005) 'Local Community on Trial'. *Economy and Society*, 34(4): 612–633.

Atkinson, R. and G. Helms (2007) *Securing an Urban Renaissance: Crime, Community and British Urban Policy.* Bristol: Policy Press.

Barker, K. (2006) *Barker Review of Land Use Planning: Final Report – Recommendations*, December. www.gov.uk/government/uploads/system/uploads/attachment_data/file/228605/0118404857.pdf (all websites in this list were last accessed November 2018).

Boughton, M. (2018) *Municipal Dreams: The Rise and Fall of Social Housing.* London: Verso.

Bradley, Q. (1999) 'The Birth of the Council Tenants Movement: A Study of the 1934 Leeds Rent Strike'. *Critical Place Blog.* http://criticalplace.org.uk/research-into-rentrikes/leeds-rent-strike-1934/.

Brownill, S., Y. Cho, R. Keivani, I. Nase, L. Downing, D. Valler, N. Whitehouse and P. Bernstock (2015) *Rethinking Planning Obligations: Balancing Housing Numbers and Affordability.* York: Joseph Rowntree Foundation. www.jrf.org.uk/report/rethinking-planning-obligations-balancing-housing-numbers-and-affordability.

Cantle, T. (2001) *Community Cohesion: A Report of the Independent Review Team.* London: Home Office.

Clarke, N. and A. Cochrane (2013) 'Geographies and Politics of Localism: The Localism of the United Kingdom's Coalition Government'. *Political Geography*, 34: 10–23.

Davis, J. (2001) 'Rents and Race in 1960s London: New Light on Rachmanism'. *Twentieth Century British History*, 12(1): 69–92.

DCLG (2014) *Understanding Troubled Families*. London: Department for Communities and Local Government. www.gov.uk/government/uploads/system/uploads/attachment_data/file/336430/Understanding_Troubled_Families_web_format.pdf.

Dorling, D. (2010) *Injustice: Why Social Inequality Persists*. Bristol: Policy Press.

Dorling, D. and J. Pritchard (2010) 'The Geography of Poverty, Inequality and Wealth in the UK and Abroad: Because Enough is Never Enough'. *Applied Spatial Analysis*, 3(2–3): 81–106.

Early, C. (2014) 'S106 Affordable Homes Deals Rewritten'. *Planning*, 17 January.

Farha, L. (2017) *Report of the Special Rapporteur on Adequate Housing as a Component of the Right to an Adequate Standard of Living, and on the Right to Non-Discrimination in this Context*. Geneva: United Nations. https://digitallibrary.un.org/record/861179.

Foster, J. (1990) 'Strike Action and Working-Class Politics on Clydeside 1914–1919'. *International Review of Social History*, 35(1): 33–70.

Garner, S. (2017) *Racisms: An Introduction*, 2nd edn. London: Sage.

Glennester, H., R. Lupton, P. Noden and A. Power (1999) *Poverty, Social Exclusion and Neighbourhood: Studying the Area Bases of Social Exclusion*. CASE Paper 22, Centre for the Analysis of Social Exclusion, LSE, London.

GMCA (2013) *Greater Manchester Strategy 2013–2020*. Manchester: Greater Manchester Combined Authority.

Gray, N. (2018) 'Spatial Composition and the Urbanization of Capital: The 1915 Glasgow Rent Strikes and the Housing Question Reconsidered', in N. Gray (ed.), *Rent and its Discontents: A Century of Housing Struggle*. London: Rowman and Littlefield.

Gov.uk (2018) *A New Deal for Social Housing*, 14 August. www.gov.uk/government/consultations/a-new-deal-for-social-housing

Gurney, C. (1999) 'Pride and Prejudice: Discourses of Normalisation in Public and Private Accounts of Home Ownership'. *Housing Studies*, 14(2): 163–183.

Harloe, M. (1995) *The People's Home: Social Rented Housing in Europe and Mexico*. Oxford: Blackwell.

Heath, S. (2013) *Rent Control in the Private Rented Sector (England)*. London: Houses of Parliament Standard Note SN/SP/6760. http://researchbriefings.parliament.uk/ResearchBriefing/Summary/SN06760#fullreport.

Henderson, A. and L. Maddock (1930) *Henderson and Maddock's Housing Acts 1925 and 1930: A Treatise on the Housing Act 1930 Including the Complete Text of the Act*. London: Eyre and Spottiswoode.

IPPR (2014) *The Condition of Britain: Strategies for Social Renewal*. London: Institute of Public Policy Research. www.ippr.org/publications/the-condition-of-britain-strategies-for-social-renewal.

Johnstone, C. and G. Mooney (2007) '"Problem" People, "Problem" Places? New Labour and Council Estates', in R. Atkinson and G. Helms (eds), *Securing An Urban Renaissance*. Bristol: The Policy Press.

Kemp, P. and S. Kofner (2010) 'Contrasting Varieties of Private Renting: England and Germany'. *International Journal of Housing Policy*, 10(4): 379–398.

Lord, A. and M. Tewdwr-Jones (2014) 'Is Planning "Under Attack"? Chronicling the Deregulation of Urban and Environmental Planning in England'. *European Planning Studies*, 22(2): 345–361.

Lukes, S., N. de Noronha and N. Finney (2018) 'Slippery Discrimination: An Analysis of the Drivers of Migrant and Minority Housing Disadvantage'. *Ethnic and Migration Studies*, DOI: 10.1080/1369183X.2018.1480996.

MacLennan, D. and A. O'Sullivan (2013) 'Localism, Devolution and Housing Policies'. *Housing Studies*, 28(4): 599–615.

McKenzie, L. (2015) *Getting By: Estates, Class and Culture in Austerity Britain*. Bristol: Policy Press.

May, T. (2017) Grenfell Inquiry Chair: Statement to Parliament by the Prime Minister, 29 June. www.gov.uk/government/speeches/grenfell-inquiry-chair-statement-by-the-prime-minister.

Morphet, J. (2011) 'Delivering Infrastructure Through Spatial Planning: The Multi-Scalar Approach in the UK'. *Local Economy*, 26(4): 285–293.

Murray, C. (1990) *The Emerging British Underclass*. London: IEA Health and Welfare Unit.

ONS (2011) '2001 Census Aggregate Data'. May 2011 Edition. UK Data Service. DOI: http://dx.doi.org/10.5257/census/aggregate-2001-2.

Parliament (1942) *Social Insurance and Allied Services: Report by Sir William Beveridge*. London: Parliament.

Parliament.uk (2015). The Benefits of Britain. www.parliament.uk/business/publications/research/olympic-britain/incomes-and-poverty/the-benefits-of-britain/.

Perry, J. (2012) *UK Migrants and the Private Rented Sector: A Policy and Practice Report from the Housing and Migration Network*. York: Joseph Rowntree Foundation.

Powell, R. (2015) 'Housing Benefit Reform and the Private Rented Sector in the UK: On the Deleterious Effects of Short-Term, Ideological "Knowledge"'. *Housing, Theory and Society*, 32(3): 320–345.

Putnam, R. (2000) *Bowling Alone: The Collapse and Revival of American Community*. New York: Simon and Schuster.

Rex, J. and R. Moore (1967). *Race, Community and Conflict: A Study of Sparkbrook*. London: Oxford University Press.

Rolnik, R. (2013) *Report of the Special Rapporteur on Adequate Housing as a Component of the Right to an Adequate Standard of Living, and on the Right to Non-Discrimination in this Context*. Geneva: United Nations. www.ohchr.org/EN/HRBodies/HRC/.../A_HRC_25_54_Add.2_ENG.DOC.

ROTA (2017) *Submission on behalf of ROTA and others on the Terms of Reference for and the Composition of the Inquiry into the Grenfell Tower Fire*. Accessed from personal correspondence and signed by Bramley House Residents

Association, Silchester Tenants Association, Kensington Residents Alliance, Joint Council for the Welfare of Immigrants, Migrant Rights Network, Voice4Change England, Runnymede Trust, Black Training and Enterprise Group, Race Equality Foundation as well as individual tenants, barristers, activists and academics.

Rowlands, R., A. Murie and A. Tice (2006) *More Than Tenure Mix: Developer and Purchaser Attitudes to New Housing Estates*. York: Joseph Rowntree Foundation.

Sampson, R., J. Morenoff and T. Gannon-Rowley (2002) 'Assessing "Neighbourhood Effects": Social Processes and New Directions'. *Annual Review of Sociology*, 28: 443–478.

Simon, E. and J. Inman (1935) *The Rebuilding of Manchester*. London: Longmans.

Slater, T. (2013) 'Your Life Chances Affect Where You Live: A Critique of the "Cottage Industry" of Neighbourhoods Effect Research'. *International Journal of Urban and Regional Research*, 37(2): 367–387.

Slater, T. (2018) 'The Invention of the "Sink Estate": Consequential Categorization and the UK Housing Crisis'. *The Sociological Review*, 66(4): 877–897.

Somerville, P. (1998) 'Explanations of Social Exclusion: Where Does Housing Fit in?'. *Housing Studies*, 13(6): 761–780.

Taylor, M. (1998) 'Combating the Social Exclusion of Social Housing Estates'. *Housing Studies*, 13(6): 819–832.

Tyler, I. and T. Slater (2018) 'Rethinking the Sociology of Stigma'. *The Sociological Review*, 66(4): 721–743.

UN (1966) *International Covenant on Economic, Social and Cultural Rights*. New York: United Nations.

Wacquant, L. (2008) *Urban Outcasts: A Comparative Sociology of Advanced Marginality*. Cambridge: Polity.

Wilson, W. (1987) *The Truly Disadvantaged: The Inner City, the Underclass and Public Policy*. Chicago, IL: University of Chicago Press.

Wrack, M. (2018) 'The Real Grenfell Scandal: Over a Year on Nothing has Changed'. *The Guardian*, 18 July. www.theguardian.com/commentisfree/2018/jul/18/real-grenfell-scandal-72-people-died-cladding-privatisation.

Photo Essay[1]

Yolanthe Fawehinmi

Note

1. For a commentary on these photos, see blog post: Yolanthe Fawehinmi, 'The Grenfell Tower fire unveils how power operates in Great Britain: The tale of the have and the have-nots.' https://blog.politicsmeanspolitics. com/the-grenfell-tower-fire-unveils-how-power-operates-in-great-britain-163ae2e424e5.

10

ComeUnity and Community in the Face of Impunity

Monique Charles

Poverty is violence. Poverty inducing structures force people to survive in plain sight, yet they are often vilified when drawing attention to their plight. North Kensington, in West London's Royal Borough of Kensington and Chelsea (RBKC), has experienced generational struggles against the dehumanising coagulation of racisms, corporate, local and national state forces as they intersect housing and land ownership; from the signs 'No Blacks, No Irish, No dogs' to ward off potential tenants/lodgers/home seekers in the 1950s (BBC, 2017), to the application for the Independent Republic of Frestonia, to the *Notting Hill* movie (1999) and subsequent encroaching redevelopment and gentrification, to the Grenfell fire. Remaining in the area for the poor and/or racialised has been fraught with battles. Space and volume is shrinking.

This chapter outlines some ways communities and groups of North Kensington have applied organic, self-organising methods in the area. It explores historical struggles over home security before examining the responses to the Grenfell Tower fire from those involved with and in the community themselves. Through interviews, observation and explorations of primary and secondary sources, this chapter gives space to first-hand experiences of working and being together, and community interaction with the local and national government to *re-humanise* and make vivid the experiences of those involved in the day-to-day challenges associated with the area and particularly the fire. As part of this process, this chapter includes a playlist for further exploration.[1] It includes musical tributes to Grenfell by artists in the area and community videos from people organising, raising awareness and documenting the efforts they have done or are continuing to do on the ground in pursuit of justice, healing and community.

The chapter serves to highlight community organisation and spirit in the face of such horrors. It also draws into sharp focus the danger of neoliberalism to those marginalised by class, the abuses it directs towards racialised groups and the dispersal of responsibility and accountability attributed to officials and those with the most power. These dangers work together to form necropolitics (the politics of dictating how people live and die) that systematically dehumanises, endangers and kills the very people the state (officials), through the premise of social housing, should protect.

Wild Wild West: Decades of Struggle

RBKC in West London is a diverse area. It is diverse because of its multi-ethnic residents and its socio-economic groups. Non-white and/or poorer residents are found in higher concentrations in the north of the borough – North Kensington. This area has a history of residents reclaiming and protecting their homes and community spaces. Grenfell tower is located here.

For decades, this multi-ethnic region of North Kensington, while shrinking in size, has remained what Hall (1978) calls an 'internal colony': an area where 'Others' have been confined within Britain. These 'Others' originally formed part of a reserve army of low-skilled workers. Internal colonies are densely populated subaltern inner-city areas of social housing and council estates, where young black, white working-class and multi-ethnic people live. The terms black and multi-ethnic include their working-class position; this is implied. I refer primarily to the white working classes residing in inner-city areas to make a distinction from white middle and upper classes. White working classes lose their whiteness dependent upon their proximity to 'Others' (Hollingworth and Williams, 2009; Nayak, 2003; Garner, 2007), even if they have racist or bigoted views towards 'Others' (Watt, 2006). Hall elaborates that internal colonies are considered parts of the third world *within* the first world and are treated by the authorities as crisis areas where criminality resides. To the authorities, internal colonies are places of scrutiny, suspicion and management.

Scrutiny, suspicion and management form part of North Kensington's history. The community, over decades, has resisted this and worked together to secure and/or reclaim space. In the 1950s and 1960s, this area was a slum (Silchester Residents Association, 2016b; Johnson, 2014). Poor migrant communities, predominantly people of African-Caribbean descent arriving since what is now known as the Windrush period, lived there. Their presence was met with hostility leading to race riots in 1958. In 1959, Claudia Jones founded the Caribbean Carnival, which later developed into the Notting Hill Carnival (in 1966), in response to racist attacks and tensions in the area towards the newly settled Caribbean community. The carnival became a way, along racial and cultural lines, to assert one's right to space and place and celebrate culture.

In 1964, Greater London Council (GLC) actioned plans to build a raised motorway (the Westway, A40) over the North Kensington area where poor people lived (built 1964–1970). The community fought back over the destruction of land and homes. Their actions resulted in the formation of the North Kensington Amnesty Trust, managed by both the government and the community, in 1971. The trust agreed that a mile strip either side of the Westway throughout RBKC should be protected for use by the community as compensation for the damage and destruction to the area. It was agreed that land use in protected areas should be determined by the community (Westway23.org). It is now known as The Westway Trust.

In 1977, a land mass close to the Westway, around the Freston Road area of North Kensington, had abandoned derelict housing that was inhabited by squatters. The area had fallen into such disrepair that previous residents were rehoused into nearby Trellick and Grenfell Towers (Frestonia). The GLC, which had already demolished homes to construct the Westway, wanted to demolish these houses despite having no plans to develop the area. Demolition would make the squatters homeless. In the spirit of Punk and with the ideology of anarchy popular at the time, the social activist Nicholas Albery appealed to the United Nations (UN) for protection from the state, requesting to secede from the United Kingdom to become '*The Free and Independent Republic of Frestonia*,[2] to govern themselves as an independent nation. This was known as the Frestonian movement. All members in the movement added the same surname 'Bramley' to their pre-existing names to present themselves to the government as one family. The name change to present as one family enabled the *Frestonian Movement* collective to organise and mobilise to push for housing security from RBKC. The council eventually built suitable housing on the land that some descendants of those involved in the Frestonian movement still live in today (Sword, 2014). Bramley Road is located in the Frestonia area of North Kensington.

Since Thatcherism in 1979, poverty, as violence, has become increasingly widespread as successive British governments adhered to neoliberal ideologies of minimal government. Minimal government occurs through mechanisms such as outsourcing and privatisation of state services; the result is the government own and manage a minimal amount of services on behalf of the people it governs. Simultaneously, this leaves those governed and the government more vulnerable to forces of the free market. Ultimately, this model enables oligarchs and multinationals to use their capital and power to dictate the terms for masses of people *and* the government as they adhere to maximising profits for themselves. Under neoliberal models of government, authority and control over the agency of those governed is intensified. The root of modernity is founded on the control and exploitation of the poor and racialised and, as such, it is the poor and racialised today that continue to suffer the most under this political shift.

Battles with governing bodies (RBKC, GLC) helped create a strong sense of community in the area, akin to what Back (1996) calls the 'our area' semantic, that is, people having close ties with community and place. The community are defensive about where they live and are sensitive to the external changes made by the government that excludes them from the land they share and the homes they live in. Gentrification, alongside race and ethnicity, in the particular case of the Grenfell fire are important points of consideration that are integral to understanding how the fire unfolded and what motivated the community to push for justice. This diverse area has formed into a community over generations (as different groups of people were housed in the area), connecting people to each other, the area they live and the public communal areas they share. External pressures on an internal colony (Hall, 1978) (such as those listed in this chapter) forge allegiance, culture, knowledge, resistance and subversion. Those subjected to the harsh realities of neoliberalism and its *profits over people* rhetoric, understand experientially that it costs lives and life chances.

Contemporarily, under neoliberal frameworks, the rights of the poor, marginalised and/or racialised in accessing and utilising communal land and housing continue to be an issue. Westway23 continues to work to protect land entrusted since 1971 to the community and raise awareness about some of the protected land being sold off by RBKC without community consent.

In 2015, residents in the Silchester estate and surrounding area, which is adjacent to Grenfell Tower, received letters from RBKC informing them about the Silchester regeneration project. The premise was that RBKC wanted to 'identify locations in the area with the potential to build new homes for local people' (Silchester Residents Association, 2016a). Concerned residents, headed by Piers Thompson, responded collectively to challenge this proposal at its earliest stages. I interviewed, Lowkey, an RBKC resident, hip-hop artist and non-executive director at '*Kids on the Green*'.[3] He informed me that before the fire, Grenfell Tower was the only building that was safe from demolition in the Silchester regeneration project proposals; all the other tower blocks in the area were supposed to be knocked down.

Before the fire took place, members of the community were concerned about their homes and community spaces being under threat. Community members set up websites and blogs about the Silchester regeneration, including Save Our Silchester and Silchester Regeneration, to document developments, including council meetings (Save Our Silchester, 2017). The community were already mobilised a year before the fire because many were fearful of the proposed changes. Lowkey also mentioned a community protest relating to the proposed leasing of the North Kensington Library a year before Grenfell fire. He recalled that once the community became aware of plans to lease North Kensington Library to the private school next door, the community protested, came together to march and storm the town hall chambers. Protests and marches took place in April and June 2016 (Micklethwaite, 2016; Cooper, 2016). The community wants the library, a community trust space, open and 'available to the public in perpetuity'.[4] As of October 2018, the community's campaign has safeguarded the library from being leased and it remains accessible to the public (Shadwell, 2018).

I attended a community event in October 2018; the Master of Ceremonies addressed the crowd informing them about the struggles the community has had with RBKC over the decades and spoke about the continued struggles. They touched upon the detrimental effect redevelopment had had in the Ladbroke Grove area in the 1990s; it removed the black population. They felt that current 'redevelopment' projects are just as dangerous for the remaining poor and racialised residents, mentioning Agenda 21.

They spoke of the cultural damage redevelopment does, stressing that musical bands such as The Clash and ASWAD would rehearse and perform in the area cheaply, Subterranea (nightclub) being sold for £1 – depleting the area of a local venue, the steel pan yard (carnival industrial enterprise) located in the heart of Notting Hill Carnival festivities, being moved from under the Westway; they reiterated that the land lost was land for the community. They spoke about institutional racism at The Westway Trust and drew attention to the fact that the trust was not working for the interests of community spaces. The space where this event took place was a space of contention. RBKC want to take it and the community have been fighting to stay there for three years. The community have occupied the space to ensure that it is not taken. Importantly, this space was crucial in the immediate aftermath of the Grenfell fire. It provided shelter and refuge from the physical effects of the fire and smoke, but also the media frenzy and the thousands upon thousands of people that descended on the area.

With regards to Grenfell specifically, residents expressed concerns about safety in their tower block before the fire happened in June 2017. The sense of concern around housing and home security is long standing. The Grenfell Action Group (GAG) was formed by residents of Grenfell Tower and surrounding areas in 2010 to challenge government plans to build a leisure centre in the green space next to the tower. Edward Daffarn, a resident of Grenfell, and Francis O'Connor, from nearby Verity Close, set up a blog to document the happenings around 'regeneration' in the area. Four or five years before the fire, residents raised concerns about safety through appropriate channels (Lancaster West Management, Kensington and Chelsea Tenant Management Organisation [KCTMO], Notting Hill Housing Trust [NHHT]), who functioned as the landlord at Grenfell owing to RBKC outsourcing (Grenfell Action Group, 2013; 2016b; 2016c; 2017). After repeated appeals to the landlords, GAG co-founder Edward Daffarn predicted that something devastating would have to happen before the landlords would act in the year before the fire:

> It is a truly terrifying thought but the Grenfell Action Group firmly believe that only a catastrophic event will expose the ineptitude and incompetence of our landlord, the KCTMO, and bring an end to the dangerous living conditions and neglect of health and safety legislation that they inflict upon their tenants and leaseholders.
>
> (Grenfell Action Group, 2016d)

Concerns and mobilisation around Grenfell and fire safety started in October 2012. Residents noted that the fire exits were blocked by cleaning contractors' vehicles over a weekend. They were parked in an area where vehicles were not permitted. The issue was raised with KCTMO but residents' concerns were not taken seriously or handled with urgency and documenting the problems via the blog began.

RBKC outsourcing and legislative changes to the regulations measuring the efficacy around safety may maximise the opportunity for profit/savings, but it erodes the possibility of responsibility, liability and accountability if things go wrong. This erosion is deadly, particularly for communities marginalised by race and/or class who are subject to free-market forces *and* state controls. Simultaneously, the management of Grenfell Tower has ripped open wider national debates around social housing stock safety and the impact of corporate, local and national state forces, new regulations and outsourcing.

No Smoke Without ... June 2017

Prime Minister Theresa May (Conservative Party) called for a snap General Election to take place in June 2017. The residents in North Kensington, like many others elsewhere experiencing the effects of neoliberalism, saw voting as an important 'low personal cost' moment in changing the trajectory in politics and their lives (Charles, 2017b; Ottewill, 2018). Self-organising in North Kensington to push for social change and justice around land and housing was already underway. However, it connected with the intersecting social movement of Grime music, culture (Charles 2016; 2017a; 2017b; 2017c; 2018a; Ottewill, 2018) and its overt interest in politics nationally. I interviewed a spokesperson from *Grime4Corbyn* (G4C, 2018). They stated that the 'grass-roots' campaign, in response to the snap election, was organised by friends in a North London kitchen. It was set up to encourage people to vote for or support Jeremy Corbyn (Labour Party Leader). The G4C collective drew upon their cultural and social capital to network with friends and/or artists across London. It culminated in a major event attracting mainstream and national attention just days before the General Election on 8 June 2017. The G4C provided a platform for Grime artists' political position to be taken seriously outside of their own circles. Artists living in RBKC, whether independently or under G4C, encouraged people to engage with the political process. Lowkey reflected, 'in the lead up to the [general] election I said if we lose the election people are gonna die that didn't have to die' (2018).

He saw and understood the impact that neoliberalism had directly on his North Kensington community through passive violence, such as the closing of public services and regeneration projects. Seeing this, he, alongside other artists resident in the borough, used their cultural and social capital to speak to local people directly about voting and the difference it could make to their community:

In the build up to the election I actually said ... for the record we got Emma Dent Coad (MP for Kensington constituency) elected here. Myself (other artists names), all residents of the borough, came out in support of Labour. I know many many youth that I directly – directly told them, go register, let's do this. We got Labour in. The rappers got Labour in in this borough, now that's unbelievable and I'm not sure if it will ever happen again. I don't know how likely it is because I think next time, when you look at the balance of, insanely wealthy and people that live more like the rest of the country live in this borough, we're actually outnumbered.

(Lowkey, 2018)

Also, in June 2017, Bush Theatre was working on a project (alongside a community organisation) to support vulnerable families (primarily mothers and children who experienced home insecurity) in North Kensington and neighbouring areas. I interviewed Holly, Community Producer at the Bush Theatre, who runs a number of community-led events (and support sessions in the aftermath). Families involved in the project starting in June 2017, included members with migrants and/or refugee status, largely from North African backgrounds. The month-long project provided (mostly) mothers with disposable cameras to take a photograph each day to capture what was important to them in their everyday lives. The photographs would culminate in an exhibition and showcase of the images captured.

Grenfell's fire happened in the middle of that month. The project became a way for some mothers to document what happened. The magnitude and shock of the fire (for those involved in the project) changed the trajectory of the photography project, and future projects, discussed below.

It is important to note that the fire happened:

- 6 days after the General Election
- 10 days after the culmination of G4C high profile campaign and event
- 14 days into Bush Theatre's photo project
- In the midst of the Save our Silchester campaign
- 1 year into the campaign to save North Kensington library
- 2 years into the fight to save a vital and much loved local community space

- Years after Grenfell Action Group had raised concerns about safety; including fire safety.

The '*apocalyptic*' (Lowkey, 2018) magnitude of the fire traumatised local residents, shocked the nation and gained international attention. Without a swift and coordinated response through any authoritative channels (local and national government), and mounting concern over the practices of charities, thousands upon thousands of people descended onto West London wanting to help, show their grief and stand in solidarity with those affected (which in itself affected local residents).

ComeUnity: People Coming Together

The word ComeUnity, and its heart shaped London Underground inspired symbol, was designed by local artist Sophie Lodge.[5] The image is highly visible in the Notting Dale area of North Kensington where Grenfell is located. It embodies how people have come together to assist in helping each other in the push for justice and healing.

The G4C spokesperson (23 August 2018) recalls faith groups – Muslim, Jewish, Christian – were some of the first organised responders to help in the aftermath. Holly (Community Producer), recalls the fire happening during Ramadan. She saw a big red carpet was laid out along the road and anyone was welcome to come to eat and break the fast together. There was a national outpouring of aid. Upon attending to help in the immediate aftermath, my cousin and I saw a local pizza company deliver stacks of boxes of pizza to a centre; multiple crates of water had been delivered, with some crates distributed throughout North Kensington. People had brought food to share and distribute to break the fast after Ramadan. Community centres, halls and spaces remained open to feed people, accept and organise donations of clothing and other household items.

The G4C spokesperson asserts that the campaign that led up to the General Election #GE2017 and the impact on the outcome cleared space that enabled artists to be taken seriously in the mainstream media after the fire, and be political and not be attacked for it. The #GE2017 outcome confirmed to artists and wider publics that people will stand behind them. Artists from RBKC such as Piki (Peaky) Seku and Akala used their new, 'mainstream accepted' political position to shed light on what was happening in the area, uncovering the gentrification and neoliberal practices that led to the tragedy on national and international media platforms (BBC, CH4, Sky News).

Burnout London, the West London production company who worked on the G4C media campaign, used the G4C format to organise a Grime4Grenfell (G4G) fundraising event in the immediate aftermath to raise money for the families affected. It was community led in the sense that 'They were leading themselves' (G4C spokesperson, 23 August 2018) to raise money for survivors. Attendees were young people from diverse backgrounds. It was a solemn, cathartic event with performances about the fire and the affected community.

Over time, people returned to their own lives across the nation. However, a lot of work continued to be done by, and for, the community. Lowkey says one outcome of the fire was that it created a 'phoenix that has risen, in terms of many different organisations', helping each other and playing to their strengths for the benefit of the community. A combination of new and pre-existing organisations such as Lowkey's *Kids on the Green, Grenfell Action Group, The Curve, Women's Centre, Harrow Club, Rugby Club, The Village, Resisting Westway 23, Faceoff, Grenfell Speaks, Save our Silchester* and others responded to support the community. These organisations and the wider public come together each month to do the Silent Walk. There may be some differences between organisations, both in approach to the challenges ahead and in function, however, all organisations are focused on achieving justice for residents of Grenfell Tower and housing safety/security in the wider area. The shared pain has bonded people and entwined lives in a substantial and sustained way.

After the fire, Bush Theatre, already working on the June month-long photo project, used their premises to create space for weekly Sunday meetings for the entire summer of 2017. Holly informed me it made space for community organisations and leaders, local people, mental health charities, therapists etc. to come together and discuss what the response to the fire would be and the long-term response in particular. It became a space for attendees to build 'a plan' together and enable people to help in the ways that they could. Importantly, the theatre was also a place to relax and have time out – including for families still in temporary accommodation. The attic space was made as welcoming and as homely as possible.

By working with different community organisations and members of the community, Bush Theatre made a programme, almost like a directory that served a dual purpose, listing what was available by locating people and their expertise; and helping people locate the services they needed. It encouraged engagement from the community for the community and was updated as more people and expertise came forward. The theatre was sensitive to and prioritised community-led solutions. The magnitude of the fire and the trauma it caused meant people needed (and still need) rehabilitation. Music, art and creativity helped residents begin to work through the trauma and were also methods of fundraising, contribution, solidarity and support. Upon direction of community organisations and local people, Holly informed me that Bush Theatre put on a 'happy' event. By August 2017, community members needed to come together and think about something other than the tragedy and grief. The event involved people in music, dance and workshops.

Since the 'happy' event, Bush Theatre continues to work with community organisations and has created new artistic projects to help families process what happened. In January 2018, Holly ran a project enabling children to explore the concept of 'home'; what do 'home' and safe spaces mean? Mothers took part in creative free writing, to write about the fire or anything else of significance to them, which, Holly reports, encouraged and empowered them (Holly, 2018). After the project finished, many reported that they would continue to write. Writing enabled some mothers to express things they had never told anyone! Holly is in the process of starting another set of sessions to continue assisting the wider community to heal.

Musically, outside of the mainstream charity single, *Bridge over Troubled Water*, Stormzy's challenge to Theresa May at the Brit Award in February 2018 (Beaumont-Thomas, 2018) and G4G, grime and-hip hop artists and poets living in and around North Kensington made tributes of their own. Some of these included Lowkey's *Ghosts of Grenfell I & II*, tower resident Shocka's *Grenfell Tribute*, Big

Zuu's *Grenfell Tower Tribute* and Potent Whisper's *Grenfell Britain*. SantanDave, from South London, raised questions about Grenfell in his song *Question Time*. All songs powerfully illustrate commitment to community, with most videos showing the community's diversity and unity. Artists use their creativity to tell the stories from the community perspective. All challenge and question the government on their role, behaviour and conscience. Companies connected to the tragedy are named and shamed. Artists are seeking justice. They speak of continued injustices, and reference trauma, grief and mental health. Some warn listeners about gentrification and redevelopment policy and how these cost and negatively impact lives.

Kamitan Arts is a local non-profit community arts company that provided space for people to begin working through trauma artistically and creatively. Community members were encouraged to write, perform, speak, rap, photograph, film and draw, regardless of ability. Kamitan Arts responded immediately, setting up workshops and running performances throughout the borough. Out of community creative expression came an award-winning, short art film and 'bi-lingual compilation poetry' book, both presented at the Poetry4Grenfell (P4G) event held at Bush Theatre. P4G included community members and guest artists to mark the one-year anniversary of the fire. Importantly, the book and film were by the community for the community, unmitigated by mainstream media. Again this approach shows how the community reaches out and supports its members.

Wider Publics? Shhhh, Nou té ka katjilé kont sa
(We Were Thinking About That)[6]

The Notting Hill Carnival, which sees upwards of 500,000 people attending throughout August Bank Holiday weekend (CoW/RBKC, 2018), takes place on the streets of North Kensington. Notting Hill Carnival organisers worked with the local community and the authorities to orchestrate 72 seconds of silence at 3pm on Sundays and Mondays to honour those who perished. The carnival now has a dedicated quiet area for reflection, has closed off access to residential areas around Grenfell and has included space for community-led creative projects and artwork for carnival attendees. Carnival goers could also wear green to show solidarity (Hayden, 2017).

The carnival going ahead and the implementation of the quiet zone in August 2017, two months after the fire, suggests that a diverse community, with different backgrounds and traditions, respect shared space. They will stand by each other and honour each other. Carnival attendees are diverse yet the Notting Hill Carnival is rooted in largely African-descended Caribbean tradition. The people that perished at Grenfell were diverse, but were disproportionately Muslim and/or of North African origin.

Another significant event that happens on the streets of North Kensington is the *Silent Walk*. The *Silent Walk* happens on the 14th of each month, marking each month since the fire. Walking in the community, in remembrance of those who perished, and survived, is a symbolic reminder of the continued pursuit of justice. The Notting Dale area in North Kensington, around Grenfell, where September 2018's Silent Walk began, has many signs and symbols of unity and remembrance. Posters, banners and T-shirts are attached to resident and organisation windows and walls, lampposts, railings and fences. Images of those who perished, tributes, flowers and teddies occupy community space. The local school and Methodist church each have large installations erected, displaying unity and honouring those impacted by Grenfell. Lowkey mentions this in our conversation: 'The fire that happened there is now reflected on a lot of the walls from around the area, so, it's hard for us to not see Grenfell in our own future' (2018). The Methodist church where the Silent Walk started was undergoing refurbishment. The scaffolding on the church was embellished with a large green Grenfell poster. The blue boards at the base of the scaffolding were populated with children's artwork showing how and why '*Everyone is special*'. The visual symbols give a sense of community, a shared connection to public/community space and a 'determination' for those who perished and the incident to be remembered.

The September 2018 Silent Walk had approximately 150–250 people. Some 'Walkers' wore Grenfell shirts, others wore green. Before setting off, placards were handed out by crowd members. Some were stewards, in high visibility jackets. Others were photographers who organised themselves in and around the crowd to capture the journey. Crowd members were a combination of new faces and regular Walkers. Those present were diverse in age, background, race and wore different styles of dress. Whilst waiting for Walkers to congregate and the walk to start, a young man played Grime artist Big Zuu's *Grenfell Tower Tribute* loudly on a Bluetooth speaker.

Before we walked, the crowd stood together to mark the beginning and silence fell, creating a heavy presence. We walked together, we held placards, we walked slowly. We stopped on occasion, stopping traffic and taking up space. The pace of the walk ensured *everyone* present could make the journey, in silence, together. From the Methodist church, along Ladbroke Grove to Lancaster Road and the Westway underpass closest to Grenfell Tower where the *Wall of Truth* is located.

The speeches at the end of the walk, at the *Wall of Truth* 'dedicated to documenting our community's first hand witness accounts ...' and in the presence of Grenfell, bring unity and centres *ComeUnity*. Speeches are used to motivate those who walk each month to keep strong; to provide updates about Grenfell to the organisations and public in attendance, including the developments and challenges with the inquiry. It is as a platform to show national solidarity with other social housing tenants. It is a space and ceremony to remember those who perished, by calling their names. Significantly, it is a space to seek support and encourage all who need 'to reach out to one another and remain connected' (Lowkey, 2018).

What is poignant in the symbolism of the walk is that those directly involved in acquiring justice for Grenfell understand it is a local *and* national issue. Whilst pushing for justice and remembering those who have perished at Grenfell, they also allow support from wider publics, remain centred and provide space for unity with others in similar situations nationally. Those present know, Grenfell's fire could have happened anywhere in the country (pertaining to the outsourcing of housing management and interpretive approaches towards housing safety standards in the process of reducing costs in social housing maintenance). However, Thompson highlights that Grenfell 'was particularly vulnerable and this council was particularly callous to those ordinary people who lived there' (Sky News, 2018). Wider politics around the internal colony (Hall, 1978) (i.e. race, class, gentrification and profits) all play a role. North Kensington is an area of high-value land. It has the potential to generate vast sums of money for the council and private developers, if the poor and racialised are removed and the land is sold.

Smoke and Mirrors: Local and National Government

The interaction between community and local and national government has been precarious since the fire owing to the slow, guarded and defensive response by officials. One of the first hurdles for the community was to access a route to justice, accountability and enable their voices to be heard. The community had appealed to have a criminal inquest rather than a public inquiry to achieve this (Baynes, 2017; Coleman, 2017). It was essential that community accounts would be heard and taken into consideration, especially as the community had self-organised and were already mobilised around housing safety and security, land and community spaces before the fire took place.

The fire generated interest from media outlets all over the world. However, it amounted to little more than an opportunity for the RBKC and authorities to show concern and promise of action. Lowkey reports that, in reality, emails and letters sent to the government by the community remained unanswered. In addition, to date, the housing minister has changed three times since the fire. The result of these changes is a slowing of addressing the issue as each new housing minister orients themselves about the circumstances pertaining to Grenfell.

Those held accountable for any crime to date have been individuals and residents in the community; those governed by the state. Nobody from the state, or any organisation, in their role as having responsibility for the safety of the residents at Grenfell Tower, have been charged and many are still in post.

Gren-Fail Pants on Fire Awards:[7]
New Nominees for Accountability

Kate Davies is the CEO of Notting Hill Genesis (formerly, Notting Hill Housing Trust – NHHT and Genesis Housing), a housing association with stock in London and the Southeast (NHHG, 2018). The housing association had tenants living in Grenfell Tower, eight of whom died in the fire (Doughty 2018). In the lead up to the merger of NHHT and Genesis Housing, Genesis residents posted concerns on their website about Davies' suitability as CEO (Admin, 2017), owing to her lack of compassion or perceived interest around social housing and her privatisation of profit generated from redevelopment. After the fire, newspapers reported her lack of sensitivity towards the tragedy (Doughty, 2018). On the one-year anniversary of the fire, Davies launched both her new book titled *Making Life More Beautiful* and fashion career, posting these announcements on social media. The launch celebrations took place at the Notting Hill Genesis offices (Doughty, 2018). Meanwhile, thousands congregated to complete the *Silent Walk*, and loved ones commemorated family and friends who died.

Former council chief and Conservative councillor, Nicholas Paget-Brown caused outrage and anger for his comments in the immediate aftermath of the fire, effectively *blaming* residents for not having a sprinkler system installed (Horton, 2017). He later resigned. The former RBKC council Chief Executive Nicholas Holgate also resigned from post with six months' pay.

KCTMO, which acted as landlord for Grenfell Tower, is now defunct. RBKC have retaken responsibility for housing management. From 1 March 2018, RBKC took over the

> running of all day-to-day services including repairs, cleaning services and looking after the estates. In December 2017, the TMO Board recognised that it was no longer possible for the TMO to offer tenants and leaseholders the levels of service they deserve.[8]

Despite some changes being made, through choice rather than following a penalty, no one has been held accountable. 'Necropolitics', the politics of systematising who lives and dies (impacting the racialised and poor the most), is spread through capitalist and corporate systems that are intertwined with the government. Neoliberalism enables corporations to enter minimal government, creates tangled webs of unaccountability that puts profit over people. 'This is necropolitics and what we're dealing with is a bipartisan orthodoxy of necropolitics, they have policies that cause people to die. In passively violent ways and this was one of them' (Lowkey, 2018). Through neoliberal frameworks, the ability for citizens, particularly the most vulnerable within this framework, to push against this structure democratically (even economically) is extremely limited.

Simultaneously, since the aftermath, in an attempt to help, RBKC has funded some community organisations that were already doing important and effective work on the ground to help survivors and local residents. Lowkey also notes that RBKC has backed away from Silchester regeneration plans since the fire (Silchester Residents Association, 2017). However, RBKC has contacted a tenant about removing green hearts from the side of her 7th floor flat claiming they are a safety hazard (Duggins, 2018). This is painfully ironic since the green hearts are a symbol of solidarity with those who perished in and survived the fire as a result of flammable cladding attached to the side of the building under RBKC's care (Booth, 2017).

Fohat al-qanaas[9] (Snipers Scope): Trauma and Racialisation

Grenfell Tower residents have been moved, and some are still seeking permanent accommodation as of October 2018 (Yeginsu, 2018). In addition to trauma from the fire, some are more isolated having been relocated far away, outside of the borough or even the city. Remaining residents, who live in close proximity to the tower, were faced with the uncovered carcass of the building for a year afterwards. Holly (2018) stated some families she worked with were scared to open the curtains in their home as they didn't want to see the carcass outside their window. Thompson reported seeing the tower at the end of his garden was 'very difficult to live with' (Sky News, 2018). Lowkey's account makes clear that the uncovered building was a daily reminder that induced psychological terror. He said residents in the area could still 'see' the people screaming at the windows. He says covering the building made a big difference to the psyche and it doesn't look like the same building (Lowkey, 2018). The fire has caused local residents trauma and some experience PTSD-like symptoms. Thompson reported that a year on from the incident members in his household have 'regular, quite serious counselling' including, for his daughter, the use of anti-depressants (Sky News, 2018).

The uncoordinated responses and lack of accountability from those who have a duty of care, in conjunction with the arbitrary application of the law to residents, exacerbates trauma, creates fear, anger and upset. Lowkey asks:

How can you expect youth that saw their friends, that saw the expendability of their lives directly demonstrated *to them* to not become nihilistic, it's, it's an inevitability; not everyone. Some people use it to motivate them to bigger and better things, moving forward and enjoying and appreciating the good in life but other people, you know, especially in the first year and a half have got nihilistic about things, they don't see any possibility of accountability.

(Lowkey, 2018)

Survivors sought engagement with the inquiry to seek accountability from first responders and official responses to the fire, but also social and housing issues (Booth and Bowcott, 2018). Lowkey recalls people being pushed about by riot police *whilst* the fire was happening, for example. The ways officials have interacted with residents since the fire has also been problematic and dehumanising.

A riot is the language of the unheard (King, 1967). Lowkey believes a significant factor that has prevented riots from happening to date is that the majority of those who died were Muslims. The discourse around Muslims in Western narratives is such that they are presented as a potential threat to civility, social order and 'our' (read 'Western and Eurocentric') way of life. The war on terror narrative is central to this. Lowkey asserts Muslims occupy a position of 'Barbarians in Rome'. Racialisation is such that this narrative perpetually and continuously raises question marks over loyalty and alignment to 'our' way of life and ideology. Violence enacted by Muslims, under any circumstance, is amplified, magnified and presented as inherent to the Muslim character. Suspicion itself can become evidence of a threat to civility and justification for any actions taken against Muslims. The controlling narrative around Muslim residents in particular ensures they do not want to do anything that allows them to be called a terrorist, particularly when examining the legal and social implications of being labelled as such.

Controlling narratives reduce the responses one can have under 'normal' circumstances or when experiencing traumatic events. Media press has already connected North Kensington with radical Muslims (Lockett, 2018; Herrmann 2014). This narrative increases scrutiny and suspicion, causing additional fear and terror to those already traumatised. It works to 'muddy the narrative and minimise the pain felt' of those affected by the fire (Lowkey, 2018).

Conclusion Ghosts of Grenfell *and Grenfellised Lives*

What I find so sad is that people died because of forces that they had no hope of really having the time to understand. You know all of the stuff that has been said in this interview by me, is stuff I've learnt since the fire ... how is it that those invisible forces can act in ways that can literally cause you to die.

(Lowkey, 2018)

Official reports say 72 people died. The community *Wall of Truth* and testimonies under the Westway say it's hundreds. According to Lowkey, 'All of a sudden their lives are just Grenfellised' (2018). Those who died are forever tied to 'Grenfell', '... *what does that do to a person's life?* What does it do to those not recognised or not counted? Where do they exist now? Their lives are subsumed by Grenfell and the tangled webs of necropolitics that surround it. They are flattened to a quantifiable number. Even in the flattening, official narratives differ from the community testimonies of the *Wall of Truth*. The way they died takes precedence over the lives they lived. Thompson states that everyone in the area lost someone they knew in the tower (Sky News, 2018). What does uncounted lives and deaths 'do' to those grieving 'unknown' losses? Those who survived and those affected and living in close proximity to Grenfell, are forever changed. How are those who have died later, or may die from conditions attributable to or exacerbated (Hopkins, 2018) by the fire be remembered? Is there justice, acknowledgement and accountability there?

we see it now as our past and, I think one of the saddest things is that it then becomes definitive of your memories. So, it's impossible for me to have memories of (friend) which are divorced from the way in which he died ... the area itself is kinda tinged by this event and I think what's quite sad is that the way people who died in there, their lives, the necropolitics of the situation is bigger than their lives, and we have to kind of deGrenfell them in a way, to bring them back to humanity?

(Lowkey, 2018)

Issues around Grenfell's safety were understood and acted upon by some residents before the fire (Grenfell Action Group, 2013; 2016b; 2016c; 2016d; 2017), but they really had no way of knowing the extent of necropolitical reach. More than a year later, the community is still trying to heal, access the truth, locate who is liable, and, in hindsight, they are beginning to understand the magnitude of what is to be faced.

In a way, you become ghouls; you become ghosts of the past and in some cases harbingers of the future. But people aren't really paying attention to you because they say that infrastructure is always invisible until it malfunctions and that's what happened that night.

(Lowkey, 2018)

Justice? Just Us?

The lattice that Grenfell residents and the North Kensington community find themselves in the midst of has left little alternative other than to continue self-organising for justice as they had done before. Community responses to the fire and neoliberal necropolitical violence has been anarchic; self-governed, owing in part, first, to lack of responsibility and accountability by corporate, local and national state forces and second, to a historical connection to a community spirit, 'our area' (Back 1996) where people have had to work, support and rely on each other for the common good, healing and justice. Going forward, the community of North Kensington and wider publics have a new understanding that the outcome of this battle impacts social housing residents nationally. Through art and creativity, people heal each other. In making space to plan, people come together and as Holly stated, seeing first hand 'the people care for each other and the people will stand up for each other' (2018).

This chapter elucidates and makes vivid the work of those 'on the ground', their pain and the important everyday activities and experiences on the road to healing and justice. It illustrates that, in the face of insurmountable forces, tragedy and unaccountability, the human spirit in the internal colony, faces their own fears and the state. The community turn to one another, despite their differences, to heal. Members do their part in the pursuit of justice, playing to their strengths in the face of dehumanisation and impunity. The chapter drew attention to the importance of symbolism in presentation and practice (posters, performances, walks) and the importance of community-led activity to move forward, while welcoming support from wider publics. It sheds light on the impact of marginalisation, poverty and racialisation on community members and drew attention to how the fire Grenfellised lives, reducing people to how they died. It speaks to the power of community and respect for humanity to which neoliberal necropolitical systems cannot relate. The chapter is a humble attempt to honour and elucidate the lives of those affected. As such, the chapter has a corresponding playlist, complete with community resources to enable further engagement and insight from the people on the ground and to enable others to listen to the community speak for themselves.

Notes

1. The playlist: www.youtube.com/playlist?list=PL1sdDFLh_rXfvPDTDooF-d17j9RsphLYsn.
2. The Frestonian movement, www.frestonia.org.
3. Director of the performing arts programme.
4. See the Public Amenity Map on the Westway23 website, https://westway23.org/public-amenity-map.php.
5. Also the founder of the #24Hearts – videos in playlist.
6. This is the Kweyol language used by Eastern Caribbean people. People from this region have significantly contributed to Notting Hill Carnival sharing their heritage and culture with wider publics. The title shows that those associated with NHC (and the wider public) were thinking about those affected by the fire and how best to balance tradition with respect for

community members. This title also speaks to the historical diversity in the area.

7. This was an award the Grenfell Action Group (2016a) issued to the TMO chair Fay Edwards for not taking resident concerns seriously.

8. See the front page of the KCTMO website, 2018, www.kctmo-development. co.uk/.

9. Lowkey informed me this phrase refers to being a target, as if being watched through a snipers scope.

References

Admin (2017) 'Is Kate Davies a Person Who Should be CEO of a Housing Association? Even less a "Mega" Merged Housing Association?'. *Genesis Residents* website, 30 November. http://genesisresidents.org.uk/merger/is-kate-davies-a-person-who-should-be-ceo-of-a-housing-association-even-less-a-mega-merged-housing-association/ (all websites in this list last accessed September–October 2018).

Back, L. (1996) *New Urban Ethnicities and Urban Culture: Racisms and Multiculture in Young Lives.* London: UCL Press.

Baynes, C. (2017) 'What is an Inquest, and How is it Different to a Public Inquiry, and Why are the Victims of Grenfell Calling for One?'. *The Independent*, 17 June. www.independent.co.uk/news/uk/what-is-an-inquest-different-public-inquiry-grenfell-tower-victims-a7794661.html.

BBC (2017) 'Private Passions – No Blacks, No Irish, No Dogs'. Loftus Production for BBC Radio 3, produced by E. Burke, 20 August. www.bbc.co.uk/programmes/b0831bt2.

Beaumont-Thomas, B. (2018) 'Stormzy asks "Theresa May, Where is the Money for Grenfell?" at Brit Awards'. *The Guardian*, 21 February. www.theguardian.com/music/2018/feb/21/stormzy-asks-may-wheres-the-money-for-grenfell-at-brit-awards.

Booth, R. (2017) 'Flammable Grenfell Tower Cladding "Passed" by Council Officer in 2015'. *The Guardian*, 14 July. www.theguardian.com/uk-news/2017/jul/14/grenfell-tower-cladding-passed-by-council-officers-in-2015.

Booth, R. and O. Bowcott (2018) 'Where do we Stand a Year after the Grenfell Tower Fire?'. *The Guardian*, 14 June. www.theguardian.com/uk-news/2018/jun/14/where-do-we-stand-a-year-after-the-grenfell-tower-fire.

Charles, M. (2016) *Hallowed be thy Grime?: A Musicological and Sociological Genealogy of Grime Music and it's Relation to Black Atlantic Religious Discourse.* Doctoral Thesis. Warwick University.

Charles, M. (2017a) 'Grime Launches a Revolution in Youth Politics'. *The Conversation*, 12 June. http://theconversation.com/grime-launches-a-revolution-in-youth-politics-79236.

Charles, M. (2017b) 'Generation Grime', in M. Perryman (ed.), *The Corbyn Effect.* London: Lawrence & Wishart.

Charles, M. (2017c) 'Roundtable: Conference Conversations'. *Renewal: A Journal of Social Democracy*, 25(3–4): 111–120.

Charles, M. (2018a) 'Grime Labour'. *Soundings: A Journal of Politics and Culture*, 68 (Spring).

Charles, M. (2018b) ComeUnity, Community, Impunity playlist www.youtube.com/playlist?list=PL1sdDFLh_rXfvPDTDooFd17j9RsphLYsn.

City of Westminster/Royal Borough of Kensington and Chelsea (CoW/RBKC) (2018) Notting Hill Carnival 2018: Residents' booklet. www.rbkc.gov.uk/sites/default/files/atoms/files/notting_hill_carnival_2018_residents_booklet.pdf.

Coleman, C. (2017) 'London Fire: Inquest Versus Inquiry'. *BBC News*, 23 June. www.bbc.co.uk/news/uk-england-london-40353738.

Cooper, G. (2016) 'Watch Protestors Storm Kensington & Chelsea Council Chamber to Disrupt Meeting'. *GetWestLondon*, 30 June. www.getwestlondon.co.uk/news/west-london-news/watch-protesters-storm-kensington--11550602.

Doughty, S. (2018) 'Grenfell Tower Housing Boss Turned Fashion Guru will hold Book Launch Party on the Anniversary of the Disaster Today While Survivors, Neighbours and Politicians Attend Memorials'. *Daily Mail*, 14 June. www.dailymail.co.uk/news/article-5842005/Grenfell-Tower-housing-boss-turned-fashion-guru-hold-book-launch-party-anniversary.html.

Duggins, S. (2018) Twitter feed, 20 September. https://twitter.com/sued62/status/1042732393520607238?s=20.

Garner, S. (2007) *Whiteness: An Introduction*. London: Routledge.

Grenfell Action Group (2013). 'More of Fire Safety'. 30 January. https://grenfellactiongroup.wordpress.com/2013/01/30/more-on-fire-safety/.

Grenfell Action Group (2016a) 'Pants on Fire Award – TMO Chair Fay Edwards'. 9 January. https://grenfellactiongroup.wordpress.com/2016/01/09/pants-on-fire-award-tmo-chair-fay-edwards/.

Grenfell Action Group (2016b) 'Grenfell Tower Still a Fire Risk'. 24 January. https://grenfellactiongroup.wordpress.com/2016/01/24/grenfell-tower-still-a-fire-risk/.

Grenfell Action Group (2016c) 'KCTMO – JUSTICE IS COMING'. 17 July. https://grenfellactiongroup.wordpress.com/2016/07/17/kctmo-justice-is-coming/.

Grenfell Action Group (2016d) 'KCTMO – Playing with Fire'. 20 November. https://grenfellactiongroup.wordpress.com/2016/11/20/kctmo-playing-with-fire/.

Grenfell Action Group (2017) 'KCTMO – Feeling the Heat!'. 14 March. https://grenfellactiongroup.wordpress.com/2017/03/14/kctmo-feeling-the-heat/.

Grime4Corbyn (G4C) (2018) Personal Interview with spokesperson on 23 August.

Hall, S. (1978) *Policing the Crisis: Mugging, the State, and Law and Order*. Basingstoke: Macmillan.

Hayden, S. (2017) 'Notting Hill Carnival to Pay Tribute to Grenfell Tower Victims'. *The Independent*, 27 August. www.independent.co.uk/news/uk/

home-news/grenfell-notting-hill-carnival-pepe-francis-sadiq-khan-green-a7915016.html.

Herrmann, J. (2014) "'It's a Wake Up Call ... We Need to do More": Why do so Many Jihadists Come from the Streets of North Kensington?'. *Evening Standard*, 17 October. www.standard.co.uk/lifestyle/london-life/it-s-a-wake-up-call-we-need-to-do-more-why-do-so-many-jihadists-come-from-the-streets-of-north-9801125.html.

Hollingworth, S. and K. Williams (2009) 'Constructions of the Working-Class "Other" Among Urban, White, Middle-Class Youth: "Chavs", Subculture and the Valuing of Education'. *Journal of Youth Studies*, 12(5): 467–482.

Holly (2018) Personal Interview with Community Producer at Bush Theatre, 14 September.

Hopkins, N. (2018) 'Huge Concentrations of Toxins Found in Grenfell Soil, Study Finds'. *The Guardian*, 12 October. www.theguardian.com/uk-news/2018/oct/12/toxins-found-in-grenfell-tower-soil-study-finds.

Horton, H. (2017) 'Anger as Leader of Kensington Council Appears to Blame Grenfell Residents for Sprinklers Not Being Installed'. *The Telegraph*, 16 June. www.telegraph.co.uk/news/2017/06/16/anger-leader-kensington-council-appears-blame-grenfell-residents/.

Johnson, A. (2014) 'Alan Johnson on Notting Hill before it was Notting Hill'. *The Telegraph*, 23 May. www.telegraph.co.uk/travel/destinations/europe/united-kingdom/england/london/west/notting-hill/articles/Alan-Johnson-on-Notting-Hill-before-it-was-Notting-Hill/.

King, M.L. (1967) 'The Other America' Speech'. www.youtube.com/watch?v=m3H978KlR2o.

Lockett, J. (2018) 'How ISIS Beatles Recruited Brit Jihadis from Tiny Corner of West London'. *The Sun*, 25 February. www.thesun.co.uk/news/5667342/isis-jihadis-beatles-alexanda-kotey-west-london-notting-hill/.

Lowkey (2018) Personal Interview with hip-hop artist and Non-Executive Director at Kids on the Green, 14 September.

Micklethwaite, J. (2016) 'Council Accused Over Plans to Lease Kensington's Oldest Library to Private School'. *Evening Standard*, 29 April. www.standard.co.uk/news/london/council-accused-over-plans-to-lease-kensingtons-oldest-library-to-private-school-a3236501.html.

Nayak, A. (2003) "'Ivory Lives": Economic Restructuring and Making of Whiteness in a Post-Industrial Youth Community'. *European Journal of Cultural Studies*, 6(3): 305–325.

NHHG (2018) Presentation to Investors on the Amalgamation of Notting Hill Housing and Genesis Housing. Notting Hill Genesis. www.nhggroup.org.uk/sites/notting-hill-genesis/files/2018-06/18-06-26%20Investor%20Presentation%20for%20website.pdf.

Ottewill, J. (2018) '10 Things we Learned About UK Grime with Dr Monique Charles'. *Institute of Contemporary Music Performance Blog*, 18 June. www.icmp.ac.uk/blog/10-things-we-learned-about-uk-grime-dr-monique-charles.

Save Our Silchester (2017), 'Piers Thompson's Estate Regeneration Consultation Response'. 14 March. www.saveoursilchester.org.uk/2017/03/14/piers-thompsons-estate-regeneration-consultation-response/.

Shadwell, T. (2018) 'North Kensington Library Campaigners Triumph as Kensington & Chelsea Council Seek to Rebuild Trust after Grenfell'. *GetWestLondon*, 26 October. www.getwestlondon.co.uk/news/west-london-news/north-kensington-library-campaigners-triumph-15333117.

Silchester Residents Association (2016a) 'Regeneration: The Story So Far'. February. www.silchesterestate.org.uk/2016/02/regeneration-the-story-so-far/.

Silchester Residents Association (2016b) 'Notting Dale History'. www.silchesterestate.org.uk/about-us/notting-dale-history/.

Silchester Residents Association (2017), 'Minutes of Extraordinary "Open Forum" Meeting held at Silchester Residents' Rooms'. 9 August. www.silchesterestate.org.uk/our-meetings-minutes/809-2/.

Sky News (2018) 'Grenfell Tower Debris Still Falls into my Garden'. *Sky News*, 11 June. https://news.sky.com/story/grenfell-tower-debris-still-falls-into-my-garden-11399675.

Sword, H. (2014) 'The Notting Hill Squatters Who Declared Independence from the UK'. *Vice Magazine*, 28 October. www.vice.com/en_uk/article/4w7pxq/republic-of-frestonia-tony-sleep-032.

Watt, P. (2006) 'Respectability, Roughness and Race: Neighbourhood Place Images and the Making of Working Class Local Distinctions in London'. *International Journal of Urban and Regional Research*, 30(4): 776–797.

Yeginsu, C. (2018) 'Grenfell Tower Survivors Still Displaced 10 Months After Blaze'. *The New York Times*, 4 April. www.nytimes.com/2018/04/04/world/europe/uk-grenfell-tower-survivors-fire.html.

Equity

Tony Walsh

Definition:

1. The quality of being fair and impartial.
2. The value of a mortgaged property after the deduction of charges against it.

They say "the swinging sixties" but for most they never swung
The reality was poverty, my parents married young
And they moved their new born baby to a rented terraced home
Where it wan't the lack of heating that would chill us to the bone
There were The Beetles of a different kind, a classic Classic Slum
Cathy Come Home, pregnant, crying, teenage wasteland, Mum

If they catch cold in the black mould then a child's in trouble soon
And *this* child lay there dying as a man walked on the moon
Aged three, Rheumatic Fever, in a damp home, but alive
With my baby sister crying, I was fighting to survive
And I was saved by penicillin, our amazing NHS
And a change in my life chances from a change in our address

A council home! A tenancy! An indoor loo as well!
Three bedrooms and two gardens and, as far as we could tell
It was a home for life, respectable, presentable and clean
It was civilised and dignified, my Mum kept it pristine
Well, as best she could, with four of us, she'd make do and she'd
    mend
And the neighbours did you favours, and we kids played out as
    friends

Is that too much to ask for in the Britain of today?
Why is homelessness and hopelessness and heartlessness ok?
Who decided that providing social housing can't be done?
That we won't look after others, we'll look after number one?
And where's this "Big Society?" Is it shrinking like the state?
Is it not collectivism that has made this country great?
If "we will build a new Jerusalem" in this green and pleasant land
Well then who's the "we" we speak of? Do we fail to understand
That we need happy, healthy workers if our nation is to thrive
But most are barely managing, and many can't survive
With no safety net beneath them or no roof over their heads
Or their children now lay hungry with black mould above their
    beds
In a modern, wealthy country this is in a word obscene
Still in poverty. In Britain. Now, in 2017

And it has to start with housing, social housing from the Latin
"socialis" meaning allied, there are other words with that in
Socialist and socialism but, of course, that is the target
To wrap up our post-war progress and to flog it on the market
Always stocks and shares not housing stock, not sharing but
    demeaning
Does it take a council kid to point out equity's two meanings?

While they're cutting, cutting, cutting, cut – but now we've people
    adding
Family members to remember in the embers of their cladding
Let this *be* the day we see the way to honour all their names
Inequality and poverty, austerity in flames

Afterword
The Fire and the Academy
Robbie Shilliam

I have done it myself. Unwittingly, I have on occasion turned the living communities of Lancaster West and of Notting Dale into a noun: Grenfell. The problem is that when communities are turned into a noun they can be enclosed and owned. Communities-under-pressure have warp and weft; they are tenaciously held together by delicate lattices of lives and existences; regardless of precarious futures, they have pasts and presents; and yet, reduced to a noun, they can be compressed into a particular classification and freely conjoined to any politics, discourse, or analytical framework. At a workshop in April 2018, Daniel Renwick cautioned us against producing a Theory-of-Grenfell. I hope that the stunning diversity of positionalities and investments that authors (both singular and collective) provide in this book will forestall the production of such a Theory. Having reached these pages, no reader will find it easy to slip the Grenfell Tower fire into the jacket of a noun. Resisting that slippage compels us – and by 'us' I mean primarily critical scholars of the academy – to ask difficult questions about our ethics of intellectual engagement. In what follows, I provide three brief thoughts on this challenge.

1. When I took my undergraduate degree in International Relations and Development Studies, I was quickly introduced to Robert Cox's proposition that 'theory is always for someone and for some purpose'. Cox wished to question the putative neutrality of 'problem-solving' theory, and with good reason. But I have since realised that it is much harder to ask questions of 'critical theory': who is it for, and for what purpose? In the humanities and social sciences, we critical theorists present our worth in terms of a sceptical inquiry into knowing and being. We do not wish to accept the world as it is or is made to appear, and we teach our students to do likewise. However, in my limited experience, communities-under-pressure do not primarily

require critical theorists to shed light on their affairs but scholars and students to share resources: time, access, influence, money, transport etc. This is not to say that critical theory has no place in – or no value for – such communities. It is rather to suggest that 'critique' might not be as urgently required as the boring and painstaking pursuit of 'problem solving' research – for example, the search through records for exculpatory or inculpatory evidence. Given all this, I wonder who benefits from critical theory, at least in so far as it is held aloft as the lodestone of emancipatory academic inquiry.

2. Every locality is its own world. It is always unclear where that world begins and ends, but it is usually quite clear where its centres of gravity lie. Immanuel Kant was a local boy; he never left Königsberg. But we scholars utilise Kant (as friend or foe) to demonstrate the universality of our critique. Could we, just in principle, accept the salience of the knowledge traditions, intellectuals and activists of the Notting Dale locale? Or is that salience always destined to be submerged under the proclaimed universality of sages from other locales? Accolades only await the first academic who translates Grenfell into the universal language of, for example, Fanon, Foucault, Agamben or Lefebvre. To be clear: I am in no way arguing against the practice of making connections, the reaching out and the drawing together; rather, I am concerned with the way in which such translations in academia usually authorise (require?) a cavalier treatment – or even abandonment – of locale. In particular chapters of this book you will have discerned embedded histories, knowledge repositories, dispositions and grammars, all working to provide salience on the key political issues. Yet fluency in this salience takes time to cultivate, with no reward. Such a familiarisation requires a respect and humility on behalf of the scholar. And this kind of edification challenges the impact agendas and public engagement fads of the higher education sector. Even if we use impact and engagement as redistributive resources, we should make no mistake about the extreme instrumentalities that undergird their metrics. Inevitably, resources committed must translate into 'outputs'; but not all engagement can or should bear recognisable value.

3. Whether justice will ultimately be served, or partially served, or betrayed, the aftermath already stretches on indefinitely. What

does it mean to have scholarly solidarity with those who must live in and through the aftermath? Are we only interested in the terror? Heroes and blameless victims are the easiest figures to animate via social and political theory. In 2015, at the height of the European refugee crisis, well-meaning scholars demanded that their academic institutions open up to those fleeing the wars in Syria and beyond. But what of the children of those asylum seekers? After having lost their humanitarian shine, these children will find few scholars committed to their uplift. Let us not forget that there exists in our societies children and grandchildren of long-arrived refugees and asylum-seekers, many of whom right now suffer from exclusion, racism, poverty, alienation. Some of these people no doubt resided in Grenfell Tower. The moment will arrive when the survivors of the fire will be rendered once more profane, unimportant, background, non-heroic, non-exceptional, a dull, diffused social problem. I worry that scholars will only once more discover the children come the next catastrophe. Politics always callously moves on. But we need to figure out what a sustained scholarly commitment might consist of, across a geographically and institutionally diverse academy. And for that task, an intra-academic conversation might be insufficient.

This Afterword is not an endorsement of liberal stand-off-ishness, or an excuse for self-aggrandising distance, or a post-whatever-paralysis. My purpose in writing it is to suggest that we critical scholars in/of the academy must proactively refine and redefine our terms of engagement with the communities that surround our institutions. In this respect, our scholarship must support and not sublate all those who think and work and survive on front lines.

Contributors

Parveen Ali is a photographer and former resident of North Kensington. She lived very close to Grenfell Tower at the time of the fire. Parveen's work has been featured in several exhibitions, as well as in the *Evening Standard* and *Huffington Post* (https://parveenali. com/).

Sam Boal is an Irish media photographer, specialising in Irish news particularly based around Dublin. He works for an agency (Photocall Ireland) and his work covers all aspects of Irish life, both national and international. At the time of the fire, Sam was in England visiting family.

Gracie Mae Bradley is a writer and campaigner interested in critical human rights, state racism and data/surveillance. She is Policy and Campaigns Manager for Liberty where she leads opposition to the 'hostile environment'. She is involved with grassroots migration struggles, including the Against Borders for Children campaign.

Dan Bulley teaches at Oxford Brookes University and is Director of the Global Politics, Economy and Society Research Centre. He has written about the international ethics and politics of migration, hospitality and foreign policy.

Monique Charles is an independent researcher. She writes about Black music, music analysis, class, gender and race. She is currently working on her first book and is exploring the uses/possibilities of music and sound.

Nigel de Noronha teaches at the University of Nottingham. His research interests are in housing, race and migration with a focus on the way people have been excluded from access to adequate housing. He believes an important role of academics is to contribute to the broader struggle for social justice.

Jenny Edkins teaches at the University of Manchester. She has written about missing people, trauma and aid, and her latest book is about whether academic work helps or hinders in the struggle for change. She is experimenting with fiction and life writing.

Nadine El-Enany teaches at Birkbeck School of Law and is Co-Director of the Centre for Research on Race and Law. Nadine writes about race, colonialism, migration, refugee law, European Union law, protest and custodial deaths.

Yolanthe Fawehinmi is a London-based digital journalist who advocates for innovation in storytelling and technology. She is currently a journalist at *The Telegraph*.

Becka Hudson is an organiser and writer, who is currently working on a variety of projects. She has written for *The Independent* and *Verso* on issues regarding race and gender. Until recently, Becka worked as Coordinator for the Radical Housing Network.

Sarah Keenan teaches at Birkbeck Law School and co-directs the Centre for Research on Race and Law. She writes about how law takes effect in time and space, and how those effects reproduce structures of race and gender. She is involved in a range of anti-racist activist campaigns.

Lowkey is a rapper, Grime and hip-hop artist based in London. He has a long history of political activism, including with the Palestine Solidarity Campaign, the Stop the War Coalition and Grime4Corbyn. Lowkey was hailed in Parliament as the 'poet laureate' for Grenfell Tower by Kensington MP, Emma Dent Coad.

Ben Okri is a multiple award-winning poet and novelist. He is widely considered to be one of the world's most important post-colonial authors. Born in Nigeria, Ben grew up in London and Lagos, living in North Kensington in the late 1980s.

Radical Housing Network is a networked collective of over 30 housing groups and campaigns across London. Grenfell Action Group, who have worked for many years to expose the contempt with which residents were treated by their landlord and the council, and the dangerous standard of their housing, were members of the network in the years leading up to the fire (https://radicalhousingnetwork. org/).

Daniel Renwick is a videographer and writer who made *Failed by the State – the struggle in the shadow of Grenfell* (with Ishmael Francis-

Murray and Redfish). He has worked as an advocate and youth worker in the North Kensington community. His writing has been published by *The Institute of Race Relations, Verso, Red Pepper* and *The Guardian.*

Anna Viola Sborgi currently works at King's College London, researching screen representations of East London and Urban regeneration. She writes on cinema, television and the city and is particularly concerned with media representations of social housing. She recently co-edited the special issue of *Other Modernities*, titled 'LondonIsOpen'.

Phil Scraton is a widely published critical criminologist at Queen's University, Belfast. His hugely influential book, *Hillsborough: The Truth*, is recognised as the definitive analysis of the Hillsborough disaster. Appointed to the Hillsborough Independent Panel, he headed its research and was primary author of its damning extensive report leading to new inquests and the verdict of unlawful killing.

Robbie Shilliam teaches at Johns Hopkins University in Baltimore, USA. He writes on colonialism, race and international politics. He works with community groups on co-curated projects, such as the Rastafari In Motion exhibition at the Black Cultural Archives (London) in 2016.

Pilgrim Tucker is a community organiser and campaigner who has worked for many years on social justice and inclusion related issues. She has been working with residents of the Lancaster West Estate, and has supported the Grenfell Tower residents' campaign, the Grenfell Action Group, in getting their voices heard.

Patricia Tuitt is a legal academic, who runs an online resource (patriciatuitt.com). She is author of *Race, Law, Resistance* (2004), and other publications on race and law. She has written several commentaries on the ongoing judicial inquiry into undercover policing.

Tony Walsh is a professional poet, performer and educator who grew up in social housing in Manchester. He had an 18-year career managing inner-city council estates and urban community regeneration programmes. Tony achieved global renown when he performed his poem, 'This is The Place' at the vigil for the victims of the Manchester Arena bombing in May 2017 (www.longfella.co.uk/).

Index

far-right groups 28–9, 55
Fawehinmi, Yolanthe *xxiv,* 165–6
Feilding-Mellen, Rock 32, 33, 38–9
Ferrante, Elena 1
films and TV programmes 99–114
　Cracks in the System 41, 117n16
　Failed by the State xvii, 100, 110
　The Fires that Foretold Grenfell 116n15
　grass-roots 100, 103–5
　Grenfell 97, 101, 102, 108–11
　Grenfell Our Home 101
　On the Ground at Grenfell 102, 103–5, 111
　on housing crisis 113–14
　The Listening Post report 100
　news 99–100
　Panorama 10, 29
　Searching for Grenfell's Lost Lives 101, 102, 106–8, 111
financial crisis 'of 2008' 51
fire department 23, 25–6, 143–4
Fire in Grenfell (Lowkey/Khalil) 100
The Fires that Foretold Grenfell (documentary) 116n15
Forensic Architecture agency 97–8
Francis-Murray, Ishmael *xvii,* 34
Frestonia 169–70
FRONTEX 85
Fuel Poverty Action 71

general election (2017) 174–5
Genesis Housing 182–3
gentrification *xxi–xx,* 57, 170–1 *see also* redevelopment
Georgiou, Myria 112
"Ghosts of Grenfell" (Lowkey/Khalil) *xxiii–xxiv,* 75–8, 100
Gizbert, Richard 99
global cities 3–5
global links, of Grenfell residents 104–5, 107, 135–6
global reasons for fire *xvii,* 8–12
　accountability and *xxii,* 12–14
government *see* Kensington and Chelsea Borough Council; national government, failures of; *specific prime minister or party*
Greater London Council (GLC) 169–70
Greece, uprisings in *xix*
green heart symbol *xiv–xv, xx,* 41, 176, 184
Green Paper on social housing 160
Grenfell (documentary) 97, 101, 102, 108–11

Grenfell Action Group
　blog post on safety fears 31–2, 33, 65–6, 115n7, 173
　Fay Edwards, award to 189n7
　formation of 19–20, 172–3
　on local development 26, 27–8, 37
　role of 62, 65–6
　see also Grenfell Unite; Radical Housing Network
Grenfell, origin of name *xx–xxi*
Grenfell Our Home (documentary) 101
Grenfell residents
　discourse on *x, xi,* 26–9, 31–2, 70, 135, 183, 186
　justice vs law for 119–29
　marginalisation/dehumanisation of *x–xi,* 26–9, 55–6, 58–9, 135, 138–9, 183
　muting/ignoring of: after fire 40, 68, 158–9; fire safety fears beforehand 9, 19, 51, 58, 81; blog post on fears 31–2, 33, 65–6, 115n7, 173; general concerns about refurbishment 9, 19–22; on local redevelopment 19, 26–8, 171–2; silent vigils as protest 19, 36, 40, 106, 108, 143, 177, 179–82
　see also Grenfell Action Group; Grenfell Unite; Grenfell United
'Grenfell Speaks' local channel 99, 109–10
"Grenfell Tower, June, 2017" (Okri) *x, xxiii, xxvii–xxxi*
Grenfell Unite 20–2
Grenfell United 23, 24, 68, 74
'grief tourism' 110–11, 130
Grime4Corbyn (G₄C) 174–5, 176–7
Guardian 124–5

Hackitt, Judith 24
Hailstones, Niles 'Asheber' *xxiv,* 27, 35
Hall, Stuart 85, 168–9
Hammond, Philip 23
Hanley, Lindsey 82
Haraway, Donna 82
Harley Facades Ltd 9–10, 12
Harvey, David 51
heart symbol *xiv–xv, xx,* 41, 176, 184
Herman, Didi 121
Hillsborough disaster *xxiv*
Holgate, Nicholas 183
Holland Park School 21
home ownership 150, 155, 156–7
homelessness 156
Hopkins, Katie 28–9
Hopkins, Keith 116n12